Managing a
Veterinary Practice

SECOND EDITION

For Elsevier:

Commissioning Editor: Joyce Rodenhuis
Development Editor: Rita Demetriou-Swanwick
Project Manager: Morven Dean
Designer: Andy Chapman
Illustration Manager: Merlyn Harvey
Illustrator: Hardlines

Managing a Veterinary Practice

SECOND EDITION

Caroline Jevring-Bäck BvetMed MRCVS

Nordic Veterinary Affairs Manager
Hill's Pet Nutrition, Denmark

with

Erik Bäck MSc

Frodo Consulting, Salsjö-Duvnas, Sweden

Foreword by

Debbie Delahunty BVSc (Hons)

President, Australian Veterinary Practice Management Association
Horsham Veterinary Clinic & Animal Hospital
Horsham, VIC, Australia

Edinburgh   London   New York   Oxford
Philadelphia   St Louis   Sydney   Toronto 2007

SAUNDERS
ELSEVIER

© Elsevier Limited 2007. All rights reserved.

First published 1996
Second edition 2007

ISBN-10 0 7020 2820 7
ISBN-13 9780702028205

British Library Cataloguing in Publication Data
A catalogue record for this book is available from the British Library

Library of Congress Cataloging in Publication Data
A catalog record for this book is available from the Library of Congress

Notice
Knowledge and best practice in this field are constantly changing. As new research and experience broaden our knowledge, changes in practice, treatment and drug therapy may become necessary or appropriate. Readers are advised to check the most current information provided (i) on procedures featured or (ii) by the manufacturer of each product to be administered, to verify the recommended dose or formula, the method and duration of administration, and contraindications. It is the responsibility of the practitioner, relying on their own experience and knowledge of the patient, to make diagnoses, to determine dosages and the best treatment for each individual patient, and to take all appropriate safety precautions. To the fullest extent of the law, neither the Publisher nor the Authors assume any liability for any injury and/or damage to persons or property arising out or related to any use of the material contained in this book.

The Publisher

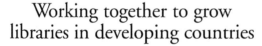

Contents

Foreword

Those of us who work within the veterinary profession are truly fortunate. Not only do we interact with the varied species which come under our care but we have the opportunity to form relationships with the wide variety of people who are their owners. As a caring member of the veterinary health care team we become a vital link in the relationship between people and their beloved pets. This is indeed a privilege and opportunity.

However, the veterinary profession is facing many challenges: either relative surplus or deficit of available veterinarians; the changing needs of the younger generation of veterinarians; increasing responsibilities of veterinary nursing and other support staff; declining pet populations in some countries; changing vaccine protocols, etc.

We cannot ignore these changes and expect our businesses to thrive. We need to pro-actively manage our businesses and the role of the veterinary practice manager is becoming a vital part of practice.

Whether we are a sole practitioner running our own business or a Practice Manager of a large multi-vet practice, *Managing a Veterinary Practice* provides valuable insights to the skills required to successfully lead and manage a veterinary practice into the next decade and beyond.

Generally, we come to practice management with either a purely veterinary background (as veterinarians or veterinary nurses) or possibly a purely administrative or business background. Both groups bring valuable skill sets to the role they play but it is important to develop sound business and marketing skills in parallel with an intimate knowledge and understanding of the veterinary profession. *Managing a Veterinary Practice* enables the reader to develop both areas, having detailed insights into the profession. There are valuable sections on understanding the importance of communication, vision setting, how to lead change and provide an elementary overview of economic principles.

The traditional view of the veterinarian as a healer of ill animals is challenged. Dr Jevring-Bäck urges us to review our role and become partners with owners in providing comprehensive programs to **prevent** illness in their companion animals. Chapters on 'Understanding our Clients' and 'Improving Compliance' are vital if we are to know and meet the needs of our clients and be able to make effective recommendations. There is a good discussion on the importance of the bond between humans and animals which takes the next step to look at the role of the veterinarian in this relationship. Our patients rely on us to be their advocate; to educate and make recommendations to their owners so they receive the best possible care.

The role of the entire health care team for the delivery of excellent patient care cannot be understated and Chapters 7 and 8, 'Understanding Your Staff' and 'Developing the Practice Team' discuss motivation, personality types, recruitment and the importance of training. There is also an important section on stress in the veterinary profession. It is becoming more and more apparent that those of us in the 'caring' professions need to look after our own physical and mental health and well-being. Failure to do so results in burn-out, depression, poor financial performance and disillusionment. It is important for owners and managers of veterinary businesses to be aware of this, not only for themselves but also for staff members under their care. Unhappy, stressed staff cannot meet and exceed client needs in the same way as staff who are fulfilled, challenged and happy.

The concept of quality and excellence in customer service is evaluated. We are challenged to consider quality not as something we choose to deliver but rather as an evaluation only our clients can make. They are the ultimate judges of our success in delivery of customer service. It may come as a surprise for us to find out what is truly important to our clients when we compare it to our own pre-conceived ideas. The distinction between satisfied and loyal clients is made. Is satisfaction enough to keep our clients coming to us? How do we develop loyalty amongst our clients? How do we market to our clients without seeming pushy? Questions such as these are addressed throughout the book, particularly in Chapter 9.

A chapter dedicated to 'Professional retailing' discusses why we should consider retailing as a service to our clients who tend to prefer 'one-stop shopping' in their busy lives. They want their trusted veterinary practice to recommend and sell the best products. This chapter helps us understand the emotions and feelings behind an owner's decision to purchase either products or services from us and how we can enhance their decision making process.

Managing a Veterinary Practice is a very useful addition to the library of veterinary practice owners and managers. It has relevance to **all** employed within the veterinary profession because of the clarity of insights into why we do what we do. Management skills are no longer an 'optional-extra' for veterinary practices, they are an absolute essential. This volume provides a comprehensive overview of the wide-ranging areas of knowledge required to operate a veterinary business in the ever-changing veterinary market. It will prove valuable to managers who are veterinarians trying to run their business 'in their spare time' and also to members of the newly evolving profession of Veterinary Practice Managers.

Debbie Delahunty
August, 2006

Preface

A clever person once said: *Never mistake knowledge for wisdom. One helps you make a living; the other helps you make a life.* In the course of their professional lifetimes, veterinarians accumulate a broad and deep knowledge about the successful management and treatment of animal disease. Over time they learn more complex surgical methods, keep abreast of medical advancements, learn new non-invasive diagnostic techniques, develop time-saving procedures, and often become increasingly specialised in one species or even one system. Of course, they also learn that every animal has an owner, and that to be able to treat the animal the vet has first to be able to establish a trust relationship with an owner. This requires being empathetic to an owner's needs, learning skills in communication, and being able to work as part of a team. These are survival skills without which a veterinarian cannot progress in practice.

But there is one area of knowledge that still seems to elude veterinarians, and that is a willingness to understand the relationship between using the scientific and client skills knowledge they have and expressing these in business terms. This missing link is what converts veterinary knowledge into wisdom and turns vague resignation and resentment about life as it has become, into the deep-seated satisfaction of living a life of the quality you truly want.

In the course of a year, I visit many, many practices. It is heartwarming to meet the veterinarians and staff in these practices and experience first hand the dedication and genuine commitment to their work of treating and curing sick animals and healing the human–animal bond. It is heartbreaking to see how vets are struggling to maintain a living standard and life quality that reflects their knowledge, skills and the caring service they offer. Many practices generate well under their potential income, are overwhelmed with staffing issues, are afraid to charge properly for their services and are struggling to provide the level of care to which they are committed.

Since this book was first published a decade ago, veterinarians have experienced many changes ranging from a much greater awareness from animal owners – our clients – of what can be done for their animals, to the profession becoming female dominated. Even practice management has become a much more acceptable term than it was, with an increasing number of practices in North America, the UK, and Australia employing dedicated, qualified managers. These practices, in general, are doing well. However, there are still many practices who either are resistant to working systematically with business management principles or feel they are too small to employ a manager. These practices are, in general, struggling.

This book is written for people who want to deepen their understanding of why business management is so important – even for a small business such as a veterinary practice. It is not a 'how to' book – there are several good examples of these already on the market. It is a book about principles and understanding why it is necessary to apply these principles to run a successful business. It contains a lot of new, updated information which is reflected in the greater length, and increased number of chapters. There is also a great deal of emphasis on clear leadership and good communication as these, I believe, are they key to any successful business.

I hope you find the ideas in this book – many of which have been adapted to veterinary practice from the great management thinkers of our time – of help in your daily work. I hope they will also help you achieve your practice and personal goals, and provide some of the steps towards the wisdom needed to give you the life quality you deserve. In the words of the great Mahatma Gandhi:

***You** must be the change you wish to see in the world.*

Caroline Jevring-Bäck
July, 2006

Acknowledgements

My deepest thanks go to family and friends who have helped and encouraged me to update this edition of the book. In particular I would like to thank friend and colleague Anne-Marie Svendsen and her husband Chris for providing many of the photos, as well as Susanne Max from Helsingborg Regional Animal Hospital. Marita Stigelius and Anne-Lie Franklin of Blue Star Animal Hospital in Gothenburg provided generous and invaluable input to the newly written chapter on economics. And finally I would like to thank my husband and fellow contributor, Erik, whose love, support and wise guidance have kept me going through thick and thin.

Caroline Jevring-Bäck

Acknowledgements

1 Leading change

The assumptions on which the organization has been built no longer fit reality. These are the assumptions that shape any organization's behaviour, dictate its decisions about what to do and what not to do, and define what the organization considers meaningful results. The organization's theory of business no longer works.

Peter Drucker, 2001

The one consistent feature of today's business environment is change. There are three primary ways to deal with change – ignore it, manage it, or lead it. The first is doomed to failure: organisations that cannot adapt to change become monoliths and die. The second, managing change, creates a business that is flexible and adaptable – the responsive organisation. The third, leading change, is the stuff of visionaries: a few, and only a few, businesses fall into this exceptional category. They are the market leaders, the trendsetters, the people at the cutting edge of their field who are willing to stick their necks out, to take risks, and to *create* change.

The business of veterinary practice is no less exempt than any other from the challenges of change. In recent years, these have ranged from a world recession and new European Union legislation, to the demands of more knowledgeable clients, changes in patterns of animal ownership, and altered expectations of new graduates. Indeed, one of the greatest challenges has been to recognise and accept that the veterinary profession is a *service* profession, serving the needs of the animal owner and their animals. Selling services requires knowledge of the needs and wants of the client – needs and wants which change over time. The successful practice must therefore be a responsive practice: *the practice that makes every effort to sense, serve and satisfy the needs and wants of its clients and the animals they care for within the constraints of the ethical standards of the veterinary profession, and the financial resources of the practice.* The responsive practice proactively works with change rather than passively having change forced on it. The responsive practice knows that change starts from inside out – from making changes to attitudes and behaviours within the practice to best respond to the external changing needs of the clients.

The impact of resisting change

> *If you keep on doing what you've always done, you'll keep on getting what you've always got.*

But we all make efforts to change, don't we? We introduce a new health programme into the practice, upgrade a nurse to office manager, attend day courses on how to be better at people management. So why is the healthcare programme not more successful? Why do you still have as much administration as before? Why are the new people skills you have learnt not creating the super productive team you had hoped for?

The problem is that these are not real changes – they are superficial, sticking-plaster sort of changes that may solve a problem temporarily but do not make a big, deep-down change in how the practice is managed and run. To make real changes with the practice requires time, energy, planning, commitment and, above all, a clear vision of the future for which you are striving. And real change requires that people behave differently – which is uncomfortable, because it is a threat to familiar patterns of behaviour as well as to security, status and financial rewards.

Real change is difficult, which means that resistance to change is natural. Resistance arises for the following reasons:

- *Preference for stability.* People seek to maintain their equilibrium.
- *Habit.* Once established, habits provide comfort and satisfaction.
- *Conformity.* For many people anything that diverges from the accepted norm in their environment is disruptive and disturbing.
- *Perceived threat to own interests.* People focus on their own best interests and think that any change must be for the worse. Often, they only take the short-term view of the immediate difficulties to be overcome.
- *Misunderstanding.* People may not understand the implications of change and believe it will cost them much more than they will gain.
- *Fear of the unknown.* Ambiguities in goals, roles and the methods of achieving the new goals and measuring the response create fear and uncertainty.

In addition, change is hard. It requires not only knowledge but also motivation and behavioural changes. For example, how many of us know how to lose weight? It's easy isn't it? – eat less and exercise more. But how many of us *successfully remain motivated and consistently employ the new behaviour patterns required* to effectively lose those extra few kilos? I think you know the answer!

According to management guru John Kotter, there are eight reasons why change does not happen in organisations (Table 1.1).The effect of resistance to change, or if change is not properly managed, is decreased morale, and loss of motivation and commitment within the practice. This results in conflict, frustration, and an ultimately destructive inertia: employees do the minimum they need to in order to survive.

Change and the veterinary profession

So, what are some of the change challenges facing the veterinary profession? I have broadly divided these challenges into three areas: external ('world') factors, external (client) factors and internal factors (Figs 1.1 and 1.2). The external ('world') factors are things such as a world recession or advances in general technology over which the profession has very little or no influence. External (client) factors include the changing demands clients make on the profession, and represent the most important area of opportunity and progress for the profession through client education and marketing leading to increased client compliance. The internal factors reflect the attitudes, feelings and traditions within the profession itself, and are often the major source of limitations.

External ('world') factors

World recession and natural catastrophes

Changes in the fortunes of global industry due to political or natural forces can create changes in the world economy that can even filter down to the level of your practice. Clients, fearing for their own finances, may choose to make cuts in their spending which may even affect how much they choose to spend in your practice. Natural catastrophes, such as the prolonged drought in Australia, have created change that has forever left its impact on rural veterinarians: the dairy industry has been forced to its knees, pushing once flourishing dairy farmers out of business, and

Table 1.1   Why change does not happen

Reason	Comments
1 Allowing too much complacency	It takes enormous energy and effort to force people out of their comfort zones. Too much past success, a lack of visible crises, low perform-ance standards, insufficient feedback from clients, etc., creates complacency and a lack of urgency to instigate change.
2 Failing to create a sufficiently powerful leadership	Organisations develop their own culture: 'this is the way we do things around here'. Individuals alone, no matter how competent or charismatic, seldom have all the assets to overcome tradition and inertia.
3 Underestimating the power of a clear vision	A vivid picture of where the practice is going plays a key role in producing useful change by helping to direct, align, and inspire action in people, turning a group of like-minded individuals into a productive team.
4 Not communicating the vision sufficiently	A vision can never work if it only exists in the mind of a few individuals or 'the boss'. To achieve a vision requires making personal sacrifices which people will not make – even if they are unhappy with the current situation – unless they really believe a transformation is possible.
5 Permitting obstacles to block the vision	Obstacles to achieving the vision can be unwilling individuals, the prevailing culture (*'We've always done it like this'*) or parts of the existing organisational structure. If obstacles are not confronted and dealt with, they disempower employees and undermine change.
6 Failing to create short-term wins	Transformation takes time. Complex efforts to change 'the way we do things around here' risk losing momentum if there are no short-term goals to meet and celebrate.
7 Declaring victory too soon	Until changes sink deeply into the culture – which may take upwards of 3 years – new approaches are fragile and subject to regression.
8 Neglecting to anchor changes firmly in the new organisational culture	Until new behaviours are rooted in social norms and shared values, they are always subject to degradation as soon as the pressures associated with a change effort are removed.

Adapted from Kotter (1995).

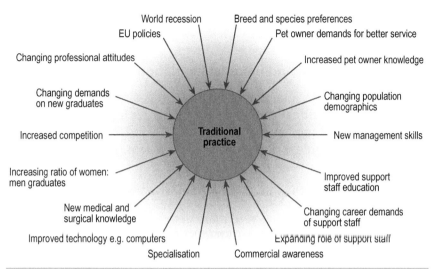

Figure 1.1 The need for change: some of the factors influencing traditional practice.

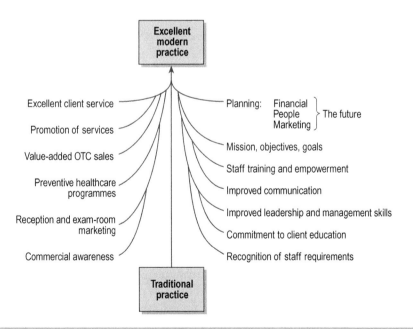

Figure 1.2 Some of the management factors needed to convert the traditional practice to the excellent modern practice.

causing the loss of a whole way of life for the veterinarians who served them.

International and national legislation

Throughout the EU, practice standards, drug dispensing legislation and standards of animal care as well as slaughter legislation, and animal transport and movement regulations, are under review. Although this may, for example, bring benefits to the client, who can now take their pet on holiday with them, not only does it require careful management of the required vaccination and worming requirements by the practice, it also requires knowledge of new or unusual diseases brought back from abroad. National veterinary associations constantly update and revise veterinary legislation, changes which affect management of the practice, for example with requirements for health and safety in the workplace, and employment regulations.

Modern technology: computers

Computers are an essential modern business tool, and although most practices are now computerised, few use the information their computers can give them to their full capacity. Computers are an invaluable aid for managing the practice accounts, payroll analysis, stock control and costings, clinical records, word processing, reception control, preventive health programmes, marketing and much more besides. Chapter 3 looks in more detail at the role of computer software in your practice.

The value of the pet industry

The pet industry is Big Business. In the USA and Japan, pet ownership is at an all time high, with 63% of all US households and around 30% of Japanese households owning pets. Studies clearly show that most of these dog and cat owners see their pet as an integral part of the family and want veterinary healthcare that reflects this. In the UK, the British pet industry was valued at nearly £4 billion in 2005, an increase of 30% over the previous 6 years, despite the declining pet population and the fact that less than 50% of the British population own pets. This level of growth was achieved through increased sales of premium foods, more frequent visits to the veterinarian for healthcare procedures such as pre-anaesthetic screening and healthcare services such as obesity, senior, behaviour and dental programmes, and increased purchase of more accessories.

External (client) factors

Serving the client

Veterinary practice is a service industry, committed to serving the needs of animal owners and their animals. The modern veterinarian must satisfy demands for good service from increasingly better informed, and discriminating, animal owners who gain their knowledge from a wide variety of more or less reliable sources such as popular behind-the-scenes television programmes, internet and a large number of 'experts', from horse whisperers to cat communicators. People are questioning the medical profession's attitude to their own health, often seeking a more holistic rather than a 'relief of symptoms' approach. This is reflected in the type of care they seek for their animals. Relying on expertise in medicine and surgery to automatically ensure a successful practice is no longer enough, and practices that incorporate selected 'alternative' treatments such as hydrotherapy, acupuncture, herbal medicine, chiropractic and homeopathy are examples of responsive practices that are responding to needs and wants of their clients whilst respecting the ethical standards of the veterinary profession.

Human–animal bond

As people strive to have and do more with their leisure time, pet ownership has become increasingly important. Companion animals serve many functions. A dog, for instance, can be kept as a guard, a loving companion, a pet for the children, an incentive to exercise, a child/family substitute, independence and security (for an elderly person living alone, say) and much more. Companion animals have been shown to improve human health and longevity, and serve a unique function in helping handicapped and institutionalised people.

Not only can animals have a huge personal value to their owners, but they may also be very valuable in their own right for breeding, showing, hunting and racing. Owners of these animals want to keep them in top condition.

How can practices best respond to the increasing demands of discerning animal owners and to the needs of the different categories of owners? Of course, there will always be a need for specialists in the treatment and care of sick and damaged animals, but healthcare programmes and sale of vet-endorsed quality products that will prevent or reduce the risk of disease are certainly part of the answer.

Pet preferences

Pet species preferences have altered as more single-person households and joint-income families make money and time scarce commodities. There is a distinct ownership trend towards low maintenance and/or exotic pets such as rabbits, birds, snakes, spiders and chinchillas, but the most marked trend is in the increasing ratio of cats to dogs. Cats are popular, partly because they are perceived as requiring less maintenance than dogs. Does your practice cater to the specific requirements of dedicated cat owners? Incorporating a feline-only section in your veterinary clinic shows that you recognise that the cat is not just a small dog, but that, like its owner, it has different and special needs. Expanding this idea through your whole practice with cat-dedicated consulting rooms, handling facilities, adapted cages for hospitalisation, and specialised staff, demonstrates your commitment further and encourages your cat-owning market. The ultimate in this category is clearly the feline-only clinic (Fig. 1.3).

Changing social trends

Society has altered from a predominantly rural to a predominantly urban society. Fewer people are brought up with or have regular contact with animals (wild or domestic) and, as a result, have little or no idea of animal care or husbandry. Many of the health and behaviour problems seen with horses, pets and exotic animals are a direct result of a lack of basic common sense knowledge about the species and its requirements for normal life. Much of the 'natural horsemanship' movement reflects this need for a return to an understanding of and common

Figure 1.3 Part of the waiting room in the 10 Lives cat clinic in Oslo, Norway.

sense management of the needs and wants of the animal. With their broad knowledge base and experience, the veterinarian is often the best qualified person to help potential owners choose an appropriate animal for their lifestyle, and to advise existing owners on behaviour, nutrition, housing, breeding and general care. How many practices promote this 'animal husbandry' aspect of their business?

Increased choice

Clients choose their practices based on convenience of locality, cost of the services, the perceived value of the services, and the quality of client service they receive. Discriminating clients are prepared to travel to get the level of service and care they want – and are noticeably less loyal than previous generations if they are not satisfied. In many areas, the standard of client service has become the major differentiating factor in determining which practice they will visit. How do you influence your clients' choice?

Internal factors

Traditional practice image

For many animal owners, a traditional image of practice persists: the dedicated, caring veterinarian who works selflessly all day and night fixing sick and injured animals, working miracles because 'animals can't talk, can they?'.

Veterinarians know that modern practice simply is not like that. But how many take the time to explain this to their clients? Yes, practice is peopled by dedicated caring professionals who often do work that appear to be miracles, but this is because modern practice is so well equipped, and professional work standards so high. How many veterinarians take the time to show clients around the practice premises and show them what they do, show them the advanced equipment and facilities in the practice, the preventive healthcare programmes, the value of employing well-trained staff, the level of expertise at which the practice works? By perpetuating the myth of practice, veterinarians are performing a grave disservice to themselves because they reduce and limit the expectations of their clients.

Changing professional attitudes

Young professionals have a different set of professional and personal values from their predecessors. Enthusiastic, creative and energetic, many are crushed into cynical apathy only a few years out of university because the profession refuses to recognise their needs. For many graduates, becoming a veterinary surgeon is no longer a vocation, it is a job. Twenty-four hour dedication 365 days of the year is not acceptable; young veterinarians want quality time off to enjoy family and leisure activities.

Increased mobility offers the modern graduate a much greater chance of trying out a variety of practices in different parts of the country, or even abroad, and so develop a wider range of experiences. If and when they do settle in a practice, many veterinarians do not then want the heavy financial and emotional commitment of a full business partnership; they want instead to retain the freedom to make choices, especially if their spouse also has career decisions to make.

Practice can be exciting and interesting; it can be routine and boring; and it can be lonely and frightening. Young veterinarians need support and help when they graduate to ensure they learn how to manage the sometimes nearly overwhelming problems of demanding owners, learning to function in the practice team, managing difficult non-textbook cases, and making a living – to name but a few of the challenges they face.

How do you accommodate the needs of young professional and support staff in your practice?

Women in the profession

Women have accounted for well over half of new veterinary graduates for the past 15 years, yet many women still face sexual discrimination from male colleagues and clients. Young women graduates are paid on average nearly 10% less than their male colleagues and there are far fewer female principals and specialists. Women veterinarians tend to be less commercial and business minded than their male colleagues. They have additional demands on their time often due to family pressures and often prefer to work part-time. Women will shortly form the majority of the veterinary workforce and the management challenge this creates will not go away. How adaptable and supportive is your practice to the career needs of women veterinarians while balancing their needs for flexible time to care for a family?

Stress and stress management

Stress arises from an inability to balance high professional standards with personal fulfilment. It can lead to alcoholism, drug abuse, 'burnout' and suicide, and is an increasingly serious problem among members of all the caring professions.

The veterinary profession has the highest suicide rate of all the professions. Stress starts early as a survey of young graduates conducted by the Society of Practising Veterinary Surgeons (SPVS) showed: 15.6% of those who answered said they were discontented and more women graduates were discontented than men. Elkins and Elkins (1987) in their survey of professional 'burnout' amongst American veterinarians, found that those in the 10–14 years-in-practice group had significantly higher scores for predisposition to 'burnout' than other groups. Although ultimately the individual is responsible for his or her own life, how does your practice culture help your staff achieve a healthy work–life balance?

Veterinary knowledge

Twenty years ago, the doubling rate of knowledge was measured in years, today it is only a few months, by the year 2030 it will be measured in minutes. The rapid increase in the volume of veterinary knowledge makes specialisation at a species and even a systems level essential.

Continuing professional development (CPD) maintains professional expertise and is an essential part of excellent client service as clients trust their veterinarian to provide the best possible care for their pet. Legislation in some countries now makes a minimal requirement for annual CPD an essential part of keeping your licence to practise. How can CPD requirements for both veterinarian and non-veterinarian staff be managed in such a way that they fulfil the needs of the practice itself to grow and develop, and help differentiate the practice in the client's eyes?

Competition

> *Most people see life as a finite pie: if somebody gets a big piece of the pie then it means less for everybody else. People with a scarcity mentality have a hard time sharing recognition, credit, power or profit. They also have a tough time being genuinely happy.*
>
> Stephen Covey, *Seven Habits of Highly Effective People*, 1989

There are more veterinarians and veterinary practices than ever before. Additional competition comes also from other animal care 'experts' such as breeders, pet-shop owners, alternative therapists and animal communicators.

Veterinarians are often frightened of what they see as competition because they have a scarcity mentality: they believe there isn't enough 'pie' to go around. Many fight colleagues by under-pricing services, against the pet shop by slashing profit margins, and against the breeder or alternative therapist by categorising them as ill-informed and therefore dangerous. 'Pies' are usually bigger than they seem, and competition can often be converted to opportunity – the opportunity to work cooperatively, and ensure everyone gets a nice big piece.

How can you convert local competition to an opportunity to develop your business and serve your clients better?

Making a difference: leading *real* change in practice

There are many factors causing change in practices but, as we have already seen, it is not enough to make only superficial changes to the way of doing things – for example, half-heartedly start up a weight management programme and call this 'commitment to pet health', put an advertisement in the local newspaper and call this 'marketing', or put your head nurse, who has no previous business management qualifications, into an administrative position and call this 'improved practice management'. People who have been through difficult, painful and not very successful change efforts often end up drawing both pessimistic and angry conclusions. They become suspicious of further change efforts, resigned to mediocrity, and fearful that they will be made to do something they don't want to do.

For real and effective change to occur a commitment is required at leadership level. Change is also a multi-step process that takes time and dedication, and that creates sufficient power and motivation to overcome all the sources of inertia. The model I have successfully used in driving change in veterinary practices is based on John Kotter's powerful eight-step process summarised in Table 1.2.

For this model to work:

1. each step must be followed in the correct order, and
2. there must be clear and effective leadership.

Trying to go faster by skipping over a stage does not work. It slows down and undermines the change effort. Change can be messy, especially in larger organisations where many people are involved. Strong leadership maintains the forward momentum whilst handling this complexity. Note that to achieve real change requires not *management* of change but *leading* of change.

Table 1.2 **The eight-stage process of creating major change**

Stage	Actions
1 Establish a sense of urgency	Identify and discuss current crises and potential crises, weaknesses, threats, strengths, and opportunities.
2 Create the guiding coalition	Put together a group with enough power to lead change. Get them to work as a team.
3 Develop a vision and strategy	Create a vision to direct the change effort. Develop strategies to achieve the vision.
4 Communicate the change vision	Constantly communicate the vision in every possible way. Model desired behaviours and actions.
5 Empower broad-based action	Get rid of obstacles. Encourage risk-taking and non-traditional ideas and thinking.
6 Generate short-term wins	Plan and create visible improvements/ short-term wins. Reward these wins.
7 Consolidate gains and produce more change	Change all system, structures and policies that do not fit the transformation vision. Employ and encourage people who can implement the change vision.
8 Anchor the new culture	Create better performance through client-related behaviours, more and better leadership, more effective management. Reinforce the connections between the new behaviours and organisational success. Develop ways to ensure leadership development and succession.

The difference between management and leadership

Management is necessary in any organisation. It is about planning and budgeting, organising and staffing, and controlling and problem solving to produce a degree of predictability and order, and consistently produce short-term results.

Leadership is about establishing direction through creating a vision of the future, aligning people to that vision, and then motivating and inspiring them to achieve that vision. It is these latter activities – the actions of a leader –that produce change.

With this in mind, let me explain how I have used the eight-step model for leading major change in veterinary practices.

1. Establish a sense of urgency

For change to happen requires a high level of cooperation from all concerned. However, if complacency is high, people will find a thousand ingenious ways to withhold cooperation from a process they sincerely think is wrong.

I have visited many practices where complacency is high – *despite* awareness of ineffectual and time-wasting systems, frustration over not being able to do a good job, client complaints, dissatisfaction with salaries, and poor and limited facilities. A feeling of resignation permeates the practice ('This is the way it is here') coupled with cynicism about change ('We tried that, but it didn't work').

Where does this complacency originate? Some of the most important reasons are highlighted in Figure 1.4 and managing – or, better – avoiding them will be discussed in more detail in Chapter 8: 'Developing your practice team'.

Increasing urgency means removing sources of complacency or minimising their impact. This can be achieved by, for example, setting higher performance standards and an effective performance measurement system (how many clients treated per vet per day? Income generated per consultation), talking facts ('Sales of Hill's products increased by 10% since we started our new weight loss programme') rather than woolly 'happy talk' based on gut feelings ('I'm pretty sure we sell quite a lot of Hill's r/d diet'), and giving lots of external feedback ('This is what our clients are *really* saying about us'). It requires bold moves that shake up the practice team and create conflict and anxiety – at least at first. It is

Figure 1.4   Why change does not happen.

only by getting people to move out of their comfort zones that change can begin to happen.

In a large hospital I managed that was on the brink of bankruptcy at the time I took over, creating urgency required actions such as opening up the financial records to the staff and explaining what the negative figures meant for the future of the hospital; showing, with figures, how few client visits actually took place compared to how many we needed each day (hereby providing clear evidence to counteract the common objection of 'But we are so busy ... .'); explaining that an old policy of not employing more veterinarians 'to save costs' had the effect of slowly strangling the organisation; and demonstrating how ineffective paper management systems wasted time and energy.

However, although creating a sense of urgency is required to shift people out of complacency, it is very important they do not become scared. Being afraid causes people to react unpredictably and, for example, to suddenly resign, or to freeze and become paralysed in their actions. This is why it is so important to show people facts and figures rather than rely on emotion and feelings. It is also important to bombard people with information on future opportunities, on the wonderful rewards for capitalising on these opportunities, and on the organisation's current inability to pursue those opportunities.

2. Create the guiding coalition

Creating change is not about achieving one man's vision, but about creating what is best for the practice and its future. Major change is difficult to accomplish, so a powerful force is required to sustain the process. Even in a small practice, the practice leader alone is not enough to make change happen. It is important to build a strong guiding team consisting of the right people who share a high level of trust, and a common objective.

Characteristics of the team members include:

- Leadership skills: those practice members who are the natural leaders whom other staff members respect and follow.
- Position power: include those who have key roles within the practice so that they cannot subversively block progress.
- Expertise: those who can represent the various points of view in terms of role within the practice, work experience, and discipline so that informed, intelligent decisions can be made.
- Credibility: those who have the most credibility so that any decisions made will be taken seriously.

In the hospital, which had a staff of 85 people, we identified a team includ-ing the practice principal, and vice-principal, the financial manager, the staff manager, and a nurse representative from each division of the hospital. In a small practice, the practice principal, manager, a veterinarian and the head nurse may be sufficient.

People to avoid are those with large egos who dominate others, and those who create enough mistrust to kill teamwork. Trust is an essen-tial component of teamwork: without it, little will be achieved.

3.   Develop a vision and strategy

Change in organisations is not achieved by authoritarian decree, nor by micromanagement, but by creating a sensible vision of the future that inspires and excites people to go into action (see Chapter 2 for a more detailed description of how to create and use your practice vision).

In a change process a good vision serves three important functions:

1. It clarifies the general direction for change, in effect saying 'We need to be south of here in a few years instead of where we are today', thus simplifying hundreds of smaller decisions.
2. It motivates people to take action in the right direction even if the first steps are uncomfortable.
3. It helps coordinate the actions of different people in a remarkably fast and efficient way.

A good vision acknowledges that sacrifices will be necessary but makes clear that these sacrifices will yield particular benefits and per-sonal satisfactions that are far superior to those available today – or tomorrow – without attempting to change. The sort of sacrifices we are talking about include the discomfort of change, for example intro-ducing computerisation into a practice currently on a paper record system. The vision is used to create strategies, plans and budgets (Table 1.3).

*Who creates the practice vision? **All** the staff should contribute to the cre-ation process. Not only does this increase understanding of the role, function and value of the vision it also gives increased ownership and therefore com-mitment to the final vision.*

4.   Communicate the change vision

For the vision to work it must be alive for *everyone* in the practice, not just a select few. This means it needs to be constantly reinforced through talk-ing about it, applying it on a daily basis, and actively using it to guide

Table 1.3 **Relationship of vision, strategies, plans and budgets**

Leadership creates	Vision	A sensible and appealing picture of the future
	Strategies	A logic for how the vision can be achieved
Management creates	Plans	Specific steps and timetables to implement the strategies
	Budgets	Plans converted into financial projections and goals

decisions in the practice. It also needs to be simple so that it can be easily communicated. The most effective method of all is to 'walk the talk and lead by example'. Nothing undermines the communication of a change vision more than behaviour of the key players that is inconsistent with the vision.

We prepared framed copies of the vision for the hospital which were hung at strategic points throughout the hospital including the staff meeting room and the reception area. The vision was mentioned at most staff meetings, and once a year was revisited and discussed in depth at the annual staff retreat.

5. Empower broad-based action

In many practices I have visited employees feel powerless – that they are not allowed to make necessary decisions that would improve how they perform their roles. Sadly, this is always a reflection of the leadership style which is typically controlling and disempowering.

Empowering people means trusting them to make the right decisions at the right times. This may involve additional training to ensure confidence and competence, but ultimately results in a far more productive and happy organisation.

There are four major barriers to empowerment:

1. Weak leadership: bosses who discourage actions aimed at implementing the new vision by needing to control everything.
2. Formal structures that make it difficult to act such as 'All decisions must have the agreement of the practice principal', or salary systems that reward doing more of the same rather than innovation.
3. Personnel and information systems that are outdated and inefficient such as complex patient admission systems that waste time for clients, or poor financial management systems that make it difficult to monitor financial performance.

4. A lack of skills which undermines actions, typically associated with someone getting promotion to a role they are ill prepared to manage, or being asked to perform tasks for which they have no training.

Why do these blocks happen? Sometimes we are so accustomed to 'the way we do things around here' that we are blind to alternatives. Sometimes we are afraid that the changes will be so great that we no longer have a place in the practice. Almost always, it is because we are not convinced that change is really necessary.

Three of the many blocks we identified in the hospital were:

- *'The way we do things around here' which reflected nearly 20 years of dominant paternal-style leadership where the only decisions that could be made were by the practice principal.*
- *Inefficient financial recording and monitoring systems meaning that economic reports were not only generated too late to be helpful but also contained information that was downright wrong.*
- *Work rotas for the veterinarians that caused increasing levels of stress and exhaustion.*

In other practices in which I have consulted that have been built up from scratch as a family business, a common strength which becomes a block is the 'every client is welcome *now*' attitude. This works well when you are building up the practice and want as many clients in as possible to establish and build the client base, but can become a tremendous source of stress at a later stage in the practice's life where quality of service to pre-booked clients and thorough investigation of cases is compromised by having to squeeze in non-acute, drop-in patients.

6.   Generate short-term wins

Major change takes time, sometimes lots of time. An important part of driving a change process is to ensure that people really see that change for the better – and in line with the vision – is happening. Generating and celebrating short-term wins reinforces the value of the change process.

For example, one of the wins we constantly shared was the economic performance of the hospital. The challenge was to turn a history of increasingly negative results into a win by the end of the first year and this was achieved through several different actions including rewriting and creating a realistic budget, better monitoring of income and costs, and sharing financial information with all the staff. Through sharing the budget plans and the monthly reports, staff members began to understand how their individual contribution – such as charging correctly and reducing wastage – made a difference to the whole hospital's economy. They could understand why some months lived up to budget and others didn't, their role in the results, and what steps leadership were taking to remedy deficits. This contrasted favourably with living with a vague but energy-sapping worry about whether or not the hospital was 'doing alright'. We celebrated with treats at tea time, and, as thanks for their contribution, bought presents for the staff (partly sponsored by supplier companies) such as outdoor clothing marked with the practice logo.

Short-term wins serve a number of important functions:

- They provide evidence that the sacrifices and discomfort people are experiencing are worth it.
- They boost morale – everyone responds to a pat on the back.
- They help fine-tune vision and strategies by giving feedback.
- They undermine the cynics and show that change really can happen – despite their interference.
- They build momentum as the sceptics and reluctant supporters get swept up in the momentum.
- They help build a feeling of team – that we are achieving this together.

7.   Consolidate gains and produce more change

Major change takes time – often years – and it is important not to get complacent too early on. Short-term wins, although valuable, are just that – short-term wins. If the change effort does not continue beyond and above these wins and complacency starts to creep back in, then the old ways of doing things will also creep back in and very little forward progress will have been made.

Changing people's habits and behaviours is not easy. In a business like a veterinary practice, employees' behaviour is held in place by bosses, previous experiences, personal habits, peer relationships, cultures and, perhaps most important of all, all the demands that are being made on that person from this employer, that colleague, or the other client.

What becomes clear over time is that you'll end up making more changes than you ever imagined at first. For example, the hospital went from circular and non-ending discussions about moving to a new location and building from scratch (discussions which had been going on for 20 years as the current building had slowly disintegrated) to an active decision to rebuild and refurbish the existing location. This not only represented a more sensible and practical investment in the hospital's physical future, it also gave the staff a much-needed boost of confidence that the change effort really was going to mean radical change and improvement.

8.   Anchor the new culture

A new culture cannot be linked only to one or two individuals at the top who, when they move on, inadvertently cause the collapse of the organisation. Unfortunately, this is relatively common in veterinary practice – that the business is built up around one or two key individuals whose departure causes the collapse of the practice.

Culture refers to the norms and shared values among a group of people. *Behavioural norms* are common or pervasive ways of acting that are found in a group and that persist because group members tend to behave in ways that teach those practices to new members, rewarding those who fit in and sanctioning those who do not. *Shared values* are important concerns and goals shared by most of the people in a group that tend to shape group behaviour and that often persist over time even when group membership changes.

Culture is the last thing to change in an organisation, not the first. It is not something that can be easily manipulated. Cultural changes only occur after you have successfully altered people's actions, after the new behaviour produces a group benefit for a period of time, and after people see the connection between the new actions and the performance improvement. Thus most cultural change does not occur until stage 8.

To achieve cultural change requires time, a lot of talk to reinforce the benefits of change, often a turnover of staff to replace key people, and consistently achieving desired results. In addition, to really achieve cultural change requires planning for the eventual replacement of the practice leaders: retaining someone from 'the old way' could lead the practice back into the old culture with all its problems and limitations.

The culture of successful practice in today's world needs to be:

- externally oriented – looking to the patient and client for the way forward
- empowering so that the people in your practice know they are making a difference
- quick to make decisions and not bogged down in 'the way we do it around here' or personal whims of the practice leaders
- open and candid so that everyone in the practice not only knows what they are contributing but also the effect their contribution makes on the success of the practice

■ more risk tolerant, rewarding innovation and tries rather than fearing mistakes.

Some final thoughts

Change is constant. Failure to manage change is common and the results are predictable: every year hundreds of businesses do not deliver promised results and are forced to close down. Even the market giants are not invulnerable to the effects of ignoring change. In the early 1990s, the Swedish airline company SAS found a winning formula of customer service that shot it to success and made it a model of excellence for service businesses the world over. Around the same period, Ericsson led the field internationally in mobile telephone technology excellence. Both companies coasted for nearly a decade on the complacency that global success brought. Around the turn of the century, both were brought to their knees by competitors through their refusal to see and respond to changes that had happened in their markets – demands for cheap, self-managed flights, and for colourful telephones that doubled as camera, accessory, and toy – and both are still struggling to reinstate themselves in markets which have nearly swept on by.

Is your practice a responsive practice?

2 Creating a successful business

Business enterprises are organs of society. They do not exist for their own sake, but to fulfil a specific social purpose and to satisfy a specific need of society, a community or individuals. They are not ends in themselves but a means. The right question to ask in respect to them is not, What are they? But, What are they supposed to be doing and what are their tasks?

Peter Drucker, 2001

A business is an organised approach to a specific market. A business is built on core values and has a core purpose. A successful business is one that has flexible strategies that change and adapt to the changing needs of its market without compromising the core principles.

The business of veterinary practice is serving animal owners through commitment to the health and welfare of their animals. The market for veterinary practice is animal owners and, as with all markets, their needs are constantly altering. The responsive practice is able to continually and enthusiastically metamorphose to serve these changing needs.

I have visited many hundreds of veterinary practices. Most are comfortably successful. Some are stagnating. Some are dying. Only a few are outstanding. These latter are the truly responsive practices. There are a number of features that characterise these responsive practices:

- *Productivity through people.* These practices recognise that their most valuable asset is their people and everyone in the practice is empowered to perform to the best of their ability. *For example, a companion hospital in southern Sweden gives complete freedom to their senior veterinary nurse to run client education evenings, puppy parties, and breeder group meetings as well as serving as a nutritional adviser to clients. Not only does*

Figure 2.1
Hydrotherapy and rehabilitation are important therapies offered by an increasing number of practices.

she create enormous good will with clients in the area around the hospital and encourages their loyalty, she also generates sales of pet foods that are paralleled nowhere else in the country.

- *Acute awareness of the needs and requirements of clients.* Practices use techniques such as active listening and client questionnaires to keep in close touch with the needs of their clients. *A practice I visited in Australia employed a staff member to phone every single client visiting the practice the day after their visit to ask them about their experience. 'Doing this keeps us in close contact with our clients' needs and wants, and enables us to provide the best possible service', explained the practice principal.*

- *Action rather than reaction.* These practices actively seek business opportunities and work enthusiastically and hard to develop them. *Improving patient recovery after surgery by offering hydrotherapy rehabilitation is increasingly popular in Sweden. Many practices now offer underwater treadmills, massage, physiotherapy and even the possibility of supervised pool swimming as part of their recovery package* (Fig. 2.1).

- *An independent attitude coupled with a willingness to be creative and imaginative* expressed as an entrepreneurial and novel approach to practice development. These practices are not limited by conventions and 'the way we've always done it' but are willing to try new ideas and find a new style they confidently make their own. *Many practices are exploring 'alternative therapies' such as acupuncture for pain relief, homeopathy, and herbal medicine as a complement to the traditional medical approach.*

- *Simultaneously flexible and adaptable.* Top practices plan carefully for the future, but as the plans are not written in tablets of stone they can be quickly adapted, modified or even discarded to suit new market

Figure 2.2 A small but attractive 'angel pet' of the appropriate breed is sent to grieving clients with a handwritten card from all the staff in the Safari Animal Care Center, Texas, USA.

forces. *A practice I visited in Oslo seized the opportunity recently to not only expand their practice but also develop a unique and much needed feline only clinic when an upper floor became available in the building in which their conventional companion animal practice was housed.*

- *An applied approach motivated by strong values.* These practices have clearly identified the values that drive them including professional and personal integrity, honesty and a commitment to improve the health of animals in their care. *The Safari Animal Care Center in Texas is committed to excellence in client service and has a truly outstanding approach to staff education. Every Wednesday morning they shut the clinic for 2 hours for training of all staff in client issues including how to behave towards clients, and technical knowledge about procedures and products to be able to inform and explain these confidently and clearly to clients* (Fig. 2.2).
- *Stick with the business they know.* Top practices establish expertise and stick to it. They don't spread themselves thinly over a wide range of peripheral services but focus on what they can do – and find ways to deliver it even better. *This is most clearly exemplified by veterinarians who develop specialist referral practices which are devoted to one or more clearly defined disciplines.*
- *Clear detailing of functions and sharing of responsibilities.* Staff in top practices have a simple hierarchical system, define roles and functions clearly, and encourage sharing and responsibility at all levels.

Chronic problems that apply to veterinary practices

So, why aren't more practices more successful? I believe it is a combination of issues which includes lack of interest in and knowledge about the complexity of business management, difficulties putting a monetary value on one's own skills and experience, and lack of leadership and management skills (summarised in Table 2.1). Business management is as much a specialist skill as training as a veterinarian, yet many vets assume they can 'do it' anyway. The thought processes and behaviours necessary for successful leadership and management in a business differ from those of the problem-solving scientist. Too many veterinarians try to run their own practices without a truly clear idea of where they want to go with their practice – an amateur approach producing predictably amateur results.

As students, veterinarians are trained in an environment where it is difficult to establish a self-value, they are not taught business, leadership and communication skills, and seldom have the chance to see good business principles in action. This results in new graduates who have difficulty in setting a value on themselves and their services, find it difficult to charge for their knowledge and time in emotionally loaded clinical situations, and do not understand the importance of business planning. Assistants are not paid salaries according to their real worth: their salary does not usually reflect the income they generate, nor do they receive profit-related bonuses. This makes it

---

Table 2.1   **Summary of poor management issues that affect practice productivity**

■ Lack of vision and purpose

■ Over-dependence on specific individuals – often the practice principal(s)

■ Poor leadership

■ Low trust between the leader and staff

■ Lack of integrity with failure to deliver on promises

■ Failure to establish and/or communicate the practice's goals both within the practice and to the clients

■ Lack of financial planning and review

■ Lack of management systems

■ Poor market segmentation and/or strategy

■ Increasing competition and a lack of market knowledge

■ Inadequate capitalisation

■ No standardised quality programme

■ Concentration on the technical rather than the strategic work in hand

difficult to charge properly as they cannot relate charging with income (and, ultimately, salary) generated. Financial information about the practice is typically not shared with its members, which means that staff do not appreciate their individual role in creating practice success. Practice principals are often technically very competent but are not very effective business leaders; so, much business in practice is inefficient and run by crisis management. Veterinarians are traditionally taught to work reactively rather than proactively – that is, wait for clients to come to them rather than seeking to generate work. This works well in a market where there is a surplus of clients to veterinarians, but is doomed to failure where the opposite applies. Finally, veterinarians are only just beginning to accept that they should regard their practices as real business concerns; so, practices lack vision, strategies, goals and budgets.

The outcome of all this is that most veterinary practices seldom fulfil more than a fraction of their business potential. How can these problems and attitudes be overcome to create the responsive practice?

The first step is to take a long hard look at where you are now by doing a thorough auditing of the practice. Performing a SWOT analysis with your staff will help identify the internal Strengths and Weaknesses of your practice, information which can then be used to guide decisions about managing and exploiting the external Opportunities and Threats (Fig. 2.3). Sometimes a strength may also be a weakness – for example, providing a 24-hour service may be very attractive to the market, but prove difficult to operate economically. A good SWOT analysis enables you to identify priority areas for practice development.

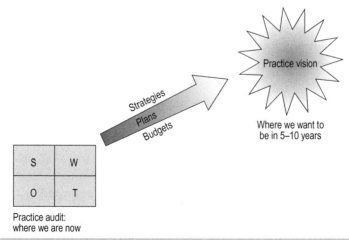

Practice vision

Where we want to be in 5–10 years

Strategies
Plans
Budgets

| S | W |
| O | T |

Practice audit:
where we are now

Figure 2.3 How a practice vision can be used to develop a practice.

What really works

A recent study published in the *Harvard Business Review* of what made 160 top American companies outperform their peers over a prolonged period showed that a strong grip of business basics was essential (Nohria *et al.*, 2003).

The four key management practices at which these companies excelled were identified as:

1. strategy: devise and maintain a clearly stated, focused strategy
2. execution: deliver services and products that consistently meet customers' expectations
3. culture: develop and maintain a performance-oriented culture
4. structure: maintain a structure that makes your organisation easy to work in and with.

In addition, excellence in business management is supplemented with mastery in any two of four secondary management practices:

- talent: retain talented employees and develop more
- innovation: make industry-transforming innovations
- leadership: develop leaders who are committed to the business and its people
- mergers and partnerships: seek growth through mergers and partnerships.

Although this study was looking at multimillion dollar corporates, the principles of good business management apply even to veterinary practices. Let's look at how.

Creating your practice vision and devising a clearly focused, stated strategy

> *Companies that enjoy enduring success have core values and a core purpose that remain fixed while their business strategies and practices endlessly adapt to a changing world.*
>
> Collins and Porras, 1996

A vision is a vivid and inspiring description of a business's future which is achieved through strategic planning (see Table 1.3 for the relationship of vision to strategy). The principle underlying strategic planning is to develop a set of actions that will make the practice's services *more valuable to clients* than the services of competing practices.

I have helped many practices define their vision and create their vision statement. There are a number of important rules to be followed in the process.

1. Involve everyone. A vision is a *shared* picture of the future so everyone in the practice should contribute to its definition, not just the practice principal or owner. Involving everyone also increases ownership of and commitment to the vision and the future it represents.
2. Take time to create the vision. An effective vision requires deep, introspective thought as well as creativity. Although a rough draft can be created in the space of a day, the true vision statement may take months to refine and clarify. As the vision will guide all the actions subsequently taken in the practice it is important to allow time for this process.
3. Keep it clear and simple. Effective visions are always focused enough to guide employees – to convey which actions are important and which are out of bounds. However, a vague statement such as 'To be the best veterinary hospital' is not motivating (to be the best at what?), and a hopelessly vague listing of positive values ('We stand for quality care and service, optimal client service …') is similarly off-putting.
4. Do not include financial measurements in the vision. Financial success is a strategy, but generally not a long-term motivator for the people working in the practice.
5. Write it down. A vision that vaguely exists in the principal's head is not going to inspire anyone (except, perhaps, the principal – when he remembers it!). To be effective the vision needs to be written down and displayed at strategic points within the practice to remind people about it all the time.

How do you create an effective vision? A model I particularly like, adapted from business management consultants Collins and Porras, defines a vision as having two components:

- core ideology
- envisioned future consisting of the BHAG (pronounced 'bee-hag').

Features of an effective vision

A vision should strive to be:

- *Feasible.* It would not be possible to combine, say, providing top quality service with rapid client throughput.
- *Imaginable.* Conveys an inspiring picture of what the future will look like.
- *Focused.* Is clear enough to provide guidance in decision-making.
- *Motivating.* People take pride in working for organisations that are unique or different. Imagine working for a practice that said about itself, 'We are just like every other practice'!
- *Distinctive.* A common fallacy among practices is that they are automatically distinctive because of the high quality of their medical and surgical care. Virtually all mission statements claim to deliver the 'highest quality' of care, but this is clearly not true and it also doesn't differentiate the practice from all the others that claim exactly the same.
- *Memorable.* The mission statement cannot be too long or complicated.
- *Communicable.* Is easy to communicate and can be successfully explained within the space of a few minutes.

Core ideology

Core ideology defines the enduring character of an organisation – a consistent character that transcends changes in market forces, technological breakthroughs, management fads and individual leaders. Core ideology provides the glue that holds the practice together over time. It consists of two distinct parts: core values, a system of guiding principles and tenets, and core purpose, the practice's reason for existence.

There are several good reasons for identifying the practice's core ideology. For example, it *guides and inspires* although not necessarily differentiates an organisation. Two practices may have the same core values and purpose but can express them, more or less successfully, in very different ways. It is *meaningful and inspirational* to people working in the practice, and also plays a role in *who* is in the practice. Attracting and retaining people who share the core ideology, although they may not all think or look the same, strengthens a business. Once the core ideology is identified anything that is not part of it can be changed. This creates a high level of integrity within the organisation.

Table 2.2 **The company's reason for being**
3M: to solve unsolved problems innovatively
Hewlett-Packard: to make technical contributions for the advancement and welfare of humanity
Mary Kay cosmetics: to give unlimited opportunity to women
McKinsey and Company: to help leading corporations and governments to be more successful
Nike: to experience the emotion of competition, winning, and crushing competitors
Wal-Mart: to give ordinary folk the chance to buy the same things as rich people
Walt Disney: to make people happy

Adapted from Collins and Porras (1996).

Core values

Core values are a small set of timeless guiding principles, which have intrinsic value to those within the practice. They are the deeply and passionately held shared values that attract people to work and stay in a particular practice and that form the basis for the transition of a group to a team. Core values are the values by which you personally live, and that you teach your children. They include honesty, integrity, empathy, service, industry, humility, patience, respect, courage and justice.

There is no universally 'right' set of values within a practice, and the number of true core values does not exceed around five. If you identify more than five then there is confusion between core values (which do not change) with operating practices, business strategies (which are nice to have) and cultural norms (which should be open to change). A practice should not change its core values in response to market changes, rather it should change markets, if necessary, to remain true to its core values.

Core purpose

Core purpose, the second part of core ideology, is the practice's reason for being (Table 2.2). This is a combination of both people's idealistic motivations for doing the organisation's work and the more selfish reasons *why* people work in this way. Somewhere in here is the important but often unacknowledged aspect of enjoying your work and having fun in the process.

To identify the practice's core purpose, ask all the practice members the following searching questions (here expressed with generic answers – clearly you need to put these into your own words):

> **What business are we in?**
> *Veterinary practice is in the animal healthcare business.*
>
> **Who is our customer?**
> *People and their animals.*
>
> **Why do we work in this business?**
> *Because we love it/enjoy it/think it is fun/get a kick out of it ...*
>
> **What business are we really in? (What needs in society are we fulfilling?)**
> *Clients come to veterinary practices to obtain **peace of mind** and **relief from worry** about their animals and they seek **self-esteem** through feeling that they are doing the right thing for their pet.*
> *We enjoy what we are doing but need to make a living from it, so how can we express client needs in business terms?*
> *Clients expect to pay a reasonable price for the peace of mind they buy; the practice needs to make money from the sale of veterinary services and products to provide us with the incomes and work – life quality we need, and to maintain and develop the business.*
> So, the reason for a veterinary practice's existence can be expressed as:
>
> > *Veterinary practice is in the business of providing animal healthcare services to the benefit of the animals in our charge and their owners (our clients), and generating a fair profit from the transaction that enables creation of a good working environment with a satisfactory reward system for its employees.*

Identifying and articulating core ideology is just a starting point. The second part of the practice vision is the type of progress you want to stimulate.

Envisioned future

The envisioned future is a challenging and audacious goal with a 5–10-year timescale that stimulates practice development expressed as a vivid description of what it will be like to achieve that goal. By painting an exciting and challenging picture of the future, practice members are motivated and inspired to make the necessary commitment and take the necessary actions to achieve the goal.

In creating this part of the vision the following questions should be considered:

- *What business **should** we be in?* Answers should take into account factors such as the life-cycle stage of the practice, the commitment to quality client service, the role of preventive healthcare, the interests and experience of the practice members, and the financial objectives of the practice. It is the practice's *idealised* vision of itself.
- *What business **can** we be in?* By considering reality – the practice's *actual* existing resources, skills, people, expertise, and so on, the 'ideal' vision can be adapted to describe the true potential for development along chosen strategic lines.

These components are then expressed as a BHAG – a Big Hairy Audacious Goal. A true BHAG is clear and compelling, serves as a unifying focal point of effort, and acts as a catalyst for team spirit. It is not simply a 'We shall do better' type of goal but something that engages everyone: it reaches out and grabs them, and requires extraordinary effort to achieve.

A BHAG is expressed in vivid, engaging and specific terms. It is a clearly articulated and inspiring goal.

So how does a vision statement look? It might be something like this:

> At ABC Petcare clinic we care about your family. Our values are integrity, empathy, and service in all we do for you, our patients; you, our pet owners; and for each other. We exist to provide good care for pets who are ill or suffering, and advice for those that are well, helping the owners of these pets make the most appropriate decisions about their family member's care.
>
> Our BHAG is to become the unequivocal Number One choice for pet care for all pet-owning families with pets in the Lingby area by 2010.

Or like this:

> At PQR Animal Hospital we stand for cutting edge technology, and a commitment to excellence in everything we do in an environment in which we thrive. Our function is to provide optimal animal care and client service to the animals, animal owners, and referring veterinarians that we serve, at a fee which reflects this standard. Our BHAG is to become an outstanding 100% referral hospital sought after by animal owners and referring veterinarians from the whole area, and a highly desirable place of employment, by the year 2008.

Developing a practice business strategy

We cannot direct the wind but we can adjust the sails.

Anon

Developing a practice business strategy is a creative activity, not a purely analytical one. It is about finding new ways of doing things that help to achieve the vision in such a way that it provides an advantage over the competition. Successful examples I have encountered include excellence in client service, commitment to serving the pet as a family member, technological excellence, commitment to serving the needs of the modern dairy farmer, being the cheapest practice in town, or being the most desirable practice in which to work. Whatever is chosen will work if it is sharply defined, clearly communicated, and well understood by employees, clients and others connected with the practice. It should reflect the values expressed in the vision statement, which are then carried out with no compromise. Of course, fine-tuning may be necessary as changes occur in the marketplace.

For example, a very successful prize-winning practice I have visited in Australia made a commitment some years ago to become the Family Practice for the area. Everything they do strikingly reflects this commitment – from the design of the logo to the hiring and training of staff, from the open, friendly atmosphere in the reception and waiting area, to the community activities in which every practice member regularly participates.

However, a strategy may not pay dividends directly as it is affected by the current stage of development of the practice. It may take years to firmly anchor all the necessary procedures for achieving a strategy. Let's look at why this may be the case.

The practice life-cycle: where are you now?

Businesses are not static – they evolve with time. David Maister, in his excellent book *Managing the Professional Service Firm*, defined a practice life-cycle for professional service firms. He suggests that clients seek three key benefits when they visit such a firm: expertise (the specialist), experience (the 'grey hair' factor) or efficiency ('cheap and cheerful'). These are points along a continuous spectrum for a professional service firm; they progress from efficiency to experience to expertise. The concept of a practice life-cycle is a crude but useful model for how veterinary practice evolves. It is illustrated in Figure 2.4 with examples of the types of veterinary practice that are found at each of the different stages.

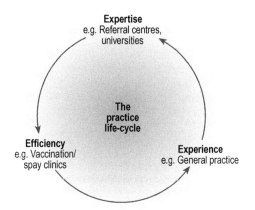

Figure 2.4 The practice life-cycle: examples of practices at different stages of the life-cycle.

The efficiency practice

Clients seeking the efficiency practice are looking for routine services such as vaccinations and spays at the lowest possible cost, with the minimum of palaver. They will phone around for the cheapest price.

The efficiency practice is characterised by having a high throughput of clients, low average transaction fees (the average fee generated per client), a limited range of basic services, and a high percentage of young and relatively inexperienced staff.

Examples of efficiency practices are spay and vaccination clinics.

The experience practice

Most clients with a sick animal would go to the experience practice where they will find a broad general knowledge of a wide variety of disease problems. These clients are neither looking for specialist skills nor, especially, to save money.

The range of services offered is much wider, the average transaction fee is higher and the throughput of clients is lower than the efficiency practice. Staff would range in skills and experience.

General practice typifies the experience practice.

The expert practice

Clients owning an exotic pet, or a valuable animal with a rare or complicated disease condition, would eventually seek specialist knowledge. They expect to pay considerably more for highly individualised, expert knowledge.

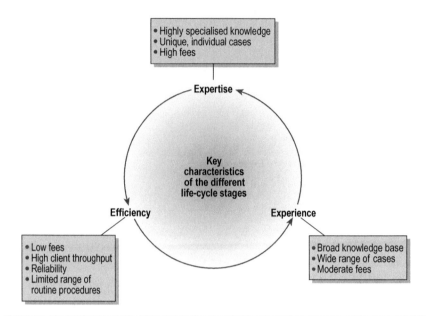

Figure 2.5   Key characteristics of the stages of the practice life-cycle.

These practices are characterised by having a low throughput of high-paying clients, and using only highly qualified staff. The specialist or referral practice exemplifies the expert practice.

Figure 2.5 summarises the key differences between each type, which are expressed in more detail in Table 2.3.

How they relate to each other

When a new practice opens it is often at the efficiency stage, offering a limited range of basic services at competitively low fees. As it becomes more established it increases its range of services (e.g. it can afford to buy an X-ray machine, laboratory equipment, computer, etc.), employs staff with a wider range of experience and skills, becomes more confident about charging for services, and develops into the experience practice. After a time, individuals within the practice identify a need for specialisation – they undertake extra training and the specialist or referral practice starts to emerge.

The time taken for the practice to evolve from efficiency to experience to expert depends on many factors, but is measured in years rather than months. Influencing factors include location of the practice, needs of the local market, personal and professional staff needs, and so on.

Table 2.3   **Important differences between the three life stages**

Feature	Efficiency	Experience	Expertise
What clients seek	■ Low cost	■ Broad knowledge	■ Specialist knowledge
	■ Speed	■ Good service	■ Highly personalised service
	■ Reliability		
Key characteristics	■ Low cost	■ Fair fees: cost related to time	■ High fees
	■ High client throughput	■ Broad range of services	■ Each case highly individual
	■ Narrow range routine procedures	■ Broad range of experience	■ Narrow range of very skilled procedures
	■ Low ratio vet to veterinary nurse		■ Highly skilled personnel
Type of work	■ Low risk	■ Broad range from routine to partially specialised	■ Highly specialised
	■ Routine		■ System/ discipline specific
Examples of practice type	■ Neutering and vaccination clinics	■ General practice	■ Referral practice
			■ Universities
			■ Species-specific clinics
Ratio of professional to support staff	■ Low. High use of trained support staff	■ Approx. 1:2. Mixture of experienced and inexperienced staff	■ Approx. 1:2 but highly trained, specialised
Ratio 'senior' to 'junior' professionals	■ Low: practice needs relatively	■ Mixture: practice wants a broad knowledge	■ High: practice needs

(*Continued*)

Table 2.3 (*Continued*)

Feature	Efficiency	Experience	Expertise
	simple skills and little experience	base	highly qualified 'seniors'
Personnel training	■ Minimal for basic needs of practice	■ Well structured and organised to disseminate information throughout practice	■ Minimal (staff already high calibre), but very specialised
Fee-setting and profitability	■ Fees low	■ Fees fair	■ Fees high, individual
	■ Often fixed fee procedures	■ Profit from fee relative to time	■ Profit per case
	■ Dependent on high client throughput		
Client throughput	■ High	■ Moderate	■ Low
	■ Short appointments or 'open surgery'	■ 10-minute appointments	■ Appoint-ment only
		■ Little 'open surgery'	
Aims of management	■ Growth of business through efficiency of the individual	■ Interdependency of practice departments to share knowledge	■ Promote quality and standards
		■ Professional and career development encouraged	
Styles of management	■ Tight, controlled	■ General small business management	■ Peer group consensus
	■ Emphasis on efficiency	■ Focus on coordination within practice	■ Leader who symbolises high standards

(*Continued*)

Table 2.3   (*Continued*)

Feature	Efficiency	Experience	Expertise
Goals and growth	■ Rapid expansion by specific targeting	■ Steady client base founded on sound trust relationship	■ Growth not a major goal
		■ Long-term commitment to improving animal health	■ New knowledge
		■ Providing quality client service	■ Frontier science
Marketing style	■ Heavy advertising of selected services	■ Mixture: newsletters, reminders, client meetings. Based on developing trust relation	■ Aimed at colleagues to promote perception as experts, e.g. publications, books, lectures
	■ Target mailing		
Type of location	■ Multiple centres	■ May have branches with different characteristics	■ One centre
	■ Franchises		
	■ Individual profit centres		
Professional salary	■ Salary scale dependent on efficiency	■ Fixed	■ Profit-sharing bonus system

The reason that this evolution is called a life-cycle is that many of yesterday's innovative and pioneering techniques (specialist skills) eventually become tomorrow's relatively routine procedures (e.g. bitch spays, cruciate ligament repairs, aural canal ablations, cancer therapies, etc.). The link between these two, though, has the longest time span.

Why is the practice life-cycle concept important?

Few practices have a clear picture of their true positioning along the spectrum, which is a major reason for failure of many strategic planning and practice marketing efforts within veterinary practices. Most practices try and provide all three types of service – efficiency, experience and specialist – to satisfy all their possible clients. This is partly a traditional attitude ('We must offer care to everyone') and partly muddled marketing. But each category has different aims, different managerial styles and requires different practice structuring (see Table 2.3). It is as much a strategy to decide to not develop beyond the efficiency practice stage as it is to decide to become the best orthopaedic hospital in town. A practice attempting to serve too diverse a set of client needs can end up serving none of them very well, which results in dissatisfied clients, poorer standards of treatment for their animals, and frustration within the practice.

The practice has the choice to go with the life-cycle, adapting and changing practice strategies as it goes, or to prevent the progression by specific actions to achieve stability.

Another option is to juggle the conflicting managerial, economic and behavioural requirements of different practice areas to combine all the different life-cycle stages. This is difficult and can only be achieved through creating artificial divisions in the practice that enable each section or branch to have its own managerial and marketing style appropriate to the marketplace it serves. Divisions in turn can create practical difficulties; for example, can the same vets that are the specialists maintain that expertise *and* take their turn in the duty roster for the broad experience branch of the practice? Or how can the practice weigh the demand for low-cost vaccinations against providing high-quality facilities and equipment for the specialist side of the practice?

In reality, this model of life-cycle stages is over-simplistic and has to be balanced by practical considerations. The average practice in Britain comprises four veterinary surgeons and 10 support staff, and it would be very difficult to divide the practice into its expert, efficient and experienced sections. On the other hand, the concept of the practice life-cycle can help clarify at what stage of evolution or development your practice is now and what you need to do next to achieve the practice vision.

Strategies, objectives and planning

Without a clear vision of where you are going and without specific behaviours to measure, it is almost impossible to achieve any goal. Goal-setting, strategies, objectives and action plans are an on-going, ever-changing part of this process, and

FINANCIAL PLAN

- Income
- Overheads
- Stock turnover
- Fee-setting

- Case volume
- Financial trends
- Economic climate

- Hiring staff
- Training and CE
- Salaries

- Advertising
- Improvement of building and of facilities

MISSION

- Management style
- People resources
- Level of expertise and skill
- Ratio professional : support staff
- Career opportunities

- Practice life-cycle stages
- Practice image (to staff)
- Staff training

- Local competition
- Local population
- Client needs
- Practice image (to clients)
- Client service

PEOPLE PLAN   **MARKETING PLAN**

Figure 2.6 Planning for success: some of the factors to be considered in developing the practice's plans.

one that will be a way of life for successful enterprises from now on.

Cannie and Caplin, Learning Dynamics, Inc., 1991

Strategies are the broad sweeps of the brush that describe how a practice will achieve its vision. Objectives express these abstractions as specific operational actions, which can be further broken down into specific targets and plans. Planning puts structure and systems to the current ideas you have in the practice and gives you control over your and the practice's destiny. There are three major, overlapping areas that require planning in practice (see Fig. 2.6 for some of the factors that need to be considered):

- financial
- people
- marketing.

Establishing objectives

Objectives are needed in all areas in which the practice's survival depends for, say, the next 3 months, 6 months, year and long-term. They are consistent with but separate from the vision statement. These objectives will, by necessity, vary from year to year, and will not all be compatible with each other at the same time. It is also not practical or wise to pursue all the objectives at once – it is better to grade them and work systematically through them. Too often practices attempt too much – and fail. The result is disillusionment and an unwillingness to try again – ever.

For example, an objective for the year might be to increase practice income by 10%. This could be achieved by:

- *increasing the income per client; or*
- *increasing the number of clients; or*
- *reducing the overheads; or*
- *a combination of all three.*

*Shorter-term objectives can then be defined within this annual objective that take into consideration these three techniques, but remember it might not be feasible to, for example, increase practice income by simultaneously increasing the average transaction fee **and** increasing client throughput, or reduce overheads **and** increase the number of clients.*

Goal formulation

Goals are objectives made into a definite plan. Of course, not all objectives will get to this stage. Goals can be expressed as SMART objectives, that is:

- **S**pecific: what exactly is this goal?
- **M**easurable: Have you achieved it? How can you measure your success?
- **A**ction-orientated: who will do it, when and how?
- **R**ealistic: can it be achieved in the given time with the given facilities?
- **T**ime-limited: when should it be completed or assessed?

I would add an extra 'R' for Responsibility: who is responsible for ensuring the plan is carried through and the results analysed afterwards?

Thus, in a practice committed to excellence in client service, objectives might be:

- To improve the telephone service (3 months).
- To increase the number of parking spaces available (3 months).
- To develop a retail pet healthcare product outlet in the practice (6 months).
- To develop a range of preventive pet healthcare programmes (2 years).
- To enhance the role of the nurse to increase the value of interaction with clients (6 months).

From these, a couple of SMART goals that the practice could start immediate work on could be:

- To improve the quality of the telephone service by reducing the time taken to answer the phone and the time spent on 'hold' by training reception staff in telephone skills (using an external expert), and employing part-time staff at peak periods so that the phone is answered within three rings, and the client not kept on hold longer than 1 minute. The effect of this will be measured in 3 months by direct observation of telephone staff, and through client questionnaires.

- To establish a vaccination programme that will achieve a 95% vaccination rate, measured at the end of 1 year, through use of increased client education, booster reminders, telephone contact and computerised client lists. This will primarily be the role of trained veterinary nurses.

Summary

Veterinary practice is in the business of serving animal owners through commitment to the health and welfare of their animals. The responsive, and therefore successful, practice constantly adapts to suit the changing needs of its market – animal owners and their animals. Creating a successful veterinary practice does not happen by chance but through careful planning.

Planning gives direction and control. Planning takes time: there is no 'quick fix' solution to running an effective business. To plan effectively requires a clear vision. The vision contains the core ideology of the practice and a vivid, exciting description of the future. From the vision the practice works out strategies to achieve the vision which are further broken down into objectives and action plans for the development of the three major practice areas – finance, marketing and people. Planning includes identifying which stage of the practice life-cycle the practice is in – expertise, efficiency or experience – and acting accordingly.

3 Managing the economics of your veterinary clinic

So now you own a veterinary clinic which is running really well. Your staff are top-of-the-line, your facilities are impressive and the clients are pouring in. Life is great! But what about managing the economics of the clinic? Is that really so important? I mean everything works well, and that must surely be the most important thing? Well, if you currently have this attitude, I suggest that you read this chapter thoroughly. Doing so might encourage you to change your view on the value of economic management in your clinic. I also ask you to carefully consider this question: What is the ultimate purpose with the business in your clinic?

The basic function of this chapter is to help you improve your skills in using economics as a tool for managing your clinic. To achieve this, I will take you through the most important areas in economic management – with a strong practical focus.

I am assuming that you are already familiar with the basic concepts of economics. This enables me to focus on the practical aspects of economic management – the issues that will really have an impact on the profitability of your practice. This means you will find very little on, for example, accounting, on annual financial statements and on taxes. However, if you feel that you would benefit from an update on economic concepts, I have included some brief notes in the appendix at the end of this chapter.

In the first section I present the most important factors that influence the economics of your clinic – e.g. its profitability. Focus on these factors and the profitability of your firm will improve significantly.

The second section, on managing the clinic, deals with the more practical processes of planning the business through the budget and what it is important to consider when you are comparing budget and actual. I also include a short note on the importance of being aware of the difference between result and liquidity. Thereafter you will be introduced to the value of key figures for managing the economy. Finally, I urge you to be generous with information to your staff.

Remember I asked you to consider the question: What is the ultimate purpose with the business in your clinic? From an economic point of view the primary purpose of your business is to generate as much profit as possible – and it is important to include your staff in this view. After all, it is their actions and contributions that make the difference to the profit of the practice. This also creates a purpose and context for them to work in the clinic over and above helping clients and their animals.

The third section, 'Business systems', looks at the importance of accounting and of business software systems in managing operations.

 Factors influencing the economics of a veterinary clinic

There are many factors influencing the economic performance of a veterinary clinic. There are, however, some that are more influential than others. These are:

- client visits
- selling medicine, food and health items
- personnel costs
- investment in buildings and equipment.

 Client visits

Without clients your business would not exist. Your clinic's source of income is what the clients are spending on services and products supplied by your clinic. So it is clear that you should always strive to attract as many client visits as possible and encourage clients to buy as much as possible on each visit. How to attract clients and make them buy as much as possible on each visit is discussed elsewhere in this book.

When your appointments list is fully booked with client visits every-thing is fine and profits are hopefully good. But what happens when a client that has been scheduled cannot be served? This happens either when the client does not show up on time, or when the vet assigned to the appointment is sick and no replacement can be found. What is the effect on the clinic's financial result when either of these two things happens?

You might assume it would not make much of a difference as there are no extra costs for the clinic. Well, let us take a closer look at this.

Let's assume that the price and thus the revenue for the visit is €50; then the clinic has lost an income of €50. How much of the cost for pro-ducing the service is variable? Assuming that all direct cost was perman-ently employed personnel – *all* cost was fixed. The implication of this is that a missed scheduled client visit has a negative impact on your result amounting to €50 – which, multiplied by a factor of a number of missed/cancelled appointments, is huge! (If you are uncertain about the concept of variable and fixed costs, see section 4 of the appendix.)

The above example is a simplification of reality, but a practical sim-plification. I have chosen to disregard the effect of missing out on sales of materials and medicine in the above example. The reason being that when you miss out on these kinds of items the actual loss is limited to the profit margin on these items. Since such items normally represent 10–20% of the total sale, the actual loss will amount to 1–2% of the total sale, which is negligible in the above context.

So, an unfulfilled client visit always represents a considerable nega-tive impact on the revenue. The loss mainly emanates from staff costs. You will, however, also incur a loss for the missed sale of food and medicine. The loss is limited to the profit margin for these items – but that is still a loss! There are two exceptions when there will not be a loss associated with an unfulfilled client visit:

- The vet and staff assigned for the cancelled visit can be reassigned to other revenue-generating activities.
- The client visit can be rescheduled to a free time.

You might argue that missing out on a client visit is not so serious, you might argue that it is fairly easy to reschedule the client, you might argue that the vet and staff can be reassigned to other revenue-generating activities … however, the reality is that a cancelled client visit will virtually always have a direct and considerable negative impact on the result of your business.

The point is that one of the most effective ways of maintaining the profitability at a high level is to make sure that booked client visits are not cancelled, and that the booking list is as full as possible.

Since there are two basic reasons for cancelling client visits let us take a closer look at how it might be possible to handle these.

The client cancels the visit

It is inevitable that some clients will choose to cancel a planned visit. There is nothing much you can do about that. What you can do is to reduce the number of cancelled visits by implementing financial consequences for late cancellations.

A client might cancel a planned visit for the following reasons:

- He forgot the appointment.
- He decided that the appointment was not necessary.
- He had a compelling personal reason for cancelling the visit.

To help avoid clients forgetting appointments, consider sending an automatically generated e-mail or text message to the client's mobile phone the day before the visit. This method has become popular with dentists and opticians, for example.

A client deciding an appointment is not necessary may reflect a need for better client education: is the client really the best person to decide if their animal needs, for example, a follow-up visit or not?

The most effective way to handle all three cases is to implement financial consequences for the client. For example, the cost of follow-up visits can be 'baked into' the initial examination costs, or a booked client visit that the client cancels less than 24 hours before the visit will be debited to the client. These consequences will act as a deterrent to cancellations whilst simultaneously reducing the negative impact on your clinic's economic result.

The clinic has a shortage of staff

If for some reason a vet is ill and therefore you have to reschedule or cancel a number of client visits, it should now be clear that this will have a considerable negative impact on the result of your clinic (since this then normally means a number of lost client visits). What resources have you got that could help avoid this?

When a vet reports sick, your first thought should not be to reschedule the booked visits, but to find out how you can replace the missing vet. Remember that for each rescheduling of a client visit you increase the risk of the client not turning up. The most effective way is therefore to have back-ups available; the second most effective way is to ask other staff currently not working if they can work this particular day/days.

There is, of course, a cost associated with replacing the ordinary vet, both in terms of the extra cost of paying for the substitute and the annoyance factor for the client expecting to meet their regular vet. This cost will have a negative impact on the result of your clinic. However, in most cases this negative impact is more than balanced by the financial and service benefits of ensuring a vet is available (Table 3.1).

This is just a simple example of how you should compare the alternatives. From Table 3.1 you can deduce that whether or not you should replace a vet short-term depends on the number of booked clients, the average revenue from the visit, the number of hours you can call in the replacement and the cost per hour of that replacement. On the downside you miss out on giving your clients the continuity of the same vet. This is an item that you can include and value as a cost on the replacement alternative or include as a revenue on the no replacement alternative.

Personnel costs

Without staff it is impossible to create any revenue. All personnel in a veterinary clinic are important for creating revenue and thus influencing the profit of the clinic.

In an average clinic the cost of the personnel amounts to 40–60% of the total cost, which is a substantial part. There are two other aspects regarding personnel costs that are worth remembering:

- Regardless of whether your permanently employed personnel are engaged in productive activities or not the clinic assumes full salary cost for them.
- The cost of permanently employed personnel is 'fixed' in the sense that the cost of staff cannot be changed until the end of the notice

Table 3.1 Comparing alternatives: It is clear that in this case it is much more profitable to replace the regular vet

	Replacement	No replacement
No. of booked clients	10	10
Average revenue	50	
Potential revenue	*500*	*0*
No. of working hours	6	0
Replacement cost/hour	−50	0
Replacement cost	*−300*	*0*
Net effect	*200*	*0*

period (which varies in accordance with labour legislation and individual employment agreements).

In a clinic typically the veterinarians generate the majority of income through sale of services. However, there is considerable potential for other staff in the clinic to generate income in their own right – most obviously through selling food and other items. For this reason it is imperative that you make sure your staff are involved in revenue-generating activities for most of their working time.

As a manager it is also your responsibility to keep an eye on the future development of incoming customers and how far you have the resources to meet the demand. If demand is rising you have to take measures to be able to meet the increasing demand. Remember that a missed client visit because your clinic does not have the resources to accept the client is very costly. It will also influence the image of your clinic if you have to decline potential clients – will they come back? What will they tell others?

Setting fees

The income to your clinic is generated from professional fees and the sale of food, medicine and other items. Determining fees is a sometimes controversial issue. However, professionally calculated fees are an important part of the well-run clinic.

Basically the idea with establishing fees is to set a price that is:

■ acceptable to the market, i.e. your customers (existing and potential)
■ covering all your costs and also generating a satisfying profit.

Please keep in mind that the most important thing with fees or prices is that the market accepts them. If your cost in the clinic exceeds the price the market is ready to pay for the particular service you offer, two basic options are available:

■ Stop offering the service (a way to cut your losses).
■ Make sure that you reduce the cost for producing the service – so that you can reduce the price of the service.

Now while all this is quite easy to understand, and hopefully also sounds clear and logical to you, there is a small but important issue remaining. From a theoretical point of view it is easy to talk about the price the market accepts and also the costs you incur for producing the service. Unfortunately, real life is more difficult: Not only will you have to work hard and still make some assumptions in order to establish the true market price for all the various services you offer, but probably you never will find the true price. What you will find, however, is your best estimate of the current price level. That will in most instances be adequate.

Still the most difficult issue remains unresolved. What is your cost for producing a certain service? Well, if you have a very well-functioning accounting department, it might be possible for you to find out what the direct costs are for producing a certain service. Then you have to find out the indirect costs, which are all other costs in your clinic that do not directly belong to a particular service. Then you also have to distribute these fixed and/or indirect costs among all of your relevant services. This is not an easy task even for the most experienced economist.

I therefore suggest the following simple and more practical approach to setting the fees:

1. Identify the services of your clinic that are the most expensive or the most sold in terms of volume – start with 30–50 services/products.
2. Estimate the market prices for these (phone other clinics or ask your clients).
3. Identify and/or assess the direct costs for producing each of these 30–50 services/products.
4. Add 30–40% of the direct costs as indirect cost. Now you have a preliminary suggested price.
5. Compare your calculated price with the estimated market price.
   - If your calculated price is higher than the estimated market price – check both prices and decide whether or not it is worthwhile to produce and sell a service that generates a loss every time it is sold.
   - If your calculated price is lower than the estimated price – go for it.

This is far from an ideal situation but it is still a more formal process of setting fees, which later on can be expanded and evolved.

Buildings and equipment

The fixed resources of your firm are buildings and equipment. The purpose of most fixed resources is to support and enable your staff to do their jobs in the most efficient way and provide good client service. Fixed resources are called fixed because they are designed for a particular size of production and can be adapted to changes in demand only by replacements. Since fixed resources normally represent a substantial investment they will often have a significant impact on your result.

Thus, to decide whether or not to invest in new buildings and/or equipment is tricky, complex and risky – and requires quite a deal of planning and making assumptions about the future. I have included a fairly simple and straightforward example in the appendix, on the basic parameters you have to consider in planning an investment. However, if you feel uncertain I strongly recommend that you contact a consultant or at least an accountant who can support you in your thinking.

So when contemplating investments you have to have a long-term perspective. For investments in buildings or equipment you normally have to consider the economic implications with a time-horizon of at least 5 years. If it is possible, in economic terms, to justify an investment in a building or equipment within one year – that is if the extra revenue that you will achieve during the first year is larger than the investment cost – then of course you should not hesitate to make the investment.

However, there will be very few cases in which it will be possible to justify an investment in equipment during the first year. Most likely you will have to look up to 5 years ahead in order to be able to justify the investment economically. You will have to look even further into the future when you are considering investment in a building – then between 10 and 15 years is a normal time-horizon.

The point is that with this type of larger investment in buildings and equipment you have to be careful when trying to assess the actual profitability of the investment and the time-horizon for your investment calculation.

In all investment calculations it is normally easier to justify investments that aim to increase profitability through reduction of costs than through increasing revenue.

Selling medicine, food and health items

So, you have a well-functioning veterinary clinic – clients and profits continue to pour in. You should focus on your core competence – shouldn't you? Well, supplying medicine is part of your core service, but why should you bother selling food and health items? There are basically two reasons for including food and health items in your offer to clients:

- to earn more profit – which is the most important aspect of all
- to tie the customer closer to your veterinary clinic – marketing your clinic.

Selling food and health items to clients will most likely have a positive impact on the result for the veterinary clinic. There are, however, a few important things to keep in mind to ensure that you will generate profit:

- Make sure that you know the size of the *profit contribution* from all these items. Calculate the actual profit contribution for these items.
- Keep track of how many internal resources (staff, square metres of space and so on) are needed to handle food and health items. Estimate the cost of these.
- Keep track of how many items in your stock become out of date. Estimate the cost of this.

Now you have all the ingredients necessary in order to calculate how much the food and health items are contributing to the result of your clinic:

Contribution to overall result = Profit contribution − Cost of resources for handling − Cost for items that are out of date

Below I give you a short description of each of these parameters:

Profit contribution

The level of profit contribution is what will decide the actual profit contribution from these items. As a rule of thumb, you should have a profit contribution on such items ranging from 30 to 50% of the selling price.

Cost of resources for handling

There is a lot of work associated with handling medicine, food and health items. You normally pay for these items, you keep them in stock, and you reserve space for them in your building and above all you handle them in your business: you unpack them, you sort them, you display them and sell them to clients and charge the clients for them – finally you have to order new items and also take care of the accounting required. Thus, there is a lot of work – costs – associated with medicine, food and health items. A final note on this parameter as well as the next – cost for out-of-date items: it is possible for you to establish an agreement with your suppliers so that they will handle your stock and/or assume the cost for out-of-date items.

Cost for items that become out of date

There is also a cost associated with items in stock becoming out of date or damaged. Whether or not this is a huge cost depends among other things on how well your business in this department works. The point is to make sure that the cost for out-of-date articles is kept to an acceptable level – that is, a maximum 3–5% of the yearly purchasing cost of these items.

By analysing articles from the out-of-date point of view you can also identify items that you should exclude from your range of goods.

Managing the economics of a veterinary clinic

Introduction

Economic management of a veterinary clinic encompasses a wide array of activities: planning, budgeting, accounting, follow-up etc. For many non-economists the most important economic activity seems to be accounting. From the accounts you obtain the necessary figures for budgeting and follow-ups – e.g. the actual management of the clinic. At the end of each year the result and economic situation of the clinic is summarised in the annual financial statement. From the income statement and balance sheet you can deduce a number of economically interesting facts.

Actual accounting has been excluded from this book, since it is such a large and complex area in itself; the same goes for income statements and balance sheets. Either you understand and handle accounting and annual financial statements yourself, or better, you employ an accountant or practice manager. The purpose of this chapter is to give some practical guidance for you as a manager and not go deep into accounting.

We will look at the following areas:

- budgeting
- follow-up
- difference between result and liquidity
- key figures for managing your veterinary clinic.

Budget

The budget is your economic plan for the forthcoming period, normally a calendar year. There are two fundamental reasons for making a budget for your clinic:

- Planning the revenues gives you an idea of the level of resources (personnel, machinery and equipment) you require in order to create the planned resources.
- Planning revenues and costs per month gives you an opportunity to compare how the actual operation is developing in comparison to

your budget, which gives you better control over the economics of your business.

One simple guide to follow when setting your budget is to use the same posts or categories in your budget as in your accounting. Budgeting is typically done in spreadsheets in Excel and then when the budget is finalised and decided, it is entered into the business/accounting system in order to facilitate the follow-up.

What is the required detail of a budget? Well, it depends on how volatile your operation is or has been. Let us take a short tour through the various types of items that you have to make a budget for.

Revenues

The level of your revenues is quite difficult to anticipate. You will have to make a best-guess effort. On the other hand, the revenues constitute the foundation for the level of costs that you are going to plan for. If you are too defensive in your assessment of revenues, you will quite likely end up with too few resources to be able to handle the incoming clients. If, on the other hand, you are too optimistic you will most likely obtain a negative result since you will have too expensive resources.

I also recommend that you break revenues down on a day-to-day basis, which means the number of booked appointments per vet per day. Through this it will be possible for you to calculate how many working days are available every month, and thus it will be easier to judge if a good or bad result is simply a consequence of the number of working days (they vary between months). You also might want to include some kind of seasonal adjustment for the revenues, e.g. if you normally have a higher flow of revenue during the summer months.

Costs

When the revenues are decided, it is easier to assess the level of resources that are required to create the planned revenues. Assuming that no investments in new buildings or equipment are required, you are basically left with the planning of the number of staff required and their individual salary levels including social costs and taxes.

This is fairly straightforward as you already know the costs of your present staff, so the only actual planning you have to do is to plan for recruiting or dismissals. An important cost which can easily be overlooked in the budgeting process is the cost of continuing education and staff development. Your staff is a key resource for your clinic's well-being, responsible for generating the major part of your clinic's revenues. It is imperative to keep them up to date and well informed.

Investments in buildings, machinery and equipment

These are important issues and require that you make a careful assessment in terms of an investment analysis before you make the final decision. Some investments are necessary, such as replacing outdated equipment; others, like buying a new ultrasound machine, require an investment analysis and longer-term repayment plan.

If it is a required investment you do not have a choice so then you just include it in your budget.

Actual

So now you have your budget, which is your planned result. Now you have to start following up the actual results of your activities.

Rule number one is to make sure that you have a good accountant or financially competent practice manager. Remember that the accounting is the last thing you want to postpone – not having your accounting available is rather like driving your car blindfold: you have no idea where you are going and whether you should accelerate or brake.

Every month you should get a month's end report from the previous month. For example, in February you should get a report from the accounting for January ideally no later than 5 working days into February. The report should contain all the actuals and a comparison with your budget. This comparison should be complete, e.g. everything you put in your budget should be there together with the corresponding actuals.

How do you follow up when examining this report? A common and practical method is to check the accounting, preferably the income statement. You start by looking for the difference between budget and actual in a separate column for a number of accounts/areas – in the following order:

- result
- total revenue
- total cost.

Note that it is a good idea to start with the result – that gives you the overall situation. Then you move on to the revenues – which is mirroring how well you have been doing in the client department. Finally you look at the costs, which are the resources you have spent in order to generate the revenues. Then you browse on through all the accounts in order to identify all deviations.

You might also choose to go through the cash flow in your clinic. The general rule is the smaller the clinic, the less the difference between result and cash flow. Sometimes your cash flow is very obvious – how much money do you have in your banking account!

If no major differences are present, everything is all right and you can go back to your surgery! So what differences should you look for and act upon? Deviations larger than ±10% and/or amounts larger than e.g. ±€500 should set alarm bells ringing. By using both a percentage and amount deviation you make sure that you identify all relevant deviations.

You need to make sure that you understand the reasons for the deviations. Depending on these you might have to take some actions and in some cases also adjust your budget. If, for example, your actual salary costs are exceeding your budget you have to understand the reason for this. If it is illness, nothing much can be done, but if it is because of bad planning, you might have to reschedule working schemes.

Difference between result and liquidity

I cannot stress strongly enough the importance of having a clear understanding of the difference between result and liquidity. Depending on your level of economic understanding these can be two quite confusing concepts.

- Result is the profit or loss in your clinic – the difference between the periodised total income and the total costs.
- Liquidity is the actual flow of cash in your clinic.

Without accounts receivables (invoices to clients that have not yet been paid) and depreciation (the yearly cost for using equipment and machinery) in your clinic's business, there should normally not be too much of a difference between liquidity and result. If, however, you have a large amount of accounts receivables and depreciations, there might be a substantial difference between liquidity and result.

Unfortunately this means that you can end up in either of these two extremes:

- The result is positive but you don't have any cash.
- You have cash but you have a result that is negative.

You should always strive to avoid getting into one of those positions. Obviously not having cash means that you cannot pay your staff their salaries or pay other invoices. If, on the other hand, you have cash, but a negative result, you can be misled into believing that everything is fine and use the cash, thus making the result even more negative.

Thus, I recommend that you also make a budget for your clinic's liquidity and follow up on that. If you don't, please be aware of the different implications of these two concepts – as I described in the previous paragraph. One of the main responsibilities for you as manager is to make sure that the result is positive while you simultaneously have cash in your clinic.

Key figures for managing your veterinary clinic

For the manager who does not feel comfortable with the figures in the monthly income statement there are other efficient methods available to monitor the practice's economy. One way to follow the operation is to use key figures. However, note that key figures are not a replacement for following up the accounting, but an important complement.

The general advantage with key figures is that it is possible to measure various aspects of the operation in one or more comprehensive areas. It is important to choose carefully the key figures you are going to use to follow up your business.

Key figures can be utilised in two ways. In the simplest context you select the key figures that best describe and represent the operation in your clinic and the direction in which you want the operation to develop. You can use key figures to set goals for the operation and then follow up the key figures on a monthly basis, thus getting a good understanding of how the business develops.

You can also use key figures for benchmarking yourself against the financial performance of other clinics. This can provide useful information – but be careful you compare 'apples' with 'apples' and that the key figures you are using are formulated and expressed in the same way.

There are two main groups of key figures that are useful:

- economic key figures
- key figures that measure operational activities.

Economic key figures
There are a host of economic key figures that can be used, so I recommend that you start by using the most common and therefore usually the most efficient:

- Actual sales/Budget sales
- Actual costs/Budget costs
- Actual profit contribution/Budget profit contribution
  Profit contribution = Sales – Direct costs

■ Actual profit margin/Budget profit margin
  Profit margin = Sales – Total costs.

Economically more common key figures are capital turnover, solidity, cash liquidity and profitability. In summary they are somewhat more complex to calculate, but nevertheless valuable. However, a more detailed description of them is outside the scope of this book.

By calculating these economic key figures for an individual month and accumulated for the accounting year, you will quickly obtain a good understanding regarding how the clinic's operation is developing from an economic perspective. If one or more of the key figures is not developing in line with budget, it is necessary to investigate why, which might mean having to look further into the accounting.

Key figures that measure operational activities

Economic key figures are valuable since they measure the output of the operation from an economic perspective. The disadvantage with economic key figures is that they only measure the *consequence* of the actual work in economic terms. In other words, it will be difficult for individual workers to appreciate how what they do on a daily basis affects the economic performance of the clinic.

Therefore it is quite valuable to also use key figures that measure operational activities in the clinic. Some examples of operational related key figures are:

■ number of booked client visits per month
■ number of actual client visits per month
■ average debiting per client visit per month (average transaction fee)
■ number of client visits per veterinarian
■ number of non-vet staff per veterinarian.

The importance of communicating economic results

It is important to communicate the economic results to your staff. The communication should start during the budgeting phase: you should preferably involve your staff in the budgeting process, thus increasing their responsibility for the result.

It is also important that you communicate the running results on a monthly basis, when it is going well and when it is not going so well. You should always try to find the reasons for success and present them, as well as the reasons why the result is not going the way it should. This indicates you have control over your business, and awareness of the factors that could affect the results. Remember, by measuring your financial performance you are in a much better position to manage it.

Business systems for your veterinary clinic

The accounting in the veterinary clinic is one of the most fundamental and important tools available for managing operations. Accounting also serves a number of other purposes:

- fulfils legal requirements for the annual financial statements
- a basis for taxation – income and VAT
- communication of results and situation internally and externally.

The basic accounting is done by posting of items to the general ledger. Items posted are the actual current events in the company, e.g. sales, procurement of materials, salaries to employees. As a manager you can then generate monthly reports.

All businesses are legally required to keep records of accounting. Today this is most effectively achieved through more or less sophisticated business systems. The heart of these business systems is the general ledger which contains all posted items. In non-economic language these are the figures for all transactions that are relevant for the operation of the firm – e.g. all revenues and costs that are relevant for the running of the veterinary clinic.

There are a large number of business software systems available on the market. These vary in terms of overall functionality available for accounting and also in the degree to which they contain pre-developed functionality for a veterinary clinic.

The main factors that should influence your choice of a business system is thus how well the system can support your staff, primarily veterinarians, in their daily work. You should also consider the size of your business in terms of: number of customers and transactions and complexity of your actual operation, when considering a new business system for your clinic.

Increased functionality and specialization in a business system is, however, a double-edged sword. On the one hand, it offers more potential for increased efficiency in your business: on the other hand, it is more complex and complicated to run, requiring more education and skills on the part of your personnel.

Remember that no system in the world can change the fact that bad input into a system generates bad output. A good rule is therefore to start simple and make the basic routines work well – that is the basic accounting. Then you can gradually expand the functionality.

In this particular section, I will list a number of the most usable functions available in all general business systems, and will conclude with some thoughts on business systems with specialised functions for veterinary clinics.

Basic functionality in business systems

The basic functions in virtually all business systems today are:

- accounting and general ledger
- budgeting functionality
- accounts payables and accounts receivables
- asset management
- customer information – customer relationship management
- functionality for handling stock
- functionality for handling production.

More sophisticated and complex business systems also contain functions for setting up portals for e-business. Through these portals customers can obtain information about services available as well as prices for these services. It is also possible to order services and pay for these services through these portals.

The key words through which efficiency by using business systems is created are integration and processes. By integrating information regarding sales, costs, customers, personnel and assets you enhance the possibilities to improve analysis of the information and to obtain reports with information of improved value that will support the management of the operations – both in the short term and long term. The system must also be capable of following the customer/pet and simultaneously supporting all staff during the overall process.

Veterinarian functionality in business systems

Depending on the size of the business and the experience and maturity within the clinic to use business systems it is possible to give the following generalized advice as to what type of functionality you should implement in your business system.

The small and inexperienced business
- Start with basic straightforward functions for accounting and budgeting.
- Include basic customer information: name of customer, address, phone, e-mail and pet type and name.

- Make sure that everyone understands how to use the system and the purpose of using the system.
- Use the system to generate reports and present these regularly to the personnel in the practice. This involves them in the result of the business, and motivates them to use the business system.

The small and experienced business

- Continue with basic straightforward functions for accounting and budgeting.
- Add accounts payables and accounts receivables.
- Add asset handling.
- Add customer information.
- Make sure that everyone understands how to use the system and the purpose of using the system.
- Use the system to generate reports and present these continuously to the personnel in the business. This involves them in the result of the business, and motivates them to use the business system.

The large and experienced business

- Continue with basic straightforward functions for accounting and budgeting, accounts payables and accounts receivables and asset handling.
- Evolve customer information to CRM – customer relationship management.
- Add functionality for handling stock.
- Consider adding functionality for handling production.
- Consider creating an integrated portal which lets customers interact with your clinic through the internet.

The functionality for supporting your vets

An interesting possibility with a business system is the ability to automate the prices of various treatments on a pet while in the clinic. The purpose of this is to reduce the quite common risk with manual pricing, that the vet ends up with a lower total price, the reason being underestimating the effort and/or simply forgetting parts of the treatments.

Another important effect of this is establishing quality assurance, since the veterinarian follows more or less predefined paths with recommended activities during the various treatments. For younger veterinarians this quality assurance can also serve as a support and reminder which will increase their speed of learning while simultaneously increasing their confidence.

In order to automate the prices of various treatments, you have to have a process-oriented business system, which closely follows the various possible treatments available for the pets. Furthermore the system must contain pre-calculated/predefined prices for all treatments. When these prerequisites are in place, you have a truly efficient business system with the following substantial advantages:

- Revenues will be higher while reducing underestimation and avoiding forgetting treatments.
- The productive time for the vet will increase since he or she will continuously during the treatment register these, thereby eliminating the need to have an administrative process after the actual treatment.
- Your clinic will have a very detailed compilation available for the customer.

An example of the alternatives available in a modern system such as Vetvision Total is shown in Figure 3.1. To the left of the menu in Figure 3.1 you find the traditional business system functions: Accounting, Assets, Sales, Business Support and so on. To the right you find the menu choices that are specific for the veterinary business.

The next screen-shot (Fig. 3.2) shows an example of the journal for a patient and the various treatments that have been predefined:

As you can see in the bottom left corner, the following types of treatments have been predefined: anamnesis, diagnosis, instructions, clinical

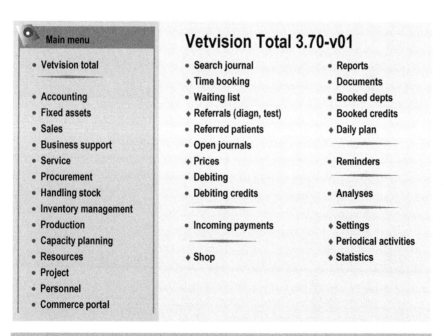

Figure 3.1 Screen-shot of menu choices in Vetvision Total (reproduced courtesy of Vetvision Software Svenska AB).

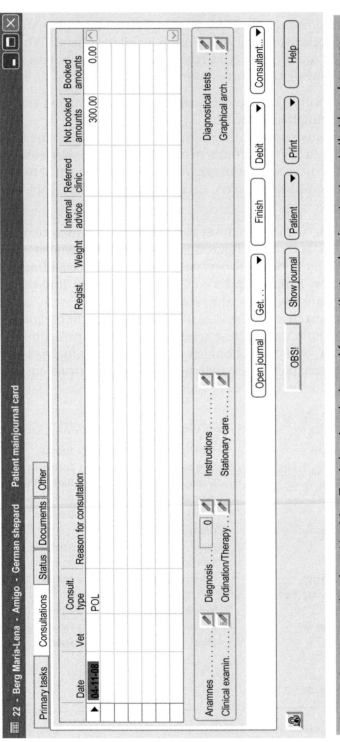

Figure 3.2 A screen-shot from Vetvision Total showing the journal for a patient and various treatments that have been pre-defined (reproduced courtesy of Vetvision Software Svenska AB).

examination, ordination/therapy, stationary care. As you can see, there has already been a polyclinical examination for which the cost amounts to 300 SEK. It has not yet been booked.

Remember that the advantage with predefined prices for treatments and actions is that you automatically debit the client for each and every treatment; furthermore your veterinarians become more efficient since they do not have to work with administration/pricing after the actual treatment.

The next picture (Fig. 3.3) is an example of a journal printed for a certain pet (a cat). As can be seen, the cat has been treated for a bite, with a basic examination and treatment of wound, anaesthesia, medicine. Please note all of the general activities that are part of the basic examination and that they are properly listed in the journal. Not only is this a good example of the administrative advantages, that everything is documented, but it is also an example of the quality assurance aspect of a basic examination. Since all the activities are listed, your veterinarians only have to go through all the steps, thus being confident that all relevant activities have been done.

Appendix: Some central economic concepts

The purpose of this appendix is to refresh the understanding of some central economic concepts that those responsible for the management of a veterinary clinic have to understand and master. For a reader eager to obtain a thorough explanation of these concepts we recommend professional literature in economics.

1. The very basic: revenue – cost = result

The most basic and important measure of any business entity is of course

Revenue − Cost = Result

However obvious this relation might seem, let us explicitly express the most basic fact that can be deduced from this relationship. Regarding how the result in a clinic can be improved:

The ONLY way to improve the result of a clinic is to INCREASE revenue or to DECREASE cost.

Another important quality with these three concepts is that they are *periodised*. The implication of periodisation is that every revenue and cost item must be associated with a specific period of time. The most common unit of time used for this purpose is the calendar month. The concept of periodising cost and revenue is most relevant when we talk

Journal (Patient no 195) (registered – cage/box H2)
Jesper – Lloyd, John

Animal type	Race	Gender	Age/Date of birth	Colour
Cat	Exotic shorthair	Castrated male	Age: 16 years 1 month 5 days	Black

Tattoo ... ... Ob 1679
Microchip ... ...
Distinctive marks ... ...
Pass no ... ...
Breeder ... ...
Pedigree name ... ...
Pedigree no ... ...
Father ... ...
Mother ... ...

Veterinarian ... ...

Medical treatment ... .
Feed ... ...

Owner
Owner (cust)... 182
　　　　　　Lloyd, John
　　　　　　Courney Rd 10
　　　　　　Westminster

Phone ... ... +46-8-717 27 08
Other owners... No
Insurance comp.
Insurance no ... ...

24/4/06 Bite sore　　　　　　　　　　　　　　　　　　4 kgs

　　　　Anamnes
CD　　　In for bite sore
　　　　Clinical examination
　　　　Basic Examination
　　　　General: Normal
　　　　General: Temperature: Normal: 37.8
　　　　General: Condition: Normal
　　　　Mucous membranes: General: Normal
　　　　Lymph nodes: General: Normal
　　　　General examination: Eyes and sight: Normal
　　　　General examination: Ears/Nose/Throat: Normal
　　　　General examination: Teeth/mouth: Little calculus, dental cleaning recommended
　　　　General examination: Cardiovascular: Normal
　　　　General examination: Respiratory organs: Normal
　　　　General examination: Abdominal palpation: Normal
　　　　General examination: Urogenital system: Normal
　　　　General examination: Locomotory system: Normal
　　　　General examination: Skin: Bite sore, left back leg about 2 cm long and 1 cm deep
　　Diagnosis
　　　　Bite sore, through skin
　　Treatment/Therapy
　　　　Treatment:
　　　　　　24/4/06 Sore treatment 30 mins
　　　　Anaesthesia:
　　　　　　24/4/06 Dormitory/antisedan cat
　　　　Products:
　　　　　　24/4/06 Rimadyl vet tablet (50 mg). 3 times every day until further order
　　Stationary care
　　　　10.00 – Temperature 37.8, General condition: gloomy, Thirst: reduced
　　　　12.00 – Urinating: Normal, Other remarks: Urinated
　　　　14.00 – General condition: painful. Hunger: Normal. Thirst: Normal.
　　　　　　Other remarks: more alert

Figure 3.3 An example from Vetvision Total of a journal printed for a particular pet (a cat) (reproduced courtesy of Vetvision Software Svenska AB).

about depreciation of investments and when a clinic pays a large debt due to a supplier.

Let us exemplify the concept of periodisation with depreciation of machinery, e.g. X-ray equipment. Assume that a clinic invests in X-ray equipment for which the price is €200 000. The clinic then pays €200 000 for the equipment on 1 January 2006. In the annual accounts for 2006 the result would then be negatively influenced by an extra cost amounting to €200 000 if no periodising was done. This would most likely have a very negative impact on the result of the veterinary clinic for 2006. The result for 2006 will be grossly underestimated.

Furthermore, it will be possible to use the X-ray equipment for at least 4 more years. However, if the equipment has already been depreciated to zero, the clinic will not incur any further cost for using this equipment over the next 4 years. The results for 2007–2010 will thereby be grossly overestimated.

Therefore the cost of the equipment should be periodised for 5 years: €200 000/5 = €40 000 per year. The actual cost per year will therefore be €40 000.

There are two important implications of this:

- You have to pay out €200 000 on 1 January 2006, which will have an impact on your cash and liquidity assets.
- The actual cost for this year will only be €40 000, which is good depending on the size of your revenue.

2. Result versus profitability

The result of a veterinary clinic is the profit or loss in absolute terms. The actual profit amount of the veterinary clinic can be compared to the interest amount paid by the bank on a deposit account. The interest amount that is paid is obtained by calculating an interest rate with the amount deposited on the account. (If you would like to compare the interest that you get from your present bank you can quite easily compare the interest rate between various banks.)

The same reasoning applies to result and profitability in a company. We just have to find the figure for the capital invested in the veterinary clinic (comparable to the amount deposited on your account). A comparison could then look like the one shown in Table 3.2.

In this particular example two companies with the same result/profit achieve different profitability due to the different amount of capital invested in the clinic. The point is that while improving result and profit in most cases is positive, it is always important to keep track of the amount of capital invested and whether it is simultaneously increasing.

Table 3.2 **Two clinics with the same result/profit achieve different profitability due to the difference in the amount of capital invested in the clinic**

Income statement	Clinic 1	Clinic 2
Revenue	90	9
Cost	−85	−4
Result/profit	*5*	*5*
Capital invested	100	50
Profitability	*5%*	*10%*

3. Some confusing terms in economics

There are three rather similar pair of terms in traditional economics which virtually always cause confusion among non-economists:

- income and expenditure
- payment and disbursement
- revenue and cost.

In most everyday conversation these terms are used interchangeably and as terms with equal meaning. In professional economics they are, however, distinctly different. They are used to describe different events associated with a sale or a purchase – particularly when they occur at different points in time.

Envisage a situation where you enter a bookshop and buy a book and pay for the book when you leave the store. When you decide to purchase the book is when the expenditure occurs. When you pay for the book the disbursement occurs. You could argue that the cost for the book does not occur until you start reading (consume) the book.

4. Variable and fixed costs

Costs are always costs, and to reduce cost will always be an important way to improve the result of the veterinary clinic. However, for analytical purposes we can divide costs into variable and fixed costs. In the very long run all costs are variable, since we can increase or decrease them. In the short run, for instance on a daily, weekly or even monthly basis, a majority of the costs within a veterinary clinic can be considered as fixed costs.

For example, the cost of permanently employed persons cannot be reduced until the end of the notice period – which often can be from

1 month up to 4–6 months. On the other hand, if there are personnel employed on an hourly basis, the cost of these people can be considered as variable, because we can reduce this cost with 1 hour's notice.

One of the challenges in running a veterinary clinic is unfortunately that a majority of the costs can be considered as fixed. The implication is that it is important for the management of the veterinary clinic to make prognoses of the future expectations of revenue – at least with a future time-horizon amounting to 2–3 months. This is in order to be able to take measures to increase/decrease the fixed resources in time.

5. Product costing and pricing

The traditional method of establishing a price for a service that you offer to your customer consists of three basic steps:

- Identify and calculate all *direct* costs.
- Identify and calculate all *indirect* costs.
- *Apportion* all indirect costs to the service.

Direct costs

Direct costs are the costs of all the resources that are directly involved in producing the service, e.g. personnel involved and the medicine and material used. To calculate all direct costs for a service you have to find the cost of the medicine and material used.

The cost of the personnel involved is calculated by measuring the time they were involved in producing the service – which could be measured in minutes. Note that you have to be careful in assessing this time. You have to find the actual and realistic chargeable time for each individual veterinarian – a common practical percentage range is 55–75% of their working time. Then you have to calculate the cost for these persons – recalculate the monthly cost to a cost per minute. Then you multiply the cost per minute with the number of minutes and add this cost to the cost of the medicine and material. This will be the direct cost.

Identify and calculate all indirect costs

Next, identify all resources that are indirectly involved in producing the service, e.g. administrative personnel, equipment and rooms. Find the yearly cost for these resources.

Apportion all indirect costs to the service

Now we have all the yearly costs for the indirect resources required to produce the service. The tricky part now is to identify a way to apportion a part of all indirect costs to this particular service. If it is a piece of equipment used only for a particular operation, then we have to estimate the total number of operations that we expect to do during a year. If it is 50 then we simply divide the cost of the equipment by 50 and add this amount to the other indirect costs.

Finally, we add the direct cost and indirect cost. Now we have an estimate of the cost of producing the service. Next, we have to add a profit (e.g. 10% of the production cost) to this cost in order to calculate the price of the service for customers.

When we thus arrive at a price, we have to compare this price with the price on the market. If it is higher than the 'average' price, we can handle this in the following ways:

- Sell the service at a price higher than the market price – maybe you have a strong brand.
- Lower the calculated price to the market price – accept selling this service on the market with a slight loss.
- Examine and analyse the price to find out whether or not it is possible to produce the service at a lower cost.
- Decide not to produce and sell this service.

Generally, it is easier to establish prices for services with a high proportion of direct costs. You should therefore strive after identifying the direct costs to obtain a correct production cost.

6. Example of investment analysis

Below you will find a typical example of an investment analysis. It is a very simplified model, but the structure and methods for evaluating investments are valid also in more complex situations.

The example below is an illustration of a situation in which a clinic has decided to purchase new X-ray equipment. The cost of the equipment including installation amounts to €500 000.

The effect of the new equipment can either be a possibility to generate more revenues, or reducing cost by allowing more efficient work with the X-ray equipment. In many cases you can identify both these effects simultaneously. Regardless of whether the effect is increased revenue or reduced cost – the effects will have a positive impact on your result. This is basically all the information you need to set up an investment problem.

Figure 3.4 shows a typical investment problem. In this particular case I have assumed that the investment is made in the beginning of year 1, and that it is possible to start generating revenue/saving costs from day 1. I have also assumed the same effects during the first 5 years, and have based this analysis on a time-horizon of 5 years.

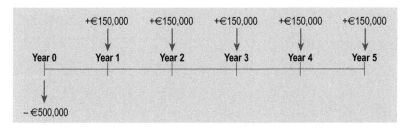

Figure 3.4 A typical investment problem.

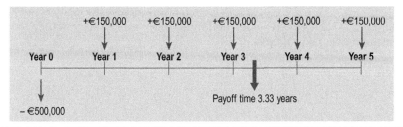

Figure 3.5 'Payoff' method used for evaluating whether an investment will be profitable or not.

The next problem is then to decide how to evaluate whether this investment is profitable or not. There are two basic methods available: a simple and a somewhat more complicated one.

Payoff

The time in years or parts of years it takes before the initial investment has been repaid (paid off). This is a straightforward analysis which is easy to calculate. Another advantage is that the result is relatively easy to understand and also to communicate (Fig. 3.5).

The time it takes to repay €500000 in the above example is 3.33 years. This can be calculated by adding 3 years' payments = €450000 (=3 years). The remaining €50000 is repaid during the first 4 months in year four (=0.33 year). Is this investment then a worthwhile investment? Well, it depends, but if your repayment criterion is 3 years, you should not do this investment since it takes more than 3 years to repay the investment. If, however, your repayment criterion is 4 years, the actual repayment time is less than that, which means that this is an acceptable investment.

Net present value

When evaluating an investment with the method net present value method, you discount (move) all payments in your investment problem to the same point in time, normally to the beginning of year 1 (Fig. 3.6).

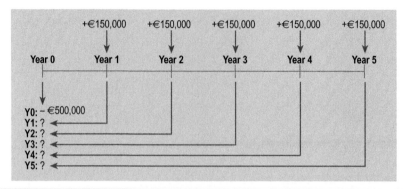

Figure 3.6 'Net present value' method used for evaluating whether an investment will be profitable or not.

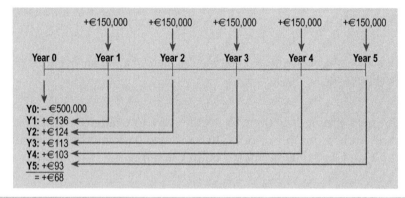

Figure 3.7 In this example the net present value is +€68 000 and should therefore be done.

Once you have discounted all the payments you sum them up, and if the total sum is positive, you should do the investment (Fig. 3.7). If, on the other hand, the sum is negative you should not do the investment.

This method is actually the most exact and correct, but also the most complicated. If you are contemplating using this method, I recommend that you seek advice from a knowledgeable accountant or a consultant.

4 What leaders really do

A leader is there to disturb the status quo.

What is it that distinguishes the responsive practice from the average? Is it having a modern building? A good marketing policy? Lots of expensive technical gadgets? Is it a feature of the number of veterinarians in the practice or the size of the retail area? Whilst many factors may contribute to success, the one characteristic shared by the responsive practices that is demonstrated again and again is the outstanding skills and behaviour of the practice leader(s).

But should practices need leaders? After all, they are peopled by intelligent, energetic individuals whom it should be possible to rely upon to be self-managing, high achievers. The simple answer is, 'Yes'. Both professional and support staff in practices lead busy lives with many conflicting demands on their time and attention. They often become so involved with the minutiae of the present that they lose sight of where they want to go with their lives. Good practice leaders provide the direction and drive to help their staff accomplish more and greater things than they would do on their own. This simultaneously builds a happier and more productive practice.

What is leadership?

As a business leader there is one thing you can count on: change. Your success as a leader will be based upon your ability to adapt, respond and bend to the conditions around you.

Bradford and Raines, Management Consultants

The function of leadership is to produce change. This involves setting a direction – developing a vision – for the future of the business, identifying the necessary strategies to achieve the vision, aligning people behind those strategies, and empowering them to make the vision happen, despite obstacles. This is in contrast to management, which involves keeping the current system operating through planning, budgeting, organising, staffing, controlling and problem-solving. The person who thinks management is leadership will *manage* change, hence keeping it under control, but he or she will be unable to provide the stuff required to make larger and more difficult leaps.

Developing good business direction is a tough process involving gathering and analysing information, thinking well beyond current limitations, and making predictions about the future. People who can articulate such visions are broad-based strategic thinkers willing to take risks. They are also focused.

Without exception, the leaders of the responsive practices that I know are well 'focused': they have clearly identified what they want to be and what they want to do, and they have established the values or principles on which this being and doing are based. By being focused they have become *effective*. By being effective they achieve more of what they really need to do.

Effectiveness versus efficiency
Effectiveness is doing the right things well. It is the goal of a leader.
   Efficiency is doing things well, but not necessarily the right ones.
A leader is needed to ensure the right things are being done.
   For example, a team may be very efficiently repairing the small hole in the bows of a sinking ship, but the water that's going to sink the ship is pouring in through the gash in the stern. The effective set of actions in this case would be to fix the hole in the stern.

A short history of the theories of leadership
Leadership started to come under close scrutiny in the middle of the last century as people increasingly realised that the model of military leadership – the hero-leader with the command-and-direct style of a large group of more or less disciplined men – was no longer appropriate for management of businesses and organisations increasingly populated by knowledge workers and women.

Originally it was believed that leaders were 'born, not made' and traits such as birthright (including socioeconomic status and birth order) and intelligence (from schooling) gave automatic leadership status.

Next, situational leadership was investigated: perhaps a leader's success was created through distinctive features of the setting in which he functioned. For example, Winston Churchill displayed extraordinary characteristics of leadership during Britain's 'darkest hours' in the Second World War, but these did not serve him well during peacetime.

Later, theories arose of 'two-dimensional' leadership (which combined concern for organisational tasks with concern for the individual and interpersonal relationships), 'contingency' leadership (where the behaviours of the leader were adaptable to the circumstances) and even 'shared' leadership (as perhaps a single-leader multi-follower concept could not apply in a larger organisation).

In the 1980s, the boom years for business entrepreneurship, the idea to separate the roles of leaders and managers began to crystallise ('Managers do things right; Leaders do the right things') resulting in the theory of the 'visionary leader' whose personal and organisational strategic vision, expressed in clearly measurable actions, created a powerful and exciting future for a business.

But this model of an inspirational individual driving change through sheer charisma no longer reflects modern requirements for leadership, and has been superseded by the current theory of the transformational leader: the leader who creates a *shared* vision that can transform an organisation by motivating followers by appealing to strong emotions.

What characterises an effective practice leader?

The conductor doesn't make a sound. The conductor's power depends on his ability to make other people powerful.

Personal characteristics that effective leaders have in common are a willingness to work hard, decisiveness, enthusiasm, and, perhaps most important of all, an ability to respond quickly to change. Leaders are proactive because they challenge the status quo of their organisation to respond to changes that affect the organisation's business. Often these proactive leaders are individuals who do not accept the rules, regulations and traditions – spoken or unspoken – that have governed the practice earlier. Leaders are also risk takers, although risks are not taken haphazardly but are regarded as opportunities that will benefit the practice.

But these characterise what they *are* rather than what they *do* – and it is their ability to get things *done* that is what makes them such outstanding leaders. How do they do it?

Leaders of responsive practices are people who are effective at making things happen for the people they employ. They are able to integrate the soft human elements with hard business actions through positively influencing other people's emotions, feelings, attitudes, and their determination to achieve their potential. They are willing to get most of their fulfilment from the success of others, are not afraid to start new things and to show others the way forward – literally to get their hands dirty. They also realise the importance of making space for the growth and development of the people they support – they do not try to do everything themselves. This type of leadership relies on creating close collaboration and cooperation between people in the practice and is known as servant-leadership: the leader serves the needs of his staff to help them achieve their full potential rather than commanding respect and ordering results.

Leading people is challenging. In veterinary practice you are most often working with highly talented people who know what to do and how to do it, but just aren't doing it. As a leader, it is not always easy to keep yourself on track, and it can be useful to have a mental picture for yourself of what you are striving to achieve.

I love gardening, and, for me, having a picture of the practice being like a flower garden where I was Head Gardener helped me visualise what I was striving to achieve as practice leader. Each practice member was a growing plant whom I had a responsibility to cultivate to its full beauty to create, all together, a glorious flourishing garden. My job was to make sure each plant had the space they needed to reach their full potential by clearing the weeds and other obstacles; to water, fertilise and prune to encourage healthy growth and development; to see they did not get too much sun or too much shade, and to enhance their beauty by placing them in the right place in the right constellations. If, in my analogy, I did not care properly for each individual, if I stood in their sun, or gave them too little water, or let the weeds grow around them, I was not doing my job well: the plants did not thrive, and the garden did not reach its full potential. I needed to be very aware all the time of the actions I needed to take to help the plants grow better – which included having the wisdom to give them appropriate individual care, and patience to let them grow at their own rate and not try to force them into something they couldn't become. This required a fair amount of inward soul-searching to recognise and manage my own barriers and blocks to achieving my goal.

Successful leaders who can create a 'beautiful garden' of the people in their practice experience a raised performance level within the practice that includes greater job satisfaction and loyalty from staff, more satisfied clients (who *doesn't* enjoy visiting a beautiful garden?) and financial success for the business. However, whilst profitability might be a goal, focusing on money is not the way to achieve it. What must be managed is the energy, drive, enthusiasm, excitement, passion and ambition of staff. *Thus, the primary skill of leaders (and the test of all their activities) is ability to raise the level of commitment, drive and productivity of those they influence.*

Who, in a veterinary practice, is the leader?

Practice principals are typically dedicated clinicians, primarily interested in animal care, who seek the autocracy of independence from being an employee. Leadership is automatically assumed an integral part of practice ownership, but many in this position lack commitment to leadership; they don't want to take on (and don't know what is involved in) the full responsibility of leadership. As a result, many principals bury their heads, ostrich-like, in the sands of clinical work and hope that all the administrative, financial and personnel problems will resolve themselves.

So, what are practice principals?

In most practices, principals have to be multi-faceted. They have to be leaders, managers, practice owners and veterinarians: different roles requiring different skills and producing different results. For the principals of smaller practices, there is often no reasonably viable alternative.

A *leader* gets things done through people by making meaning for them and a desire to achieve. A leader is *effective*. He or she requires good communication, negotiation, delegation and self-management skills, coupled with long-term perspective.

A *manager* creates the environment in which people can be more effective. A manager is *efficient*. A manager's time is more splintered than a leader's with a greater diversity of problems and situations to deal with in any one day, and the results are more ambiguous and difficult to measure.

An *owner* is most interested in the practice's *profit*.

A *clinical veterinarian* concentrates on the diagnosis, treatment and management of the consultations, operations and visits booked. His or her day ends with visible signs of progress which can be measured in a number of different ways, such as number of clients seen, and income generated.

These are all different behaviours, different expectations and different measures of progress and achievement: trying to combine these contrasting roles can only result in compromise for the multi-faceted principal, and, not infrequently, leads to personal frustration, stress and an increased risk of physical and mental 'burnout'.

Can principals learn to be better leaders?

Yes, but they have to decide what aspect of multi-faceted principalship they want to focus on and delegate much of the rest in the practice. Unfortunately, many principals are afraid of losing authority through delegation and prefer to 'do it all themselves' so they can have full control over the situation, or they lack the skills to successfully delegate, and end up doing everything themselves anyway. This is not what is best for the practice and is certainly – in the long term – not best for the principals either.

The E-myth revisited

Author Michael Gerber explains why leadership frequently fails in small businesses. Most people starting up their own businesses are actually technicians, usually very skilled at their trade of haircutting, carpentry or veterinary medicine, but people who make the fatal mistake of believing that if you understand the technical work of a business you understand the business that does the technical work. To complicate things further, everyone who goes into business is actually at least three personalities in one: the Entrepreneur, the Technician and the Manager. The Entrepreneur has the brilliant vision of the future, the Technician has the skills of the trade and wants to get on with doing his job, and the Manager can create order and systems to manage the past: different roles with different needs. The problem? All want to be Boss, all are in conflict, and one usually wins. The result? A struggling business that mirrors the leader's own lopsidedness.

Gerber goes on to explain that most businesses are operated according to what the *owner* wants, not what the *business* needs. He writes:

The purpose of going into business is to expand beyond your existing horizons, so you can provide something that satisfies a need in the marketplace that has never been satisfied before. So you can live an expanded, stimulating new life. However, if all you want from your business is the opportunity to do what you did before you started your business, get paid more for it, and have more freedom to come and go, your greed – which may sound harsh- will eventually consume both you and your business. You need to play a new game called 'Building a small business that actually works'.

The rest of the book is dedicated to clearly and simply explaining how to create a successful small business.

Practice principals are, first and foremost, veterinarians. Their primary – and economic – strength is as skilled, competent and experienced clinical veterinarians. They have no training as leaders/managers/owners responsible for the financial success of a business. Their value to the practice may be far lower in these secondary roles.

The decision that has to be made within the practice is: *for the good of the practice*, how is the practice principal most *valuable* to the practice? In which role(s) does he or she become more of an overhead than a valuable production unit? Which role(s) should be developed? The practice leader's role, responsibilities, accountabilities, and performance measures need to be agreed and written down.

What are the alternatives for a multi-faceted principal in a small practice?

For many, probably the best solution is to become a 'clinician with a vision' by hiring a manager. By delegating the responsibility for the day-to-day running of the practice to a suitably qualified person the principal can continue to perform the clinical work he or she is so skilled at (and contribute most effectively to the practice income), *and* be able to hold the vision that takes the practice forward and makes it special. Afraid the practice can't afford a manager? A good manager should have at least generated their own salary in increased income and savings by the end of the first year, so there should be no extra cost to the practice, but all the benefits of increased efficiency.

A question of ownership

Ownership of veterinary practices is changing – from the traditional one-man or multi-partner set-up to corporate, franchise and lay ownership. There are also pet superstores with in-store veterinary clinics. These different types of ownership affect many aspects of business management including responsibility for leadership, staffing and structure of the practice, and generation and sharing of profits and tax benefits. The leaders of a smaller, privately owned clinic are often more motivated to generate a profit because they can quickly see and measure the direct effect of their actions, compared to employees managing large, multi-branch corporates where decision-making is ponderous and changes are slow to be implemented, and who experience less direct impact from their actions.

Vision and focus

What do I want to be famous for?

> *Your business is a distinct reflection of who you are. If your thinking is sloppy, your business will be sloppy. If you are disorganised, your business will be disorganised. If you are greedy, your employees will be greedy, giving you less of themselves and always asking for more. If your information about what needs to be done in the business is limited, your business will reflect that limitation. So, if your business is to change – as it must continuously to thrive – you must change first. If you are unwilling to change, your business will never be capable of giving you what you want.*
>
> Michael Gerber, 2001

Veterinarians are typically highly trained, intelligent and usually ambitious people. They want to feel special and feel that the practice they belong to is special. But remarkably few are focused.

It is difficult to focus, to write down your personal mission or creed: what it is that will make you special. But by being focused and by having a clear sense of direction in your life, you become more effective; you achieve more and gain greater satisfaction from life than those who merely drift.

One method to help you focus is to ask yourself, 'What do I want to be famous for?', i.e. 'What do I want to do in my life that will make me special?'.

It will actually be fairly difficult to define the answers clearly and precisely, and it may take some months before you are able to do so. The answers can sometimes be quite surprising. Once you have defined them, work out the steps you need to take to achieve them, and a time plan for each step. Be brave! Challenge yourself! – don't limit yourself with self-imposed constraints.

What do my staff want to be famous for?

According to David Maister, being an effective leader is not about charging ahead yelling 'Follow me' but about getting your people enthused, excited and energised. Focus on what excites each of your people not (just) on what excites you (McKenna and Maister, 1996).

Good leaders not only have vision, strong personal motivation and the ability to inspire and motivate others, they also have a high level of integrity, self-discipline and very effective communication skills.

Leaders get things done through people, but the people need to know what they *want* to do – and what they *need* to do to help the business they are in. A practice leader helps his people achieve both the practice vision and their own, vision-compatible goals.

Ask each member of staff what they want to be famous for – and help them find the answer. By making them clarify their ambitions, you create a team of people that is ready to work for the practice vision and simultaneously grow their own individual skills and abilities. The effect of focusing your staff is illustrated in Figures 4.1 and 4.2.

In the unfocused practice (Fig. 4.1) people (A–F) are not working effectively because they don't know either what the practice stands for or what they want from their lives.

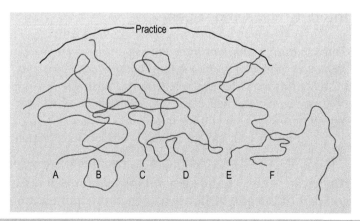

Figure 4.1 The unfocused practice.

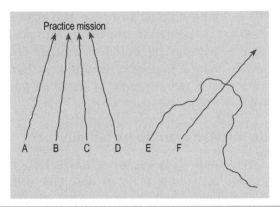

Figure 4.2 The focused practice. A–D have personal missions in line with the practice mission, E remains unfocused, F's mission is not in line with the practice mission, so he or she will probably leave.

In the focused practice (Fig. 4.2), A–D have personal missions that are compatible with the practice mission; they will grow and develop as the practice develops. Character E cannot focus and will continue to be undetermined and ineffective. Character F finds that the practice mission is not compatible with F's own aims (perhaps to work in a different type of practice, go into research or industry, or learn particular skills that cannot be got from the practice) so it would be best to leave and find a more suitable practice for his or her needs. If F remains he or she will be dissatisfied and resentful, which could affect the work performance of others in the practice.

Integrity and self-discipline

Through truth, communication and leadership you may help employees grow and open to commitment which opens your business to success beyond your vision. But in the absence of these, employees will close into cynicism, and whisper 'revolution'.

Bruce Berger, Vice President , Whirlpool Corporation

Integrity is doing what you say you will do when you say you will do it. Integrity creates trust, confidence and inspiration. Self-discipline is an integral part of integrity. One aspect of self-discipline is time management. Poor time management is a sign of disorganisation and is the limiting factor to effectivity (Drucker, 1966). You have only 24 hours in a day. There are a certain number of jobs and procedures you are required to complete in that time, plus dealing with the general problems that arise daily in practice. Much time-wasting comes from an inability to define objectives, set priorities and stick to them. By planning and organising your time you *can* achieve all you want and more. Not only will you have more time to pursue other interests and hobbies, but you can also retain your enthusiasm for and enjoyment of practice life.

So how should you spend your time?

There are numerous ways in which to manage time better detailed in a variety of self-help manuals. Some common time-wasters and a simple guide to making better use of your time are outlined below.

However, the multi-faceted principal requires a time management plan which highlights the relative importance of each of his various roles, controls the time spent on each, and makes that time as effective as possible.

Common time-wasters
- Long/unscheduled telephone calls
- Interruptions
- Unnecessary meetings
- Handling the daily mail
- Poor office desk management
- Poor medical records/record filing system
- Inability to say 'no'
- Poorly managed appointment system with unscheduled appointments
- Inability to delegate
- Poor use of trained support staff

Ways to improve your time management
1. Record how your time is spent. Compare it with your *idea* of how you spend your time – you will be surprised at the result!
2. Cut back on unproductive use of time by managing your time, i.e. making yourself accountable for all the time you have.
   - Take 10 seconds to ask yourself:
   Why am I doing this?
   Who else could do it?

Does it need to be done at all?

What priority does it deserve?

- Identify and eliminate all things that need not be done at all. Relating actions to the goals of the practice vision helps eliminate unnecessary activities.
- Delegate jobs that could be done as well or better by other members of the practice.
- Avoid wasting other people's time, and thence your own, for example, on long, unstructured meetings.
- Don't plan too tightly – allow some reactive time for events that are beyond your control (e.g. travel time between farm visits, 'breathing space' between meetings, etc.). *This can be as much as 10% of your day.*

3. Consolidate your time into the largest possible units – it is impossible to work effectively in little dribs and drabs.

- Know your limits, that is your effective working time span and your most productive working time. (*For example, I know I work most effectively with greatest focus from about 7 am to 1 pm. After that I am better doing jobs requiring less mental input. Where possible, I try to schedule my day to reflect this.*)
- Keep control of your time plan: don't be sidetracked from it by minor issues.
- Improve your effectiveness by making lists of what you want to achieve that day, with priority ranking. Don't allow yourself to be sidetracked from these.

4. Make sure other members of your practice know about and understand your time plan so that they can cooperate with you. For example, in Swedish veterinary practices, many veterinarians have a fixed daily telephone time during which they deal with all telephone queries from clients. For this system to work, staff must know when that time is, and book calls to the veterinarian during that time. Similarly, if you decide to do your clinical work three days a week, and the other days are for administration, etc., make sure your staff know about it.

Learn to say 'no'. Saying NO is actually not brutally saying 'no' but saying something like 'Tell me what you want to achieve so I can help you find a possibly better solution to your problem'. Saying NO is also the first step in delegating. However, to accept delegation staff must be prepared for it. Saying NO is also having a network of relationships so that you can refer somebody somewhere else to find a solution.

> What do you do if your receptionist asks you in the middle of a busy morning surgery to 'just have a few words' with Mrs Jones who's at the front desk? You know Mrs Jones is a very nice person, is a good client and she cares a lot about her animals – but she can also talk the hind leg off a donkey. Do you agree to chat with her, knowing this will completely ruin your scheduling, making you late for your remaining patients, and annoying the staff working with you? Or do you say, NO – and suggest some other alternatives? By finding alternatives such as asking the receptionist to book Mrs Jones in one of your telephone times, or to find out if someone else could deal with Mrs Jones' query, or asking the receptionist how she would best deal with the situation, you do not compromise yourself, your staff or your waiting patients. And you probably provide better service to Mrs Jones, who will ultimately receive undivided and focused attention.

A leader's success is measured through his people's achievements.

Maister (1993) identifies the most important role of a practice *leader* as coaching and encouraging staff to fulfil their potential. I have adapted his time plan (originally for principals of legal firms) as follows:

- *Administration*: not more than 10% of time. If it takes more time than this to keep abreast of paperwork, hire a trained administrator.
- *Clinical work*: not more than 20%. For a truly effective practice *leader*, performing clinical work is *not* the most productive use of time but it may be necessary to maintain professional respect. (However, see earlier – the problem of the multi-faceted principal/clinician. In addition, in a small practice the proportion of time spent on clinical work must, by necessity, be much higher.)
- *Marketing and selling*: not more than 10%. It is not the job of the practice leader to promote the practice through client meetings, organising the practice marketing, and so on, although it is important that the leader fully supports practice marketing. This role can be delegated to the practice manager.
- *General client relations*: not more than 20%. A certain amount of time solving client problems and, more importantly, canvassing clients

for their ideas, comments and criticisms is invaluable but should not take more than a fifth of the total time.

■ *Coaching veterinarians and staff*: up to 60%. The most productive use of a *leader's* time lies in individual coaching to get the best from staff members. By helping staff solve their problems, keep their priorities straight, and set themselves stretching goals, coach–leaders enable the individuals in the practice to achieve more than they would on their own – which has the added advantage of improving the practice's productivity too.

> Coaching is not easy: changing people's ways of working and doing things is hard because people prefer to stick to what they know and feel comfortable with, and because different individuals are motivated by different things.
>
> A good coach takes a deep personal interest in his or her coaches and structures small, simple changes, with which it is easy to attain success, and which give people confidence to try new things. A good coach also works hard to develop joint tasks so that staff gain the experience of teamwork and joint responsibility. The practice becomes much more effective if the staff function as a team rather than a group.
>
> This time plan would have to be modified for the principal of a small practice but it still provides, I believe, a useful indicator of how leaders should best focus their time.

A final word about leadership

There is no easy answer to the problem of how to make practice principals better, more effective business leaders, but much of the solution lies with the principals themselves: they need to objectively put the needs of the business first rather than subjectively hoping they'll 'wing it'. To be truly effective as *leaders* they need to learn new skills of people, business, and self management. For many principals, this is not actually what they want to do.

Think carefully about your various roles as practice principal. Where are you *really* most valuable to the practice? What do you *truly* enjoy doing most? Be honest with yourself. Look at the options available for yourself and the practice. Hiring a full-time practice manager? Remaining an assistant/salaried partner? Taking time to train and develop new professional leadership skills? Studying for an MBA? Work out what is best for you and your practice.

Where do practice managers fit in?

Although the terms leader and manager are regarded by many authors as being synonymous (and in smaller veterinary practice are often the same person), 'pure' leaders and managers have different actions and aims. *Leadership complements management, it doesn't replace it.* Both are necessary for success in an increasingly complex and volatile business environment.

The leader/manager relationship has been likened to a group hacking their way through the jungle: the manager, who typically works by rational, applied means, ensures they are hacking efficiently, but it is the visionary leader who climbs the tallest tree and makes sure they are in the right jungle. The role of the practice manager is explored in more depth in the following chapter.

5 What does a practice manager do?

Our ability to contribute to society depends as much on the management of the organization for which we work as it does on our own skills, dedication, and effort.

Peter Drucker, 2001

What is management?

Management is about coping with complexity. Without good management, complex businesses (and any veterinary practice with more than about 10 people employed is complex) tend to become chaotic in ways that hinder their health and development. Good management brings a degree of order and consistency to key dimensions such as the quality and profitability of services. To realise good management needs a good manager.

What is management about?

In any business, *results only exist on the outside* so the most important function of management is to create satisfied clients. This is achieved through activities such as:

- creating and reinforcing commitment to common goals and shared values
- improving communication between individuals and encouraging individual accountability towards sharing knowledge, skills and work
- making people capable of joint performance by enhancing their strengths and reducing their weaknesses in a common venture

---

- measuring performance to assess and continually improve the health and productivity of the business
- growing and developing the business as well as the individual.

A brief history of the development of modern management

About 150 years or so ago management as we know it today did not exist. It was not until the turn of the last century and more particularly during the crisis periods of the First and Second World Wars, when unskilled, pre-industrial labourers were required to produce precision armaments and other products rapidly, that the need for organisation, management and marketing arose. At this time, the only large-scale model for management was the Army. This command-and-control structure, with very few at the top giving orders and many at the bottom doing the hard graft, was the model for the men who put together the transcontinental railways, steel mills, modern banks and department stores. During the First World War, the scientific management principles of Fredrick F. Taylor began to be applied where tasks were broken down into individual, unskilled operations that could be learned quickly, enabling high levels of productivity from unskilled and inexperienced labourers on an assembly line. Over the next decade or so, accounting went from 'book-keeping' to analysis and control; strategic planning developed from the 'Gantt charts' used during war production planning; analytical logic and statistics were used to convert experience and intuition into definitions, information and diagnosis; marketing evolved as a way to manage distribution and selling; and the management pioneers began to question the value of production line assembly in terms of use of human resources, and investigate and develop automation. Each one of these managerial innovations represented the application of knowledge to work, the substitution of system and information for guesswork, brawn and toil. Each one replaced 'working harder' with 'working smarter'.

Modern management is relevant to every human effort that brings together in one organisation people of diverse knowledge and skills. Knowledge by itself produces nothing. By organising and managing how knowledge is used, it becomes productive.

> *Management has converted knowledge from social ornament and luxury into the true capital of the economy. (Drucker, 2001)*

What does a manager do?

A good manager manages the complexity in the business in three primary areas:

1. planning and budgeting
2. organising and staffing
3. controlling and problem-solving.

Let's look at these in more detail.

1.   Planning and budgeting

If you don't know where you're going you won't know when you've got there.

Planning involves setting targets or goals for the next month, year and, typically, 5-year period, and establishing more-or-less detailed steps for achieving those targets. Budgeting is allocating resources in an organised way to accomplish these plans.

Included in this area is tracking daily, weekly and monthly cash flow and key performance figures to monitor performance trends, handling accounts and paying bills. An important aspect of budget management is regularly updating and informing staff about business performance in relation to budget. For example, a months-end presentation to staff of the key performance figures such as income generated, number of clients seen, number of operations performed, amount of pet food sold and so on, with an explanation of why they are as they are, not only demonstrates that the practice has control over its finances but also encourages team accountability by increasing their understanding of their individual role in generating these figures.

Planning and budgeting also includes marketing and sales – the strategies and plans needed to attract and retain clients in the practice, and to profitably sell them professional services and goods.

2.   Organising and staffing

To achieve plans requires an organisational structure and set of jobs for accomplishing plan requirements, staffing the jobs with qualified individuals, communicating the plan to those people, delegating responsibility for carrying out the plan, and devising systems to monitor implementation. This key management area includes identifying the type of staff needed and hiring them; providing appropriate on-the-job and external training; setting performance criteria and ensuring the systems are in place for individuals to achieve them; developing reward systems for good performance; giving appropriate feedback and coaching; and removing or relocating staff that do not perform as needed.

Included under organising and staffing is also effective communication. This means everything from a one-to-one, face-to-face conversation to more generalised internal internet messages. Managing information technology is an increasingly complex and time-consuming part of a manager's job.

3. Controlling and problem-solving

Managers ensure plan accomplishment by controlling and problem-solving – monitoring results versus planned outcomes in some detail both formally and informally by means of reports, meetings and other tools; identifying deviations, and then planning and organising to solve the problems.

Problem-solving is often experienced as the most predominant aspect of a manager's job as much of it is 'fire engine' stuff. Much of this daily work comes under the name of 'general office management'. On a typical day in practice this might include: handling a crisis such as a break-in and drug theft, reorganising the staffing schedule because of illness, dealing with a client complaint, and implementing short-term strategies to boost client numbers.

A good manager also needs to know about the 'housekeeping' in a practice such as the rules and regulations governing employment, health and safety regulations, cleaning and hygiene requirements, and disposal of clinical waste.

What is the role of a veterinary practice manager?

Maggie Shilcock and Georgina Sutchfield, in their book *Veterinary Practice Management, A Practical Guide*, define the role of the practice manager as follows:

> *To enable the good management of the veterinary practice so that the owner or partners can continue to carry out their clinical functions without the need to devote too much expensive time to management.*

They describe how, in veterinary practice, there are often many administrators – people who carry out management tasks – but only one manager who coordinates all the activities (with the exception of very large practices where there may be several managers each with responsibility for a different area). The responsibilities involved in the different areas of management may be wide and varied, as summarised in Table 5.1.

Table 5.1 **Responsibilities involved in the different areas of management**

General management	Daily office organisation
	General purchasing
	Equipment lease, purchase, hire, maintenance and service
	Building fabric
	Banking
	Client accounts
	Policies, protocols and procedures
	Staff manual
	Internal communications
	Rotas
	Ethical and statutory requirements
	Security
Human resource management	Implementing employment legislation
	Staff recruitment and selection
	Job descriptions
	Contracts of employment
	Staff induction
	Appraisals
	Staff training
	Staff motivation and teamwork
	Staff discipline
	Payroll
	Sickness/holiday monitoring
Financial management	End of year accounts
	Monthly financial report production
	Financial and business planning
	Financial trend analysis

(Continued)

Table 5.1 (Continued)	
	Cash flow and bank account management
	Administering practice insurance, vehicles, premises and personnel
	Drug purchase
	Stock control
	Monitoring/controlling equipment purchase
	Liaising with practice accountant, bank insurers and solicitors
Health and safety management	Implementation of all health and safety legislation
	COSHH (Control of Substances Hazardous to Health Regulations)
	Carrying our risk assessments
	Fire regulations
	First aid and RIDDOR (Reporting of Injuries, Diseases and Dangerous Occurrences Regulations)
	Drawing up and implementing safe working procedures
	Waste disposal
	Health and safety training
IT management	Organisation and maintenance of the practice computer systems
	Working knowledge of hardware and software
	IT troubleshooting
	Assessment of veterinary software programs
	Website production and maintenance
	Generation and management of computerised and financial information
	Liaising with software and hardware companies
	Computer training
Marketing, services and sales management	Developing marketing strategies

(*Continued*)

Table 5.1 (*Continued*)

	Target marketing planning
	Setting up/overseeing new services
	Promoting new services
	Overseeing production of client communication materials
	Client surveying
	Advertising policies and procedures
	Media liaison
	Public relations
	Managing product and service sales strategies

Adapted from Shilcock and Sutchfield (2003).

What characterises a good manager?

The job of a manager is to help the people in his or her group achieve more than they would if left on their own. The manager must cajole, nurture, challenge and inspire each group member to stretch for achievement. Beyond this (and what is much harder), the manager must get the individuals to function as a team.

David Maister, 2003

A manager's role is to get things done, achieve goals, and get results. For this, maturity, experience and authority are favourable requirements. A manager needs to be a problem-solver, someone who follows through on actions, and someone who thrives on unravelling complexity. A good manager also needs to be someone who is interested in people – both to encourage and develop staff members and to cheerfully help clients.

> Managing people is about managing emotions. To get the best from people requires being able to take a deep interest in them and to learn about what motivates them. It is about recognising the individual's abilities and harnessing these for the benefit of the greater whole – the veterinary practice. Above all, it is about facilitating achievements not dictating results.

> ### What characterises a good manager?
> Managers achieving high financial returns were seen by their people as being:
>
> - even-keeled and even-tempered
> - genuine
> - good at reading people's characters and skill levels
> - sensitive to personal issues
> - someone of high integrity
> - apolitical
> - sincere
> - a good listener
> - accessible
> - comfortable with allowing other people to get (and take) credit
> - disciplined about standards, though open to reasons why they may not be met
> - enthusiastic
> - studied and precise in conversations
> - thoughtful.
>
> From Maister (2001).

To perform the job well, a manager needs to be given authority within her roles of office as well as a clear definition of those roles. Authority or power is needed to, for example, hire and fire both professional and support staff, to evaluate and coach staff and reward performance, to discipline staff, to train support staff, to control drug and equipment purchase, to resolve client problems, work with book-keeping, accounting and legal issues, have financial accountability for the practice and do the banking, and have responsibility for miscellaneous duties such as maintaining strict standards for cleanliness, and updating the practice library.

Where power is not defined, the potential for conflict arises ('She has no authority to tell me what to do'; 'He shouldn't be sticking his nose into my job'). Of course, power can be misused to push, coerce and generally irritate people.

In one practice in which I worked, the practice manager was the boss's wife. She abused her position of power in many ways, for example in sending handwritten notes demanding urgent (heavily underscored) attention when this was seldom necessary. The result was mistrust, irritation and dissatisfaction amongst employees.

Managers and power

One of the distinguishing characteristics of typical managers is how dependent they are on the activities of a variety of other people to perform their jobs effectively. Unlike, say, clinical veterinarians whose performance is more directly related to their own talents and effort, a manager is dependent on cooperation from the practice principals and owners, office assistants, other staff in the practice, outside suppliers, clients, banks and many more besides. These dependency relationships are an inherent part of a manager's job because of two organisational facts of life: division of labour and limited resources. Dealing with these dependencies and the manager's subsequent vulnerability is an important and difficult part of a manager's job. Theoretically, everyone would be cooperative and the manager's job would then be easy, but this is seldom the case in reality. Indeed, managers often find themselves dependent on many people (and things) whom they do not directly control and who are not cooperating. This reduces efficiency and may create frustration.

To cope with this a manager needs power within the job role. Power is often seen as a dirty word, and yet managers cannot perform their job without power – power to influence and guide others, to plan, organise, budget, evaluate and all the other things a manager does. If the practice manager is also the practice owner then that power is inherent in his or her role as 'boss', but if the practice manager is an employee then power needs to be established in other ways.

What's in a title?

There are a number of different levels of management that apply in veterinary practice:

- *The office manager* – who is responsible for implementing and coordinating the administrative directions determined by the practice owner or hospital director.
- *The practice manager* – who has greater responsibilities than the office manager which may include the overall coordination of financial activities, preparation of budgets, hiring and firing of support staff, and generally having more authority for the day-to-day running of the practice. They are still answerable to the practice owner(s).
- *The practice or hospital administrator* – a qualified, experienced person with complete authority over the running of the practice. Apart

from clinical matters, he or she is responsible for every aspect of practice activity.

Most practices have not progressed beyond having an office manager, which creates profound restrictions on the development of the practice.

Some reasons why practice managers are not successful – yet!

> *Good practice managers are rare, but so is a practice that will tolerate a good practice manager.*
> Don Dooley, Veterinary Management Consultant, 1992

This statement was written over a decade ago and yet it still holds true. Although more practices are employing a manager, few allow development of this position to the full.

Practice managers can make a very significant difference to the productivity of a practice but for many principals the abdication of the authority that ownership of the practice entails to a better-qualified third party is an almost impossible hurdle to overcome. As a result, so-called practice managers are very limited in what they can achieve. Until veterinarians have the self-confidence to truly hand over the responsibilities to a practice manager of running the practice on a day-to-day basis and to planning for its future, the best that can be achieved in most practices is learning to delegate the many duties a good practice manager could undertake to suitably trained staff members.

Managing your boss
Effective practice managers take time and effort to manage their relationships not only with other staff members, but also with their boss(es). Even if *you* are the practice owner and manager, you need to know how to manage yourself!

One of the biggest concerns in practice is a fear that a practice manager will somehow 'take over' the practice from the principal/owner and sweep control out of his or her hands. However, practice leaders and the manager have a mutual dependence on each other. Bosses can link the manager to the rest of the practice, help them set priorities and secure the resources they need. Managers can help bosses by ensuring cooperation, dependability and honesty so that they can do their job effectively.

Bosses and managers are – like us all – fallible human beings. To manage your boss requires a good understanding of yourself and your boss, especially regarding strengths, weaknesses, work styles and needs. You then need to be able to use that information to develop and manage a healthy working style – one that is compatible with both people's work styles and assets, is characterised by mutual expectations, and meets the most critical needs of the other person. Valuable understanding of each other's needs can most easily be achieved, for example, through psychometric profiling (see Chapter 7).

Veterinarian versus practice manager

As we have already established, veterinarians tend to resent taking advice from non-veterinarians and are often unwilling to hand over authority to a (non-veterinarian) manager. This reduces immediately the manager's effectivity.

However, in many practices the practice manager *is* a non-veterinarian who has either been promoted from a nursing or reception position, or is retired from a civilian position (bank manager, accountant, etc.). Of the former group, there is a risk that they may not have the maturity and confidence based on experience and understanding of the requirements of their role to exert the necessary authority; the latter may not be given the necessary authority. In addition, without a lot of support from the leaders, it is not easy to cope with the effects of being promoted and being given power over former friends and colleagues.

Some practices hire a retired veterinarian or retain a semi-retired partner as the practice manager. Although these practitioners may bring a wealth of clinical experience with them, they can have a negative effect on practice development in a number of ways:

- They retain old-fashioned ideas and policies and may not be receptive to new ideas.
- They block the development of a new culture.
- Their skills are primarily as clinicians not managers.
- They are less financially productive as managers than when using their clinical skills (but often still expect a high salary commensurate with their maturity and clinical experience).
- They do not necessarily have the people management skills essential for the job. The 'older school' of veterinarians is often a tough group of individuals who are very much self-made individuals.

Another source of practice managers is the principal's non-veterinarian spouse. This may seem the ideal solution in a small practice; for example, the boss's spouse can take the load of responsibility for all the non-clinical procedures in the practice. In reality, the close relationship of the manager to the practice owner often creates uncomfortable problems:

■ Staff are afraid/feel unable to come to the manager to discuss issues concerning the boss, or vice versa.
■ The manager is felt to have undue influence over the boss, which may spill over into management of clinical aspects of the practice.
■ The manager may abuse the position of authority and make employees' lives very difficult.

Practices like this are often characterised by a high turnover of unhappy professional and support staff.

Increasingly, however, certified veterinary practice managers are being employed in those countries where certification is available. In the UK and Australia, for example, the number of managers certified in veterinary practice management increases each year and the qualification is regarded by the profession as a benchmark of quality in veterinary management. The aims of the British Veterinary Practice Management Association (VPMA) are: 'to provide individuals who are involved in the management of veterinary practice with an effective means of communication and interaction with others with similar interests, and a forum for promoting, providing and recognising training and excellence in all aspects of veterinary practice management'. To this end, certification is available as a practice manager or practice administrator.

The Certificate in Veterinary Practice Management (CVPM)

A formal qualification which demonstrates to prospective and current employers a manager's measurable skills in administration, financial management, personnel matters and marketing of the business of a veterinary practice.

Achieving the Certificate in Veterinary Practice Management is the 'gold standard' and will acknowledge that the holder possesses a wide range of practice management skills and expertise which sets them apart as a professional.

The Veterinary Practice Administration Certificate (VPAC)

This formal qualification, introduced in 2001, is accredited via the Open College Network, and available to administrative and other staff with administrative responsibilities in practice.

Further details from the VPMA website: www.vpma.co.uk.

In Australia, the AVPMA offers the Graduate Certificate in Practice Management (Veterinary practice) to raise knowledge about and enhance the application of management in veterinary practice.

> ### *AVPMA mission*
> To enhance quality of life in Australian Veterinary Practices, by enabling AVPMA members to develop personal skills in veterinary practice management and by providing resources and networks that enhance veterinary practice management through knowledge sharing and knowledge creation and through the fostering of relationships and personal support that comes from belonging to the association.
> Further details from the AVPMA website: www.avpma.com.au.

Practice managers in the future

The role of management in veterinary practice is changing, with greater importance being put on this essential function. The increasing complexity involved in efficiently running even a relatively small, often private, business such as a veterinary practice means there is greater need for competent professionals who are trained to manage this complexity. Increased specialisation within the management field is likely as well, requiring more advanced skills sets and disciplines and thus gradually reducing the role of 'general administrator' or 'admin assistant' to a thing of the past.

6 Effective communication: the vital link

Human beings carry an ability to receive, interpret and emotionally distort every message they receive.

Hayes and Watts, Business Management Consultants

Communication is something that everyone does every day on many different levels and yet communication problems are the greatest cause of stress, job dissatisfaction, and disappointed clients in veterinary practice. Good communication is critically important because it is the foundation of a healthy business.

Where communication is not working well you have an unhappy practice. Staff complain, gossip, and come late to work. Promising new staff members rapidly become complacent and do only the bare minimum, or simply vote with their feet and leave, creating a high staff turnover. An unhappy practice is costly, ineffective and a miserable place to work. It is also not popular with clients.

Relations with clients mirror relations between employees. Relations between employees mirrors the way *you* treat *them*. A well-organised, happy staff team who are willing to help clients is an indication of sound leadership and a healthy communication system, where trust is high (Fig. 6.1). Trust is the cornerstone of good relations, so the more trust that is developed between staff and clients, the more compliance is achieved, the better care animals receive, and the more satisfaction your clients experience.

Clients visiting a practice expect professional levels of medical and surgical care, but can only measure that professionalism in terms of the service they receive. Professionalism is about being committed to serving clients and their needs to the best of your abilities within the framework of your professional values. Part of being a professional is

Figure 6.1 Happy staff are willing to serve and create happy clients.

excelling in communication, which includes visible signs such as professional dress (the white coat and stethoscope or the nurse's uniform), manner (showing concern and caring), and behaviour (working with integrity and having authority) (Fig. 6.2a & b).

Professional is not a title you claim for yourself, it's an adjective you hope other people will apply to you. You have to earn it. Professionalism means *deserving* the rewards you wish to gain from others by being dedicated to serving their interests as part of an implied bargain. Professionalism implies that you do not focus only on the immediate transaction, but care about your relationship with

(a)

Figure 6.2   (a) The green uniform of the qualified veterinary nurse is a clear symbol of her status both within the practice, and to the client. (b) A clearly printed name badge enhances communication to clients. Acknowledgement Anne-Marie Svendsen.

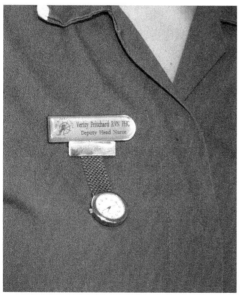

(b)

the person with whom you are working. It means you can be trusted to put your clients' interests first, can be depended upon to do what you say you will do and will not consistently act for short-term personal gain. Professionals make decisions using principles of appropriate behaviour, not just short-term expediency (Maister, 2005).

Essential to good communication skills is an aptitude in and understanding of emotional intelligence. Emotional intelligence describes abilities distinct from but complementary to academic intelligence, that is, the purely cognitive capacities measured by IQ. Emotional intelligence is defined as *'the capacity for recognising our own feelings and those of others, for motivating ourselves, and for managing emotions well in ourselves and in our relationships'*. In veterinary practice, emotional intelligence is all the elements that go into building relationships with clients, and with each other, and it is an integral part of the skills shown by good leaders and managers.

Understanding the components of emotional intelligence
Emotional intelligence consists of five emotional competencies:

■ *Personal competencies* that determine how we manage ourselves:
self-awareness – knowing one's internal states, preferences, resources and intuitions
self-regulation – managing one's internal states, preferences, resources and intuitions
motivation – emotional tendencies that guide or facilitate reaching goals.
■ *Social competencies* that determine how we handle relationships:
empathy – awareness of others' feelings, needs and concerns
social skills – adeptness at inducing desirable responses in others.

The sort of communication techniques that make up emotional intelligence include not only active listening, accurate interpretation of body language, careful use of words, and using visual and tangible support materials to aid understanding and compliance, but also *how you use* these different methods depending on what you are trying to achieve (Table 6.1). For example, conducting a clinical examination uses probing and empathetic questioning to gain information to make a diagnosis and treat the animal; managing a client complaint requires attentive listening and the authority to help the client find a mutually satisfactory resolution; performance appraisal is a formal interview to evaluate, enhance and reward desirable behaviour; whereas marketing is about using all five senses to convey a certain types of message

Table 6.1　**Communicating with colleagues and clients**		
Methods	**Purpose**	**Outcomes**
Voice and words	Create trust	***Staff/colleagues***
Active listening	Convey interest,	Happy, productive,
Body language	care and concern	creative work environment
Written material and	Convey professionalism	
visual aids		***Clients***
Touch (Smell)		Repeat business, income
		Better animal health

or messages about the practice to clients. These are specialised styles of communication, each with a specific purpose and measurable outcome.

An inappropriate style of communication in these situations – that is, inappropriate application of emotional intelligence skills – would create frustration, anger, confusion and misunderstandings. Imagine a clinical examination conducted like a third degree interrogation, or a staff appraisal which consisted of a monologue on how you see the world? These would not be likely to produce desirable results! (Fig. 6.3a & b)

In the practice environment, communication has a number of goals. These are outcomes you hope to achieve through using effective communication. Primary goals within the practice include creating the feeling of being a contributing member of a well-functioning and productive community, and being part of the growth and development of the practice as a living organisation. Goals of external communication with clients include helping them feel satisfied that they and their animals have been well cared for and that they have been able to make the best decisions regarding the health and well-being of their animal. Powerful measures of effective communication include word of mouth recommendation from existing staff that attract new staff members to the practice, indicating that it is a desirable place to work; and word of mouth recommendation from clients to potential new clients – a sure sign that the client has been *personally and positively* touched by the service and care they and their animal has received (Fig. 6.4).

A wide variety of different communication methods requiring different skills are needed in practice (Table 6.2). The major problem is that most people learn them by trial and error – few have formal training in how to build relations, how to conduct an effective client interview, or

(a)

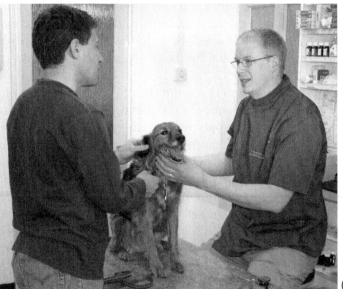

(b)

Figure 6.3a and b The simple action of being on eye level with a client helps this very tall veterinarian relate better with his client.
Acknowledgement Anne-Marie Svendsen.

how to communicate well with staff. In fact, for many veterinarians, communication skills rank second to clinical knowledge – a reflection of the comfort felt in the discipline of a fact-based training, rather than the quicksand of the art of communication.

Figure 6.4 Showing you take an interest in the pet is appreciated by the pet owner.

Table 6.2 **Some of the different communication methods needed in practice**

Internal	External with client
Recruitment interview	Recruiting advertising
Release interview	Website
Appraisal interview	Complaint management
Coaching interview	Consultation
Meetings	Bereavement management
Internal memos	Telephone booking
Intranet	Telephone laboratory results

Veterinarian Paul Manning highlights the dichotomy professionals face in interviewing clients in his recent Masters degree in Consultation Technique. In the course of his studies, which involved questionnaires to and interviews of consulting vets and their clients, he found a clear difference between what veterinarians *believe* clients want and what clients *actually* expect. He found that:

■ vets rated clinical skills as the most important service delivery, with communication skills second
■ stress associated with time management is likely to push the veterinarian into asking more 'closed' questions than 'open', which reduces opportunities for eliciting clients' concerns
■ vets tended to focus on the diagnosis rather than the prognosis, whereas the latter often had higher priority for clients ('*When* will Tibbles' diarrhoea get better?')
■ vets often make decisions on behalf of clients without asking them (for example, not recommending an X-ray examination of a lame

dog when this is what the owner would really like to have) – or don't explain why they don't offer certain options.

His overwhelming conclusion is sobering: '*Possibly the most significant finding of this whole project is that the vets put their clinical ability as the top point in their appreciation of the consultation whereas the clients put communication first.*'

So, what is communication?

Communication is the sharing or exchange of information, ideas, or feelings. It is a complex learned skill that uses all the senses (sight, hearing, touch, smell and taste).

People differ in how they use their senses. Some are primarily *visual* – 'Yes, I *see* what you mean'; some are primarily *listeners* –'I'll be *hearing* from you then'; and some are primarily *feelers* using touch and emotion – 'I need to *get a grip* on this', 'I *feel* really excited by your suggestion'. A trained communicator in a one-to-one conversation will quickly identify the favoured style of communication and adapt their style of communication to match it.

Communication is a vast and complex area and for the sake of clarity and brevity I have selected those aspects which I believe are most important in veterinary practice. Often, an artificial division is made between 'internal' and 'external' communication. In reality, the way staff communicate with clients reflects the way they communicate with each other.

Communication and trust

Effective communication is central to good business because it creates trust. J. Richard Hackman, Harvard Professor of Psychology, says about trust:

> *Trust isn't something you can mandate, a lever you can simply pull to improve an organization. Trust is an outcome, something that develops gradually in organizations that are*

> *well designed and well led. To say 'Now we must all trust*
> *one another' is to say nothing at all.*

A healthy trust relationship between colleagues and with clients is the basis for a sound business. Trust comes from many little actions, rather than one or two big ones. A trusting relationship takes time and determination to establish, and it is very fragile. Once damaged, like a cracked cup, it may be possible to use it, but it is never the same again.

When you talk to a client you are usually trying to persuade them of the value of your ideas for the care and treatment of their pet: you are literally 'selling' yourself and your concepts to them. For them to 'buy' they must believe and trust you. This trust comes through not only what you say and how you say it, but in having a confident, friendly and reassuring manner. This is demonstrated by maintaining at least 60% eye contact (would you trust anyone who cannot meet your eye?), gestures such as patting or stroking the animal as you talk (conveying you like animals), confidently handling syringes to give injections (conveying I know what I'm doing), returning the animal clean and groomed after hospitalisation (showing that we care about our patients) and so on.

Creating trust with clients comes from a willingness to help clients. It starts by having an agreed policy in the practice that the client is the most valued member of the practice. Where the client is regarded as a mere intrusion on the day, trust can never develop satisfactorily. The behaviours that make up trust are listed in Table 6.3. These behaviours are the competencies identified in emotional intelligence.

There are two key behaviours that must take place for trust to develop:

- attentively listening to clients to hear what they are *really* saying, which is explored in depth in the next section
- and being consistent.

Table 6.3 **The 7 C's of trust**

1.	*Communication* – maintain trust through clear, honest communication
2.	*Competence* – includes professional and personal abilities
3.	*Consistency* – conformity with previous attitudes and behaviours
4.	*Compassion* – showing empathy, and the ability to understand someone else's viewpoint
5.	*Costs* – a fair price for a good job
6.	*Cheerfulness* – being welcomed into a friendly, happy environment
7.	*Commitment* – to always doing the best possible job

Being consistent means conforming with previous practices and behaviours; being reliable. In your practice, by striving to *consistently* show courtesy, kindness and honesty, keep commitments, and convey an 'I care' attitude to staff and clients alike, you maintain your professional and personal integrity by matching your actions to your words and treating everyone by the same set of values. Of course, being human you will not always be consistent in your behaviour, so trust also involves being able to apologise and 'clean up' if you make a mistake or behave in a less than professional manner.

> One of the secrets of the enormous success that the McDonald's food chain has experienced globally is being consistent. No matter where you buy your McBurger, you will receive the same product served with the same level of service at a similar price.

Trust is not only important in client relations and business building: it is also essential to team building with your staff members. Putting trust in someone else's abilities is the highest form of human motivation and brings out the best in people. By giving practice members plenty of scope for professional and competency development, supporting and encouraging that development without jealousy, and coaching and encouraging them to give their best rather than accepting mediocrity, practice members will rise to the level of trust put in them.

To create trust requires a knowledge and understanding of the techniques of effective communication, and also how to remove the common barriers that block or disrupt communication. Let's look at these in more detail.

The skills of effective communication

Listening skills

How many times have you heard someone exclaim 'You're not listening to what I'm saying!'. When the person accused of listening answers, 'I am too; I can repeat everything you said', the accuser is not comforted. What people look for in attending and listening is not the other person's ability to repeat their words. A tape recorder would do that perfectly.

People want more than physical presence in human communication; they want the other person to be present psychologically, socially and emotionally.

Egan, *The Skilled Helper*, 1990

Listening is a core competence. People who cannot listen cannot relate: poor listening undermines the ability to communicate with others. Despite the fact that we spend around 45% of communication time listening, compared with 30% speaking, 16% reading and 9% writing, few people have received formal training in how to listen *attentively*.

Attentive listening involves more than just sitting and doing nothing. Attentive listening is a complex psychological procedure involving interpreting and understanding the significance of both verbal and non-verbal messages and turning this into meaning in the mind. It is an active process and conveys respect.

The four main types of listening

Comprehension listening: the listening used when conducting fact-finding interviews or attending lectures. Facts, themes and ideas for future use are identified.

Evaluative listening: used to make judgements about persuasive messages such as sales persons or negotiators are using to influence attitudes, beliefs and actions.

Empathetic listening: used in counselling, appraisal interviews, and in situations where someone needs to talk to and be understood by another. The listener demonstrates a willingness to attend to and understand the thoughts, beliefs and feelings of the speaker.

Appreciative listening: the type of listening people engage in for pleasure, for example in listening to music or children playing. The listener seeks out signals or messages she wants to hear.

Figure 6.5 Turning your back on the client cuts off communication.

Figure 6.6 Plugging in the stethoscope and making speculative noises is a very effective way to block client communication and even increase their concern levels.

The four main types of listening (see above) have in common the following components:

■ *attending* – the way the listener orients herself to the speaker both physically and psychologically
■ *listening* –receiving and understanding the verbal and non-verbal messages transmitted by the speaker
■ *empathy* – understanding the speaker's message from within his frame of reference and communicating this to him
■ *probing* – encouraging and prompting the speaker to talk about himself and define his problem more concretely and specifically.

The different styles are used in different proportions in different situations. For example, empathetic listening may dominate when talking to a grieving client, and comprehension listening may dominate in a clinical consultation.

What becomes clear is that listening is a two-way process. As the communicator speaks to the receiver, the receiver is (mostly subconsciously) making judgements about a wide variety of factors such as the choice of words, the emotionality with which they are expressed, the body language used, and the importance of the message for the receiver. The communicator, as she speaks, is getting feedback in terms of body language and facial expression, which indicate the receiver's interest and receptivity, which, in turn, affects how the communicator continues the communication. It is like a spiral dance where one strand of communication winds around the other to build a double helix of mutual understanding and respect.

> **Empathetic listening**
> *When another person speaks, we are usually 'listening' at one of four levels. We may be ignoring another person, not really listening at all. We may practice pretending. 'Yeah. Uh-huh.*

> *Right.' We may practice selective listening, hearing only certain parts of the conversation. We often do this when we are listening to the constant chatter of a pre-school child. Or we may even practice attentive listening. Paying attention and focusing energy on the words that are being said. But very few of us ever practice the fifth level, the highest form of listening, empathetic listening.'*
> (Covey, 1989)

Empathetic listening is listening actively, paying full attention to the speaker, and digesting and interpreting the true meaning of what is being said. It is not projecting your own autobiography onto someone else and assuming thoughts, feelings, motives and interpretations, nor is it simply waiting for a gap in the conversation that you can fill with your own good advice. Empathetic listening says. 'I want to understand you. I want to know you.' It is one of the most basic ways to convey a sense of respect, to treat another person with dignity. It is partly a skill, which means it can be improved with training and practice, but it is primarily a *desire* to really understand another person. Empathy is not the same as sympathy. Whereas with sympathy the listener seeks to *feel* the same as the person in pain, the empathic listener seeks to see the world through that person's eyes without becoming swamped by the other person's feelings.

Sympathy versus empathy

Sympathy: the sharing of another's emotions, especially of sorrow or anguish, compassion.
Empathy: the power of understanding and imaginatively entering into another person's feelings.
(New Collins Concise English Dictionary)

Attentive listening is critical for the effective exchange of information in a conversation. It is estimated that we use less than 25% of our listening powers in a typical exchange and ignore, forget, distort or misunderstand a staggering 75%. This is borne out by studies which show that medical doctors interviewing patients frequently interrupt them – often as early as 18 seconds in their opening statements – which results in frustration and information withholding ('because the doctor hasn't time for me') from the patient's side. In veterinary practice, not listening attentively creates irritation (e.g. from not listening to the nurse who suggests a valuable time-saving technique), loses business (not hearing the client who mentions that Bonzo has intermittent diarrhoea, a condition which might respond to dietary or medical management), and may even be dangerous (not hearing the client who says that Fluffy is drinking more, which may mean diagnostic blood tests for renal disease are advisable before giving the anaesthetic for the dental you're recommending).

Attentive listening is both active and highly skilled. Four specific skills areas are needed by medical doctors interviewing patients to develop the ability to listen attentively:

- wait time – pausing and waiting to enable the patient to assimilate and articulate their thoughts and feelings
- facilitative response – encouraging the patient to talk by making encouraging noises ('Uh-ah, tell me more about this') or signals (head nodding, a sympathetic hand on the arm)
- non-verbal skills – including eye contact, and open, interested body language
- picking up verbal and non-verbal cues – hearing the message behind the words.

Barriers to attentive listening

Attentive listening is not easy. It requires commitment, energy and focus. There are also many barriers to listening (see below) not least of which is our own internal monologue which includes our own personal views, thoughts, and our agenda. What we hear and understand is largely based on personal experience and background. We have many preconceived notions and ideas so that we often hear what our mind *thinks* a person has said, not what they actually *have* said (Fig. 6.7a and b).

We may have perceptions about the communicator and are more accepting of someone we like rather than someone who has different or conflicting views. In addition, we often choose to ignore or forget information that does not concur with our own beliefs.

Common barriers to listening and understanding
- Hearing unfamiliar words such as technical jargon or slang.
- Speaking too fast, especially if the person is hard of hearing or is herself a slow talker.

(a)

(b)

Figure 6.7 (a) A computer positioned so that the user must turn away from the client can serve as a barrier to effective listening. Acknowledgement Anne-Marie Svendsen. (b) This Danish veterinarian has found a practical solution that enables him to maintain visual contact with his client during the consultation and write the patient records. It also helps him avoid back problems!

- Doing other things simultaneously/distractions such as working on the computer or reading the patient records as you listen.
- Excess background noise from howling dogs or chatting staff.
- 'Switching off' because you are not interested, or thinking of something else.

- Being critical and judgemental about someone and the way they have behaved instead of trying to understand what they have done from their viewpoint. Criticism deadens communication and diminishes trust.
- Being compliant for the sake of comfort and agreeing to do something or follow a recommendation without really understanding what it involves.
- Using an inappropriate or incorrect form of address.
- Tiredness, hunger and other physical discomforts distract listening.

It is difficult to talk to somebody who is apparently not responding and may create feelings of confusion, discomfort and even anger on the part of the speaker that stops further communication. By using encouraging body language (such as nodding your head), eye contact, facial and auditory signals ('Yes, I see'; 'Mmmm, that's interesting') coupled with repeating or paraphrasing what the person has said ('If I understand you correctly, you think that Tibbles ...'; 'Jim, from what you've just said, the problem with the current X-ray system is ...') you indicate that you are listening, and that you follow and are interested in what the speaker is saying. On the telephone, where people can't see you nodding and agreeing with them, make agreeing noises ('Yes','Ah-ha', 'I see ... ' and so on) to show your interest (Fig. 6.8).

Figure 6.8 Eye contact helps create trust with clients. Acknowledgement Anne-Marie Svendsen.

Clients also have barriers in their communication which are particularly relevant during the clinical consultation. For example, they may have:

- *Ideas and beliefs* about the cause or effect of the illness their animal is displaying, and about health and what influences or contributes to it (*e.g. some cat owners believe it is healthier for their pet to eat a vegetarian diet*).
- *Concerns and worries* about what the symptoms might mean (*'Is this cancer?'*).
- *Expectations* about how the veterinarian will help them, and the outcomes that will be achieved from the visit (*'The vets on that TV programme could fix this problem'*).
- *Effects on life*: the effect that the animal's illness has on their own life now and in the future.
- *Feelings and emotions* coupled to the breakdown of the relationship with the animal.

I recently experienced first hand the confusion, worry and concern that happens when the relationship with your pet breaks down. Despite being a veterinarian, when one of our cats and beloved family members, Frodo, became inappetent, withdrawn, and started vomiting and having diarrhoea, turning almost overnight from an enchanting playful companion to a miserable little heap of ungroomed and unresponsive fur – I lost all contact with cool rationality and became uncharacteristically out of balance. I wanted him 'right' again but despite clinical examinations by excellent colleagues, extensive tests, treatments and medication he did not return to his old self. Terrible emotions began to run through my thoughts – anger and frustration at him not getting well (and at the vets treating him), despair that he would not recover, worry about how much it would all cost, and even a cold pragmatism – 'well, he is only a cat' – hastily swamped by a passionate love for our littlest family member. After an unrevealing laparotomy, he did make a full recovery (Fig. 6.9) and is now back to his enchanting self (in fact, he is

Figure 6.9   Frodo fully recovered after his ordeal and back to his inquisitive self.

trying to get his paw into the printer and catch the 'mouse' as I am writing) but the experience was both very uncomfortable and also a great lesson in understanding what clients go through.

Taking time to explore and understand the concerns clients have can make a big difference to levels of client satisfaction and compliance experienced. It can also largely remove the risk of client complaints as the root of almost all client complaints lies in poor communication.

Voice and words

In a face-to-face meeting less than 20% of the exchange depends on the words being spoken; most information for the receiver comes from non-verbal signals such as tone of voice, facial expression, eye contact, and body language. A cold, brusque voice is alienating, and a shrill, loud voice can be both irritating and wearing. The ideal voice is warm, friendly and fairly low-pitched.

Voice is especially important on the telephone where the caller cannot see the person and makes a judgement from voice alone. Less than 15% of the impression made on the telephone comes from the words spoken. Smiling as you talk and using gestures positively influences voice quality, pitch, and speed of speech. As receiver you are using only your listening sense, so good listening skills become critical.

Choice of words is also important. Jargon is off-putting and generally not understood by clients. Interestingly, many studies have shown that medical doctors not only use language that patients often do not understand, they actually appear to use it to control their patient's involvement in the interview. Often clients are embarrassed to ask for explanations of terms they do not understand, which means they can be very dependent on the nurse (or receptionist) to explain to them afterwards 'What the doctor said'.

Words mean different things to different people. A simple example is the English word 'chronic'. In medical terms it means a long-term condition (e.g. 'He has chronic hepatitis'), whereas in layman's terms it means something not very pleasant, rather dreary (e.g. 'It was a chronic party', 'He's really chronic'). It is important to ensure that the person to whom you are speaking understands the words you are using. Check this by asking them at regular intervals and in a non-threatening way: 'Do you follow what I am saying?' 'Does this make sense to you?'

Body language

Body language is an integral part of face-to-face communication. It is generally an involuntary and therefore truthful indicator of what the

Figure 6.10   Eye contact and even appropriate physical contact help create a trusting relationship.

speaker is actually thinking, whatever words he or she may be choosing to use. Communication research has shown that non-verbal messages tend to override verbal messages when the two are inconsistent or contradictory. Many individual components are involved in non-verbal communication, including posture, movement, proximity, direction of gaze, eye contact, gestures, facial expression, touch and physical appearance. Particularly important is eye contact (Fig. 6.10).

> Human patients felt their doctor was not interested in them if they experienced little or no eye contact. This often resulted in them proffering less information about themselves – information which might have affected their diagnosis and treatment.

Closed body language (crossed arms, looking away from the person to whom you are speaking, turning your back) shows a lack of interest, and a lack of receptivity. Many people sense this and are put off by it. Staff may feel, 'The boss wasn't really interested in my problem', and clients may comment to their friends, 'That vet wasn't really interested – he didn't listen to me' (Fig. 6.11).

> ### Simple ways to improve your body language
> - Smile when you meet the client.
> - Establish eye contact.
> - Shake hands when the client enters the consulting room.
> - Fondle their pet and show kindness to it.
> - Have a friendly, welcoming expression.
> - Look interested in what the client is saying.
> - Maintain the 'open position' (avoid crossing your arms in front of you, or sitting with your arms and legs crossed).

Figure 6.11
Appearing bored and disinterested significantly reduces the freedom and ease with which clients communicate, which may result in not being given vital information. Acknowledgement Anne-Marie Svendsen.

- Avoid turning your back on your client.
- Maintain at least 60% eye contact during a conversation.
- Don't fiddle with things or glance at your watch – it implies lack of interest or that you have 'something better to do'.
- Have clean hands and nails and keep your hands out of your pockets.
- Take pride in your professional appearance.
- Avoid habits such as nail-biting, hair-twisting, etc. – they are distracting.

Open body language, and mirroring or copying body language signals help break down barriers to communication. Copying body language conveys a very important non-verbal message: it tells others you like them or agree with them, and vice versa. You will often see mirroring when two friends are talking to each other.

Use of written material and visual aids

Visual aids are a very important part of communication between human beings because they are primarily visual creatures. Studies of patients visiting medical doctors have shown that patients retain less than 10%

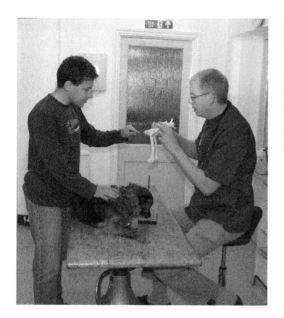

Figure 6.12 Using a model of the hip joint of a dog can help owners visualise and better understand health issues in their own pets. Acknowledgement Anne-Marie Svendsen.

of everything discussed in the consulting room immediately afterwards. Assuming our clients have the same retentive powers, there is clearly more we can do to get information across.

Writing something down helps clarify the information to be conveyed, reduces the opportunities for misinterpretation and encourages consistency in service levels. In addition, there is often an innate acceptance of the written word whereas the reliability of the spoken word may be questioned. Information sheets, newsletters and written instructions help to reinforce and enhance the verbal message and improve compliance with clients, and written job descriptions, signed agendas from meetings and written protocols assist good communication between practice members.

Slides, overheads, whiteboard drawings, models, diagrams and sections of skeletons aid explanations and presentations to colleagues and clients alike (Fig. 6.12).

Touch

Although there are many complex social taboos surrounding touch and physical contact, touch is still a very important part of communication. A welcoming handshake or a comforting arm around the shoulders of a grieving client can say far more than words alone.

Figure 6.13 Taking time to explain problems to pet owners helps to create trust.

Smell

The importance of smell is also underestimated particularly as part of the 'first impressions' a client gains of the practice. What impression does a client gain of a practice where the receptionist wears an overpowering scent, or the veterinarian smells unwashed, or the waiting area reeks of tom cat urine? After all, what are your reactions to the client who has powerful halitosis, or smells of drink, or owns a poodle soaked in scent?

People's sensitivity to smells does vary, but never underestimate the effect an odour can have on a person.

Further barriers to communication

As we have seen earlier, a major barrier to communication is our very natural tendency to judge, evaluate, approve or disapprove of what the other person is saying. Because the human mind processes words at four times the rate we speak or hear them, we often think we understand the other person before we have heard them out.

Other barriers to communication which can profoundly reduce its effectiveness are emotions and practice size.

Emotions

Our emotions often cloud our interpretation of messages. For example, if we are worried and anxious or tired and hungry we are less able to concentrate and accept ideas; if we are angry we may be totally intolerant of otherwise perfectly good suggestions. Appreciating how emotions can be a barrier to understanding is especially important when talking to the owner of a very ill or dying pet. They may be so upset they are unable to make rational and sensible decisions, and you may have to repeat things several times before they 'sink in'.

A veterinarian specialising in cancer therapy shared with me that when he first discusses the diagnosis 'cancer' with his clients he insists that they are not to make any decisions about the management of their pet until at least the following day when they have talked it over with their family and friends. By giving a 24–48-hour period for them to think about all the implications of potentially complex and costly treatments which may have profound effects on the owner's lifestyle, he finds that owners are more likely to make a rational decision which they then follow through. 'The 24-hour rule gives them time to digest what I have said, and make a decision they can stand for instead of rushing into something in the middle of an emotional turmoil and making a decision they later regret', he explains. 'For those choosing therapy, compliance with the protocol is much higher, and the quality of life achieved for both pet and owner is much better.'

Practice size

The bigger the practice and the more people in it, the greater the chance of misunderstandings and miscommunications arising. As practices get larger and communication becomes exponentially more complex, managers need to take greater and greater care that communication remains clear and that the right information gets to the right people at the right time.

The importance of first impressions ...

Within a few seconds of entering a new situation it is human nature to make judgements about it using all five senses. These 'first impressions' create so-called 'moments of truth' which colour all further experiences. First impressions and moments of truth are important because they affect each of your clients as they contact or come into the practice many times a day. First impressions generating moments of truth include telephone contact, the external view of the practice, the greeting clients receive as they walk in, and how they are received as they enter the consulting room. For example, consider the difference in the moments of truth created for a client by a friendly receptionist who gives a pleasant greeting using the person's and pet's names, compared with a surly receptionist who ignores the client and continues chatting on the phone to her friend.

The problem is, you work in the practice and become blind or indifferent to things which can have a profound impact on the first

(a)

(b)

Figure 6.14a and b What judgements might your clients make about your practice before even entering it?

Figure 6.15 What might the entrance of this practice convey to clients? Acknowledgement Anne-Marie Svendsen.

impressions clients form. The wrong first impressions may actually turn a client away, or at least ensure they do not return.

Try to see the practice from the client's viewpoint (Fig. 6.14). Take time to come into the practice through the client's entrance (What does the building look like? What does the entrance look like? How does the place smell? Did the receptionist greet you – even if it was 'only' you? What do you notice when you sit in the waiting room? What might this say to you about the practice?) (Fig. 6.15).

Improving communication in the reception area

The reception area is the first area the client sees in the practice (Fig. 6.16a, b). It is ideal for communicating some of the basic values of the practice, such as:

- *We care about our clients* – make the area as attractive, comfortable and welcoming as possible (Fig. 6.17). Remember to make it attractive for the pets too!

(a)

(b)

Figure 6.16 (a) Making the entrance area welcoming. (b) Showing who works in the practice.

Figure 6.17a and b Make clients feel welcome with a dog or cat theme in your waiting area.

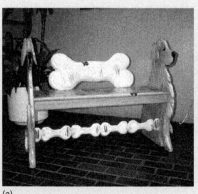

(a)

(b)

- *We are a professional team* – photograph boards with the staff (and their pets), and their qualifications tell clients who works here and that they care about animals.
- *We give top animal healthcare* – professional posters, and product displays inform clients about preventive healthcare and other services available in the practice.

The role of the receptionist in communication

The receptionist is one of the key people in the practice and is usually the first person the client meets and speaks to. A receptionist's job is far more than simply managing the front desk and the telephone; a receptionist communicates the practice's professional image to the client by manner, appearance and attitude. It is especially important to hire a receptionist who is interested in people and their animals.

... and last impressions

Equally important as first impressions are last impressions – the feelings and thoughts the client experiences as they leave the veterinary clinic or finish their telephone conversation with the vet or nurse. Studies show that satisfied clients leave the encounter with the practice feeling that they:

- were listened to
- received an explanation of the problem that made sense to them
- felt care and concern being expressed by the caregivers and others in the clinic
- left with an enhanced sense of mastery over their animal's illness or its signs.

To help achieve these, it is important to consider the following points in the final part of the encounter with the practice:

- That they feel comfortable with the prognosis or the next steps in the treatment.
- That they receive help to identify the diet the veterinarian has recommended and understand how it is to be used.
- That giving medicines is demonstrated – better still that they can try giving them themselves under supervision.

- That last questions are answered and that they know whom they can contact for more information.
- That they do not have to queue for prolonged periods to pay.
- That the bill does not come as a nasty shock, and that the items on it can be explained by the receptionist if needed.
- That a new appointment can easily be booked.
- That they receive assistance calling a taxi, or help out to the car.

In some cases, such as the first visit of a new client to the practice, the whole experience can be enhanced by sending them a letter a few days after their visit welcoming them and their animals to the clinic, and describing the services the practice can offer them.

Communication and professionalism

Successful firms are differentiated not by their different goals, clever strategies or special managerial tactics – these are all remarkably similar worldwide. Successful firms are clearly differentiated by a strict adherence to values, i.e. to professionalism.

David Maister, *True Professionalism*, 1997

Being a professional means a commitment to serving clients and their needs to the best of your ability within the framework of your professional values. This is not always easy. In addition, the public's attitude to professionals has changed. Whereas in the past, professionals were often given respect and trust automatically because of their position, now, clients question professionals' recommendations, making them justify everything they plan to do on the client's behalf and meticulously monitoring and questioning the costs involved. Trust and respect is still there – but now they have to be deserved and earned.

Professionalism is shown in the manner in which professionals conduct themselves in a variety of situations. For most people, professionalism is, at least initially, judged by appearance, so it is foolish to think that experience and ability is automatically communicated whatever you look like. Attention to professional dress helps convey the message that colleagues and clients alike are dealing with a qualified, competent veterinary professional.

The head of a top human surgical unit in Sweden, who prefers to dress casually in jeans and a sweatshirt, found that this image was totally unacceptable when he was trying to establish a new market for the clinic across Europe. Prospective clients wanted their surgeon to *look* like a top professional surgeon, which meant a collar and tie, good quality trousers and polished shoes, under a spotless white coat, with badges of office such as a name badge and stethoscope prominently displayed.

Adopting a professional dress code throughout the practice serves several functions. Uniforms:

- look smart and professional
- help identify the roles of individuals within the practice
- give a consistent feel to the practice (this *is* ABC Vet Clinic)
- help clients know who is who in a clinic
- give the staff members a feeling of belonging
- define 'work time' as different from 'personal time'
- help protect own clothes
- avoid the problem of staff wearing unsuitable clothes to work.

Use lapel labels with the staff member's name, qualification and position (e.g. veterinarian, veterinary nurse, receptionist, practice manager, etc.) clearly printed. Name badges are a simple courtesy to clients as it is arrogance to assume clients know who you are and what your role is in the practice (Fig. 6.18).

Improving communication in the consulting room

The consulting room offers many opportunities over and above discussions of medical and surgical treatment to communicate the values of the practice to your clients. As veterinary management consultant Ross Clarke comments:

> *Your exam room demeanour can bond clients to your practice – or chase them away. Improving communication in the exam room is a challenge well worth the effort, as effective communication can be not only fun, but supremely rewarding to you and your cash flow.*

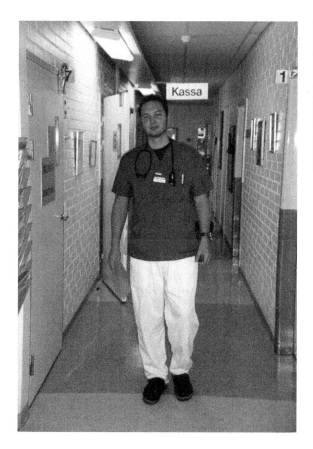

Figure 6.18
Professional clothing may vary from country to country, but it is important to present a professional appearance including having a legible name badge.

More effective consulting room communication
- Introduce yourself.
- Touch and talk to the pet.
- Present yourself as a professional.
- Be an active listener and ask good questions.
- Talk about the *benefits* of treatment/professional products/drugs, etc.
- Use visual information.
- Give educational handouts.
- Compliment the client.
- Explain the best treatment options first.
- Make sure you've answered all of the client's questions.

Improve communication by attention to detail:

- take a personal interest in each case
- get the sex of the pet right

- call pet and owner by their right names
- read the records and be informed about the case before seeing the pet
- use an assistant to restrain the pet
- ensure the room is scrupulously clean and odour free
- provide a chair for the owner to sit on.

Communication and the telephone

In almost every practice I have visited, staff express concerns about their telephone service. Questions such as 'Should we answer the phone or deal with the client standing in front of us?', 'What can I do about the client who just talks and talks – it seems so rude to interrupt them?', and 'How can we "answer within three rings" when we have so much else to do?' come up regularly.

The telephone is not only the major and often first contact with the practice for clients, it is also a powerful marketing tool. The person answering the phone represents the practice. They must 'sell' the practice by voice alone, and are responsible for creating some of the very first 'moments of truth' in the practice. This telephone response can literally win or lose clients, and thus business. Good telephone service is not only critical to good client service; it is also an indication of a well-managed practice (see Appendix 1 for suggestions on how to improve your telephone service) (Fig. 6.19).

Figure 6.19 Would you like your receptionist to have this attitude to clients phoning in?

So, how good is your communication – really?

A mystery shopper survey of 150 randomly selected UK veterinary practices conducted by veterinary marketing company Onswitch Insight
(www.onswitch.co.uk) showed that although clients' first impressions
over the telephone or meeting the reception staff tended to be good, there
were very large gaps in quality and type of information received later.

> Mystery shoppers representing uninformed owners of a new puppy
> or kitten experienced the following:
>
> - 14% found the practice smelly and off-putting
> - 38.5% couldn't identify staff and their role
> - only 4% were given information on fleas, and 11% on worming
> - 75% were not even offered an appointment with the veterinarian
> - 60% felt practices were poor to average in the interest they dis-
>   played in them and their pet when they visited personally, and
>   75.8% felt this when they phoned the practice.
>
> Further comments about telephone service include:
>
> - 74.3% had to wait 7–10 rings or more
> - 84% were immediately put on hold, 335 of these for up to 3 minutes
> - 8.4% could not get through or were timed out
> - 75% didn't know to whom they were talking
> - 89% didn't know the person's role in the practice
> - 47% experienced poor to average phone service.
>
> From Onswitch Insight, *Mystery Shopping: a unique look through your client's
> eyes*, 2005.

The role of the practice leader(s) in communication

The *responsibility* for good or bad communication within the practice
starts with the practice leader. Communication within the practice creates the attitude which is then conveyed to clients. Thus, a good
leader, who is a good communicator, creates a happy practice peopled
by happy staff, who work to create happy, satisfied clients. In practices
dominated by a bad leader with poor communication skills, staff are
typically unhappy, unsure of themselves, and have a cynical and jaded
attitude – they are not interested in clients, and the clients sense it.

It is not always easy for a leader to be a good communicator:

> *For example, the director of a residential facility for retarded people was sympathetic to complaints by staff members about their low wages, so he spoke at a meeting with what he thought was forthrightness and concern. He levelled with them by admitting that their jobs would never pay enough to support a family. He also told them they would not be able to advance to higher-paying jobs if they did not have graduate degrees. As their friend, he advised that if they wanted jobs that could lead to more lucrative careers, they would have to find different jobs. The staff did not appreciate their director's candour, because they did not receive his communication as an expression of concern for their welfare coming from a peer. Rather, they heard it as a threat from the boss: 'If you don't like it here, you can jolly well leave.'*
>
> Deborah Tannen, *You Just Don't Understand*, 1992

Sometimes communication problems have become so severe in a practice that it may be difficult to find solutions.

For example, a practice in which I did a consultancy is a prime example of the effect of severe, prolonged communication problems at every level. The principal works half-time in the practice, which is resented by all the practice members because:

- *They didn't see him as dedicated to the practice.*
- *They didn't like having to work full-time when he did not.*
- *He was not available when problems arose.*
- *He used the 'seagull' technique of management: He flew in every so often, squawked a lot, defecated on several, and flew out again!*

As a result, they were not happy in their work, they barely cooperated with each other, they gave (in his eyes) mediocre service because they didn't see why they should really bother with the clients, and took advantage of his 'kindnesses' (such as not clocking-in their working times, not controlling their usage of pet foods and other products for their own pets, and so on).

To improve this practice and sort out its many problems, the leader must lead. He must communicate his wishes and desires more clearly – and listen more attentively to his staff. They need to agree on what are desirable and non-desirable behaviours and he needs to be on site far more, modelling the behaviour he wants from his staff – or appoint a full-time manager. It is only by constantly and repetitively telling and showing them what he wants, and rewarding them for the right response that their behaviour can change.

This example highlights the need for practice leaders to be committed to improving communication, and concentrate on developing their own strengths and overcoming their own weaknesses before trying to influence their staff. This again goes back to the behaviours inherent in emotional intelligence.

Staff problems

Of course, not all communication problems are the fault of the boss. There are also a number of distinct communication problem areas common to many practices, which create friction, stress and unhappiness. These include lack of job definition, unclear expectations, lack of team spirit, lack of feedback and recognition, poor (negative) attitude, and personality and communication differences. Most of these will be covered in the next few chapters.

Personality types and communication differences

Attitudes and styles of working differ according to personality types, so communication can often be confused by individual and personal differences in interpretation of messages. For example, men and women tend to work and communicate in different ways, which is a common source of communication problems. An awareness and understanding of these differences can contribute towards maintaining a tolerant and harmonious atmosphere in the practice.

Deborah Tannen, author of the international best-seller *You Just Don't Understand*, explains the differences between how men and women communicate as follows:

> *Men function as individuals in an hierarchical social order in which they are either one-up or one-down. In this world, conversations are negotiations in which people try to achieve and maintain the upper hand if they can, and protect themselves from others attempts to put them down and push them around. Talk is primarily a means to preserve independence*

> *and negotiate and maintain status in an hierarchical order.*
> *This is done by exhibiting skill and knowledge, and by holding*
> *centre stage through verbal performance such as story telling,*
> *joking or imparting information. From childhood, men learn to*
> *use talking as a way to get and keep attention. Life is a con-*
> *test, a struggle to preserve independence and avoid failure.*
>
> *Women function as individuals in a network of connections.*
> *Conversations are negotiations for closeness in which people*
> *try to seek and give confirmation and support, and to reach*
> *consensus. Emphasis is placed on displaying similarities and*
> *matching experiences. From childhood, girls criticise peers who*
> *try to stand out or appear better than others. They try to pro-*
> *tect themselves from others' attempts to push them away. Life*
> *is a community, a struggle to preserve intimacy, and avoid*
> *isolation. Though there are hierarchies in this world too,*
> *they are hierarchies more of friendship than of power and*
> *accomplishment.*

The generation gap and communication styles

Veterinary practice, like any business, is typically a mixture of generations. Raised in different time periods with different social norms and
expectations, this generational diversity is both a source of creativity
and originality, and also, potentially, conflict and misunderstandings.

> *Matures*, born 1909–1945, tend to be guided by duty, loyalty and
> tradition. They know the need for hard graft to achieve results. The
> men of this generation tend to be highly independent individualists
> who have difficulty working in a team. Women of this generation
> tend to defer to their husband's decisions.
>
> *Baby boomers*, the largest generation produced until Generation Y,
> were born in the post-war period, 1945–1964. They are the 'me'
> generation showing drive, tolerance and self-absorption, which has
> contributed to their withdrawal from social institutions and the rise of
> divorce. Women in this generation feel pressured by struggling to
> balance careers with the major burden of household chores and
> family care.

Generation X, born 1965–1976, show diversity, savvy and pragmatism. They are a materialistic generation with much distrust towards the previous generations, so they don't listen to authority. They tend to delay marriage, but put much emphasis on family, friends and a traditional life-style. They start their own businesses at three times the rate of the baby boomers.

Generation Y or millennials, born 1977–1994, are the largest generation yet produced and are fiercely different from previous generations. Not only are they growing up with internet and mobile phones, they are also driving change in fashions and styles. They have few shared experiences, and their tastes change constantly. One in four has been brought up by a single parent, and three out of four have working mothers.

Each generation, regardless of their age, has something to offer the practice. Whereas the Xers and Yers bring technical competence, enthusiasm and the willingness to try new things in new ways, the older employees have the advantage of expert knowledge and confidence that come with years of experience. They also know about hard work – the need to 'buckle down and get on' with something that needs doing, rather than hoping for an easy short cut as the younger generations tend to do.

Managing conflict

Conflict can occur between members of a practice, or between staff and clients. It is defined as: a collision of interests, wills and/or feelings between people who are dependent on each other.

It can be a source of misery, and loss of energy and well-being. It can also be an opportunity for change and improvement.

From the above definition, solving conflict sounds quite straightforward: identify where the clash of wills occurs, or what the damaged feelings are, and the conflict can be easily resolved. However, real conflicts are usually more complex than this. Often the apparent reason for the conflict is only the tip of the iceberg. There is usually an unfulfilled need behind the source of the conflict. There can also be both a hidden agenda (what you don't want your opponent to know), as well as factors unknown to each party – often unidentified emotional baggage.

In a major conflict situation I experienced with an older, experienced male colleague for whom I had a lot of respect, the apparent reason for the conflict was simply a clash of wills: I wanted to encourage delegation of responsibility and encourage personal growth within the practice, he wanted to keep control of power. However, although we talked about this with each other we seemed unable to find a common ground. He would become aggressive and unpleasant, and I would become increasingly cowed – behaviour that is very atypical of me! With some deep introspection I realised that at some level I was identifying with this man as a fearsome father figure – and was responding as though I was about six years old. My hidden agenda was a fear that he would see I was not as experienced as him and therefore as worthy. Although the realisation came too late to resolve this particular conflict situation, it did at least forewarn me of the dangers of similar situations and enable me to cope very differently next time around.

Sources of conflict include:

- *Differing needs or desires* – as in the example above, the man's need for a patriarchal and hierarchical organisation with him holding the power clashed with my need for a cooperative non-hierarchical organisation where the power was shared. The struggle that ensued was painful and disruptive.
- *Unclear purposes or goals* – for example, not having a written job description that defines areas of responsibilities may lead to arguments over who does what and when.
- *Different life stages* and different views of life can be sources of conflict – both negative ('It was very different in our day: we were expected to work nights and weekends. The young people these days – all they want is time off ...') and positive ('I didn't grow up with computers like you did and I don't really understand them. Can you help me?').
- *Painful memories* ('Last time I tried that it went badly wrong and the boss was furious').
- *Misunderstandings* arising from attitudes and behaviours ('She turned away from me when she said that ...'), lack of clarity, and insecurities or fears.

If not promptly resolved, negative conflicts can be draining, exhausting and very time-consuming. Sometimes the solution may be to agree to differ and to move on. Usually, difficult conflict requires more input – in some cases legal or other expert advice may be called upon. To satisfactorily resolve conflict requires that both parties understand and accept the other's viewpoint.

Communication: summary

Communication is an integral and complex part of human interaction and involves all the senses. Far more than words are used to convey meaning. It is possible to improve communication by concentrating on skills such as active listening, using written and visual support material, and showing friendly, open body language. Improved communication creates happier staff and therefore happier clients, and ultimately a more successful practice.

7 Understanding your staff – what makes people tick

Businesses are people, and people are shaped as much by their emotions as they are by their intellect. The hidden resources of feelings, beliefs, perceptions, and values that make up an organisation's 'emotional capital' can be harnessed and help drive every person and every organisation forward. Emotional assets are the only ones truly capable of adding untold wealth to organisations, or, as has happened time and again, of destroying them. The key challenge in the coming decade will be the harnessing of hearts and minds, emotions and intellect/knowledge, to deliver superior service and business performance.

Kevin Thomson, 1998

The power of emotions

There exists a dilemma in managing a veterinary practice. Although there may be clear guidelines about what to do and when to do it, although staff may be highly trained, and although there may be all sorts of systems in place to measure results in indisputable numbers, in reality we cannot get away from the fact that a practice is a society or collective of people and people are largely ruled by their emotions, not by reason and logic. Emotions and internal values profoundly impact our daily lives, and affect our performance and achievement levels. And they affect the results the practice produces.

For example, who hasn't felt the pull of a warm and comfy bed on a cold winter morning when you know you ought to get up; or worked selflessly to try to save a case which you know, in your heart of hearts,

> is hopeless; or been moved to tears performing the euthanasia of a much loved family pet – despite never having met the family before and whilst struggling to maintain a professional face?

Sometimes, emotions are a handicap. For example, a fear of failure might stop you from trying out a new surgical technique; a dislike for conflict may stop you having a needed conversation with an employee; or an internal drive to always understand and resolve every case might lead to exhaustion and burnout. Where a whole practice is paralysed by its emotions – 'This is the way we have always done things round here: we can't change' – a death knell sounds.

Harnessing people's positive emotions such as enthusiasm, motivation and the desire to do better can transform a practice into a magical place to work. People want to come to work in the morning, they love their job, and they are more than willing to go the extra mile for the clients. And the substantial year-end profit shows the outcome of their enthusiasm and motivation.

Table 7.1 shows some of the emotions that exist on a daily basis in any business or practice. A predominance of the negative or 'deadly' emotions will at worst, slowly strangle the practice; at best, ensure it is not productive to the level it could be. The deadly emotions are energy sapping, and drain enthusiasm and creativity from the practice.

Practices that capture and harness the positive 'dynamic' emotions of people in the organisation can create a unique and successful business. So, how do they do this?

Emotional intelligence and motivation

In the previous chapter we talked about the importance of emotional intelligence in successful communication. Emotional intelligence is also the key to motivation and high performance. Emotional intelligence is an array of non-cognitive capabilities, competencies and skills that influence your ability to succeed in coping with environmental demands and pressures. It is the capacity to recognise your own feelings, to motivate others, and to manage emotions well in yourself and in your relationships. It is composed of four parts:

- the ability to perceive emotions
- to access and generate emotions that assist thought

Table 7.1 The emotions that make or break a business	
Dynamic emotions	**Deadly emotions**
Obsession: persistent idea that constantly forces its way into consciousness	*Fear*: feeling of distress, apprehension from impending danger
Challenge: desire to rise up, fight and win – especially against the odds	*Anger*: feeling of great annoyance or anger over some real or supposed grievance
Passion: strong enthusiasm for something	*Apathy*: lack of motivation
Commitment: dedication to a particular action or cause	*Stress*: mental, physical or emotional strain
Determination: firmness of purpose	*Anxiety*: state of uneasiness or tension
Delight: act of receiving pleasure like fun	*Hostility*: antagonistic or oppositional behaviour
Love: great affection, desire to 'give'	*Envy*: discontent, resentful feelings about another's perceived success
Pride: feeling of self-respect, personal or organisational worth	*Greed*: excessive desire for wealth or power
Desire: wish to have or be	*Selfishness*: lack of consideration of others actuated by self-interest
Trust: confidence in the integrity, value or reliability of a person or organisation	*Hatred*: feeling of intense dislike

- to understand emotions and emotional knowledge
- and to reflectively regulate emotions to promote emotional and intellectual growth.

Emotional intelligence is not the opposite of intellectual intelligence, but a unique intersection of the two. By integrating thinking and feeling you can live more effectively.

Closely coupled to emotions are values. Values dictate how we spend our time and resources. Having a capacity or skill is not enough to create real-world results. People taught skills in a vacuum without relating them to their value and belief system will not perform to the best of their ability. Relating behaviours to values – that is, by integrating thinking and feeling, and using emotional intelligence – you create more positive results and significantly enhance performance.

> *Values*: assumptions, convictions, or beliefs about the manner in which people should behave and the principles that should govern behaviour.
>
> *Morals*: values concerned with or relating to human behaviour which are based on cultural, religious, and philosophical concepts and beliefs, by which an individual determines whether his or her actions are right or wrong.
>
> *Ethics*: the science or philosophical study of morals in human conduct. The rules or standards governing the conduct of a person or the members of a profession.

Successfully relating behaviours to values and thereby harnessing the powers of the 'dynamic' emotions to achieve a high level of performance is a direct reflection of the practice leadership. Leadership needs to identify and name the values that exist within the practice (see 'Creating your practice vision', in Chapter 2) and couple these to the energy within the 'dynamic' emotions.

The culture within the practice is also important. Practice culture is the emotional environment in which people in the practice work each day. It is created by the practice leadership. Research shows it strongly influences how people do their jobs. An important component of practice culture is the level of trust that exists. People working in a low trust environment, for example, subjected to the mood swings of the boss, or the politicking of one group of staff against another, will spend more time defending their backs and protecting their own patch than contributing to the business or caring about clients. Staff in a high trust environment, on the other hand, will work well and productively together, and will enjoy helping clients.

There are five other factors that also contribute to the culture in a practice:

- *Accountability and responsibility*: how committed are practice members to taking individual and group responsibility for doing the right job well?
- *Collaboration* and problem-solving: how do team members communicate and work together to resolve issues and find solutions?
- Perception of *leadership*: how are the practice leaders and the type of leadership perceived?
- *Alignment* to the vision: how well does staff understand and work with the practice vision? How much of a daily influence does the vision have on decisions made and activities performed in the practice?

- *Adaptability* for change: how adaptable and flexible is the practice? Are people seeking change or hanging on to what they know?

The role of personality types

Before moving on to the systems and methods that exist to maximise the value of employees to the practice, there is another aspect to understanding what drives people and that is their personality types. Having the skills to do a job is not the same as having a job that is truly compatible with your personality. Psychometric profiling is increasingly used to identify strengths and weaknesses, and to better match people's skills and ambitions with the job they are expected to do.

Myers–Briggs Type Indicator

There are various formal systems available which help you identify your personality type. One of the best known is the Myers–Briggs Type Indicator, an instrument for measuring a person's preferences, using four basic scales with opposite poles. The four scales are: (1) extraversion/introversion, (2) sensate/intuitive, (3) thinking/ feeling and (4) judging/perceiving. The various combinations of these preferences result in 16 personality types denoted by four letters, e.g. ENTJ (extraversion, intuition with thinking and judging).

Developed by Jungian psychologists, over 2 million Myers–Briggs analyses are performed yearly by trained consultants worldwide. The purpose is to help improve work and personal relationships, increase productivity, and identify leadership and interpersonal communication preferences within the business.

The idea behind the concept is that it can be very difficult to separate the careers that suit your personality and abilities from the careers that would frustrate you or make you unhappy. To be happy and successful in a job, you need to ensure that your abilities, values and personality are well aligned with those needed for your chosen career and with those of the organisation you work for. By performing such analyses on practice members – especially those in key positions of responsibility – or when interviewing likely candidates for employment, matching the right person for the job can improve communication, work harmony and effectiveness.

Achieving top performance

People's performance is powerfully affected by their emotions. Emotions also influence how they express their personal values and the values of the practice, and they shape the culture of the practice. Understanding the power of emotions, leaders can use this information, deploying four strategies, to match the right person to the right job to obtain best performance. These strategies are: motivation, performance assessment, delegation and empowerment. The latter three will be considered in more detail in Chapter 8. We will now look at motivation.

Motivation

> *People who feel good about themselves produce good results.*
> Blanchard and Johnson, *The One Minute Manager*, 1982

Motivation is the degree of commitment to a course of action and is measured by the effort put into the action. It is a highly complex issue, so what motivates one individual may have little effect on another, and the effect of removing a demotivator may not always be to motivate. For example, a pay cut is usually a demotivator, but a large pay rise may not stimulate harder or better work. The role of the practice manager (principal/leader) is to build up and maintain high levels of motivation, which simultaneously builds staff effectiveness.

Understanding motivation
- *Be motivated to motivate others* – a leader must be motivated to motivate his or her team.
- *Motivation requires a goal* – it is impossible for an individual or a team to be motivated without a goal.
- *Motivation once established does not last* – motivation is like blowing up a balloon – if you don't tie a knot in the inlet, the air will come out again. Motivation is a constant, ongoing process.
- *Motivation requires recognition* – people strive harder for recognition than almost anything else in life. Ensure you reward and praise achievements.
- *Participation motivates* – feeling they are part of something gives people a higher level of motivation.

- *Personal progression motivates* – going forward, whether in a personal or business situation, motivates people to try harder.
- *Challenge only motivates if you can win* – the greater the chance of winning, the greater the effort applied.
- *Everybody has a motivational fuse* – a good leader provides the light that sparks it.
- *Group belonging motivates* – the smaller the unit, the greater the loyalty, motivation and effort given to the group.

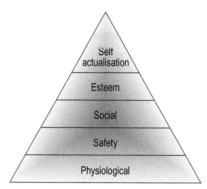

Figure 7.1   Maslow's pyramid of needs.

There are many theories of motivation, the best known, perhaps, being Maslow's theory, developed in 1943. A psychologist, Maslow described a pyramid of needs illustrated in Figure 7.1. Working from the bottom up, each set of needs must be satisfied before moving on to the next level. The desire to fulfil the needs is the level of motivation experienced. Thus a starving and cold man is very motivated to find food and warmth but is not at all motivated by self-actualisation, whereas a replete man living a comfortable life is not worried about where his next meal will come from, but will be highly motivated to earn the esteem and recognition of his peers.

Further research within factories and offices over the last 50 years showed this model was too simple as it failed to produce convincing evidence that satisfying these needs *consistently* leads to motivation and good performance. Another psychologist, Hertzberg, studying whether *satisfied* factory workers were therefore *motivated* factory workers, identified a number of what he called hygiene factors. These included interpersonal relations, working conditions and salary. Their absence created dissatisfaction, but their presence did not create motivation or satisfaction. Thus, receiving the monthly pay cheque late created dissatisfaction, whereas receiving it exactly on time was neither motivating nor satisfying.

What this meant was that *satisfaction alone* is not a motivator; effort depends on the *rewards* people expect to get. This, in turn, depends on the value of the reward to the individual and the likelihood of getting that reward (which is based on how difficult the job is seen to be and the amount of effort involved). The higher the value of the reward and the greater the probability of receiving it, the more effort that will be put in to achieve it.

Later studies have shown that other factors also affect motivation including:

- *Ability* – the individual's intelligence, skills and know-how.
- *Perceptions about the job* – the individual's interpretation of the job (which should be the same as the organisation's).
- *Influence of other people* – peer and group pressures are important as they affect social and esteem needs.
- *The job itself* – the extent to which the work itself gives people an opportunity for achievement, responsibility and satisfaction.

The problem of motivation in veterinary practice

I have visited well over a thousand veterinary practices in many places in the world. In many practices, staff motivation is well below par. Young, bright vets have become cynical and jaundiced about practice life; the turnover of competent nurses is shockingly high; and employers are frustrated and unhappy, working long hours for little return. I have found that the levels of motivation in a practice reflect a number of different factors including the level of motivation of the practice leader(s), the systems in place that encourage and reward motivation, the level and quality of communication between practice members, and the innate level of motivation within the individuals employed.

The practice leader(s)
As we have already seen, the behaviours of the practice leader(s) creates the emotional framework for the whole practice. A leader who is cynical and despondent, or despotic and over-critical, or subject to unpredictable mood swings will not be able to motivate staff to produce their best performance. A leader who is positive and encouraging, relatively consistent in her behaviour, and who can retain a sense of humour and realistic perspective on things will have far happier and more motivated staff.

In addition, the leader that does not support the actions and ideas of an enthusiastic staff member will kill enthusiasm and creativity.

Motivation systems

Young graduates need considerable support and help in their first few years in practice when they not only learn to apply their hard-gained knowledge, but also have to struggle with the realities of difficult and unpleasant animal owners, long working hours, loneliness, putting a value on and charging properly for their services, and managing inevitable diagnostic or treatment mistakes. Lack of support and care in these critical first years may even force the young graduate to leave practice life for ever.

Vets and nurses enter practice full of enthusiasm and expectations, bursting with new ideas. A few years later, many of them are dull-eyed and cynical about their work. What has gone wrong? In many cases, it is because they feel they have been tricked. Promised expectations have not been fulfilled. Life has become dull and routine. Managing individuals' expectations within the practice is an essential part of successful motivation.

People need goals to work towards to give themselves direction and purpose. Veterinarians are no exception, yet what does a veterinarian do after 5, 10, 25 years in practice? Lack of a career/personal development structure – which, in any business, would be seen as a sign of poor management – destroys motivation.

Goals need to be realistic. For example, although the mutual aim may be to produce a competent surgeon, expecting a new graduate to manage a major surgery well when they have only done a few cat spays previously is putting an unfair and potentially very demoralising pressure on them.

Studies show that veterinary nurses are capable and caring people who love their job. They are motivated by getting thanks for a job well done, and by being given the opportunity to learn more and develop their nursing competencies. They are demotivated and eventually embittered by continuing to receive low wages that do not reflect their true value to the practice, by not receiving recognition for their knowledge and skills, and by the lack of career structure. In many cases, the only significant promotional prospects for a veterinary nurse in practice are away from nursing to restricted 'managerial' positions. If the promotion is not accompanied by sufficient recognition of the authority the new position should bring and by adequate training for the role (including how to manage staff as subordinates who only yesterday were mates), demotivation and eventually loss of an excellent staff member from the practice results.

Mixing the mundane with the challenging rather then constantly being given routine, humdrum work avoids boredom, helps alleviate frustration and maintains motivation.

People need to feel wanted and important. Rewarding behaviour stimulates motivation; however, it is important that the right, i.e. the desirable behaviour is rewarded. For example, Richard Barrett, author of *Liberating the Corporate Soul* (1998), writes: 'Creativity will not blossom in a rigid culture that punishes failure. It requires a culture of trust that encourages risk taking, and in which both success and failure are celebrated. Failure must be seen as a learning opportunity if creativity is to be nurtured.'

Other common examples include:

- Do staff who work long hours and look busy get rewarded against those who get results?
- Are demands made for quality work, but no guidelines given as to how to achieve quality?
- Are staff not encouraged to be different and yet the boss always complains about lack of initiative?
- Is teamwork demanded, but one team member played off against another?
- Are the individual's needs and ambitions recognised within what the practice can offer?
- Does the boss want more creative ideas and yet severely reprimand mistakes?

Again, to be clear about the behaviour desired of staff members to be able to effectively reward it requires a clear vision of the values and goals of the practice.

Innate motivation

Selecting staff for positive attitude and high levels of motivation is the first step in building motivation within the practice. A negative attitude is much harder to convert to a positive one. Similarly, weeding out staff with a negative attitude will stop the spread of cynicism and demotivation.

Veterinarians are often described as 'type A' people – highly driven, highly self-critical and highly insecure. This somewhat neurotic combination of attributes, although contributing on the one hand to the brilliance and commitment shown by veterinarians, can on the other hand become crippling demotivators through over-harsh judgement of self, and lead to stress-related and mental illness. (This is considered in more detail in the section on managing stress, pp. 162–163.)

Young workers ('twenty-something') have been identified as a motivational challenge by authors Bradford and Raines (1992) because their perceptions and expectations are so different from older people. Compared to those in their thirties, forties and fifties, they tend to be self-orientated and cynical, materialistic, and slow to commit themselves to responsibility. They want instant recognition of skills, rapid and easy promotion, and reward in return for their input – *now*. Understanding that these differences exist is the first step for a leader in motivating both young professional and support staff.

Motivation: accepting responsibility

The purpose of motivation is to stimulate someone to work harder and better: to get performance. This is achieved not through threats and bullying but by encouraging the individual to *accept responsibility* to perform. Management guru Peter Drucker argues that responsibility is the essential internal self-motivation for performance. He also points out that the question of whether people *want* to assume responsibility is irrelevant; an organization *needs* performance which it can only get by encouraging, inducing, and, if need be, by pushing the person into assuming responsibility.

Motivation, then, is getting your staff to accept responsibility for their own performance: successful motivation is getting them to do this willingly and take pride in the results.

Most staff are motivated when they first join a practice and are willing and interested to help clients who, of course, provide the business. However, promising staff often lose that motivation over time and become less productive or even leave the practice. Why does this happen?

The importance of matching expectations

> *Failure to match expectations will have a detrimental effect on the practice in general, ultimately affecting client service and profit.*
>
> Gudrun Ravetz, Management Symposium, 2005

Recruiting of staff is often mismanaged in veterinary practice. A decade or so ago it was perfectly feasible to put an advertisement in the professional journals and expect to find a suitable vet, nurse or receptionist to hire. These days, expectations are different – from both the employer's and employee's viewpoints.

Factors affecting expectations

- *Demographics*: increasing feminisation of the profession means that employees are more likely to work part-time and have career breaks for family.
- *Technological advancement*: availability of more or less advanced technological 'tools' attract staff.
- *Scientific advances*: rapid advances in knowledge challenge staff to keep up to date.
- *Animal owner expectations*: media and internet provide unlimited information to animal owners. In addition, there are changing patterns of ownership (e.g. more pure breeds owned, generally older owners) and requirements (more advanced technology, management of age-related diseases as pets live longer).
- *Health and safety requirements*.
- *Working regulations*.
- *Out of hours and emergency care*: whereas this was formerly a standard expectation for any veterinarian, now vets are actively choosing not to have to work out of hours.
- *Financial expectations*: new graduate expectations are increasingly influenced by the size of their student debt, and comparison with salaries in other professions.
- *Mobile career*: desire for travel and experience abroad.
- *Work–life balance*: increasing importance of work–life balance as a counterweight to stress in the workplace.

Research shows that whereas employers believe staff leave primarily for financial reasons and the attraction of a better salary elsewhere, only about 12% of employees leave because of dissatisfaction with their salary: the majority leave for other reasons. These are the unmet (sometimes unexpressed) expectations.

What is the actual cost to the practice of not meeting employee expectations? Whereas expectations create hope and a willingness to work to achieve expectations, not meeting these expectations results in disengagement from the workplace. There is loss of commitment to do the assigned work, productivity decreases and the rest of the practice team is negatively affected. Unfortunately this period can extend from months to years before a 'final straw' incident stimulates the dissatisfied employee to leave. The primary effect is illustrated in Figure 7.2.

A veterinary colleague explained her situation like this: 'Although I am already a competent surgeon, I really wanted to develop and specialise my

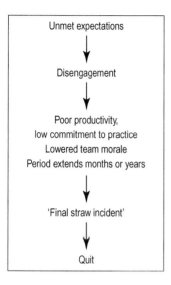

Figure 7.2 Primary effect of unmet expectations.

surgical skills in the large hospital practice in which I was employed. I have clearly stated this on several occasions. However, the practice principal has never really supported me in this, favouring another colleague for no apparent reason other than he is more clearly outspoken and 'pushy' than I am. The final straw for me was getting the latest work rota and seeing that I had – again – been assigned the same amount of operating time as the most junior of the vets whilst being expected to be so surgically competent that I am an out of hours and emergency back-up for these vets. I left the hospital and am now working in a much smaller practice where I am employed because of my surgical skills and given every opportunity to develop them. I feel far more motivated now than I have been for years.'

Direct costs to the practice for 'disengagement' include the costs of advertising for a new position, of interviewing potential employees, and paying for a locum in the interim period. However, the indirect costs are more serious because they are harder to measure and potentially much more damaging. They include:

- Revenue lost during the disengagement period. An unmotivated employee is going to do the minimum necessary to complete his job.
- Negative effect on general staff morale. An unmotivated person is often a source of a debilitating attitude of world-weariness and cynicism which drags down others around him.
- Cost of client relationships: the unmotivated employee is not going to 'go the extra mile' for the client, which may lead to client dissatisfaction and even defection (this practice is not concerned about me and my animal's problems).

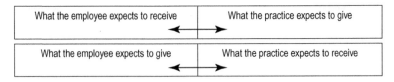

Figure 7.3 Matching expectations.

- Cost of loss of knowledge and skills that person offered.
- Cost of training new employee to replace the one that has left.

The most important of these intangible costs is the lost revenue to the practice because of indifferent client service. Just as we need to be able to fulfil client expectations to have satisfied clients that are more likely to return to us and to recommend us to others; so we need to fulfil staff expectations to be able to encourage them to perform at their best and to stay with the practice. This requires a long-term view of staff employment. (Of course, staff leave for personal reasons other than job dissatisfaction such as relocation, or career change – these we have little influence over.)

To manage employees' expectations means identifying what they are, and seeing if they can be met by what the practice has to offer. This is balanced by identifying what the practice expects to receive and clarifying that this is what the employee is willing to give (Fig. 7.3). Managing expectations is thus a contract between the team member and the practice. Periodically and frequently expectations on both sides need to be reviewed, recognising and meeting any changes that arise as an ongoing part of managing the practice team. For example, a new graduate may expect a lot of team support and 'hand-holding' in the first year of employment, and to be given time to think about and manage cases. The practice is willing to provide this because they see the new graduate as an investment for the practice's future and are willing to train up the graduate in the practice's ways, but the graduate's lower productivity will be reflected in the salary. By the second year, the young vet is expecting to perform most routine surgeries on her own, and to be able to work within prescribed appointment times – and the practice recognises this with an appropriate salary rise and the assurance that help is always at hand if needed. In the third year, the veterinarian becomes pregnant and expects the practice will be empathetic in meeting her changing capacity to work (for example, in not being able to take X-rays, or to lift patients), and by the fourth year expects the practice to understand and meet her need for reduced and flexible working hours to manage family commitments.

Problems arise where employees themselves are not clear about their own expectations as these include both obvious 'external' expectations and less obvious 'internal' expectations. These latter reflect the individual's personality and emotionality, and will vary according to maturity, experience, gender, cultural background and other factors. They include the need for support and encouragement, the feeling of belonging and contributing to the practice and being part of the team, the recognition of doing a good job or provision of supportive critical feedback where improvement is required, and so on. This support is formally provided in the structure and organisation of the appraisal system in the practice. An appraisal is defined as a constructive review of the employee's progress and development (see Chapter 8).

Expectation on the practice's side must also be clearly identified and honestly presented to the employee. This can be done by involving all the members of the practice team in defining what the job is, what skills it requires, and the sort of person they want to fulfil it.

For example, it is not enough to say 'We need a replacement veterinarian'. It is important to discuss the role and function of this veterinarian as well as the desirable personal characteristics. For example, are you seeking someone who is a good team leader with proven leadership skills? With specialist veterinary skills? Excellence in client communication? Driven and energetic – perhaps willing to develop a new area of the practice? Do you want someone with maturity and experience? A team player? Someone who is willing to work a lot on their own? What – specifically – do you want them to do in the practice? Train and develop junior staff? Attract new clients? All these aspects are then put into a detailed job description. This is compared against what the new employee's expectations are: in some cases this will eliminate most of the applicants because only a few will match those expectations. Although the final choice applicant may not be a perfect match, at least every effort has been made to get the perfect match. It is often best to wait to find the right person by hiring a locum to avoid making a panicked decision which results in a poor match.

Successful motivation

The three greatest motivators have been identified as money, recognition and happiness. Money buys things and status, so it can also provide social recognition and status, but money *itself* does not motivate. It motivates only when the person is *ready to assume responsibility*: incentive pay produces better output where there is already a willingness to perform better. Responsibility cannot be 'bought'.

Recognition, both socially and from peers, is a very powerful motivator. People will even choose recognition, in the form, say, of a title, over all other motivators.

Happiness and what is needed to achieve happiness is complex and best defined by the individual. In today's world, happiness is often increased freedom to choose working hours and conditions to be able to achieve a satisfactory work–life balance. I know many practice employees who choose less pay and increased time off in preference to a pay rise and longer hours.

To motivate successfully you need to understand what inspires the individual, what makes him or her 'tick'. When employing someone new, find out what they have outside work that excites and interests them. Dominic Monkhouse, Managing Director of Uxbridge College of Further Education, commented in an article in *The Guardian* newspaper that if a prospective new staff member could not show evidence of a passion for something outside of the workplace he would not hire them. 'If they don't have this quality already they won't be able to transfer it (the enthusiasm) to their work.' By understanding what motivates someone, you can then help them achieve both personal and practice goals.

Remember that what motivates you may be very different from what motivates other people. For this reason, 'blanket' motivation such as a practice incentive scheme often does not work well *because* different things motivate people. People's motivation needs can also change over time. *For example, when I was a single parent with two young children to support and no other income, I was very motivated to earn a good salary. Later, when my personal situation became more stable, peer recognition became more important, and now my greatest motivation is to find a harmonious work–life balance which combines economic security with time for my husband, my family and my horse.*

Incentive schemes

Incentives are rewards that stimulate greater productivity in a specific area. They can reward the individual or the team. They are frequently misused, usually because they are set up so that practice members compete against each other – which disrupts the team and can upset the whole practice.

However, incentive programmes for individuals can be made successful by adhering to the following five rules (Denny, 1993):

- Everyone must have an evenly weighted chance to win. There are two important reasons for this:
  - ☐ If there is little or no chance of winning, people will not even try.
  - ☐ If a low performing person wins through luck, it can be enormously demotivating for a high performing person (e.g. in a raffle draw).
- *Time the incentive system carefully* – short, intense competitions lasting a maximum of 3 months have a more powerful immediate effect than long-drawn-out contests.
- *Decide exactly what the scheme should achieve* – then reward the behaviour you seek.
- *Give tangible prizes* – money is not the best incentive in competitions because it so easily 'dissolves' on mundane household and personal items. A tangible prize such as theatre tickets, wine, a food hamper, and so on are far more effective – and make the tickets or weekends away for two people.
- *Ensure the scheme is fully understood* – everyone should be able to answer the following questions:
  - ☐ Exactly what do I have to do?
  - ☐ Exactly what do I get?
  - ☐ By when?

To convert this to an incentive programme for a team get members to work towards joint goals that depend on the team working and cooperating together, for example increasing the number of dentals performed in the next month, or increasing the sale of diets by 10% over the course of the year. And reward them jointly.

A word about understanding what motivates professionals

Managing professionals, in this case veterinarians, is like herding cats: it is a much tougher challenge than most people realise. Certain characteristics of professionals that allow them to do their jobs well create barriers to them being successful in the group setting. For example, most professionals are trained to be sceptical and analytical and will almost always critically challenge any new idea – which can make it tough to gain agreement on issues or for them to maintain the perspective on the big picture. Professionals often want to over-study any problem; first it satisfies their need to eliminate every last ounce of risk before they make a decision, and second, it gives some professionals an excuse to have endless conversations so they will never be required to act.

Professionals often resist accountability, fearing that it will limit their creativity and ability to find the best solution. In addition, many like working alone and are reluctant to contribute to a team or group for fear of losing their impartiality. This means keeping a group of professionals in a room is often difficult: they can always leave by saying they have a client commitment when in fact they are not comfortable in the group.

Professionals are often driven by some sort of ideal. Although this can be a powerful internal motivational force, it can make it difficult for them to accept the realities of the limitations of the real world and what they can achieve in it, which can result in stress, disillusionment and burnout.

Veterinarians are essentially knowledge workers. They work with intelligence, imagination and knowledge, skills which, by themselves, set only limits to what can be attained. It is important veterinarians receive support and guidance to work on the *right things*, which is what will make them effective and convert their skills into results. However, this is not achieved through close or detailed supervision, but through learning to direct themselves, and to be accountable for their performance and contribution.

Stress in veterinary practice

Stress-related illness, exhaustion, depression and mental illness are debilitating problems that are very over-represented in the veterinary profession. Dr Virginia Richmond, co-coordinator of the British Veterinary Surgeons Health Support Programme (VSHSP), comments in a leader in the *Veterinary Times* in 2005: 'The suicide rate is three times the national average, and addiction amongst the veterinary profession, be it alcohol, drugs or whatever, is double the national average.' She further comments that the high rates of suicide and addiction may relate more to the stigma of mental health problems than a lack of support. 'Vets seem to be frightened that if they go to their GP, or whoever they may go to for help, that once it's on their medical records that this is going to blight their career. Mental health problems still carry a huge stigma and because of the shame people feel they wait until crisis point before getting in touch with us.' So why are vets so much more prone to stress and stress-related problems. Let's begin at the beginning.

Why do vets become vets?

Studies show that the choices we make regarding which profession to train for, which client group we will work with, and in what kind of setting, are all profoundly influenced by our need to come to terms with unresolved issues from our past. Many of the conscious choices made by helping professionals are based on idealism. From a psychoanalytic point of view, the drive to affect reparation is partly conscious, but largely subconscious, and is the fundamental impetus to all creative, productive and caring activities.

Those in the helping professions inevitably and repeatedly encounter failure in their work with damaged animals and emotional owners. This arouses feelings of guilt and anxiety, and individuals have different, often primitive, ways of dealing with these painful feelings in order to maintain a precarious self-esteem and to defend themselves against the retaliation anticipated for failing to heal.

The helping professions are often regarded both by their members and by their clients as vocations requiring special qualities such as superhuman caring, and near-magical healing powers. The individual under pressure may use skills and 'technology' to defensively ward off anxiety about personal adequacy for the task whilst secretly hoping they have enough 'internal goodness' to repair damage to others that may occur. Recognising these innate problems and dealing with them through, for example, realistic task definition which, by making some overall success possible, increases the capacity to tolerate depressive anxieties, is a key function of a practice manager.

What is stress?

> ### What is stress?
> Stress is the 'wear and tear' our bodies experience as we adjust to our continually changing environment; it has physical and emotional effects on us and can create positive or negative feelings. As a positive influence, stress can help compel us to action; it can result in a new awareness and an exciting new perspective. As a negative influence, it can result in feelings of distrust, rejection, anger and depression, which in turn can lead to health problems such as headaches, upset stomach, rashes, insomnia, ulcers, high blood pressure, heart disease and stroke. With the death of a loved one, the birth of a child, a job promotion or a new relationship, we experience stress as we readjust our lives. In so adjusting to different circumstances, stress will help or hinder us depending on how we react to it. (Adapted from: www.ivf.com.)

The most common stressors are change, fear, overload (e.g. over-commitment), under-load (e.g. boredom), uncertainty and a perceived lack of control. When any or all of these stressors are present in your life you adapt by producing 'stress hormones' that enable a 'flight or fight' reaction. If the stressor continues, the body continues to adapt to the new higher levels of stress until a point is reached when the levels are too high, and exhaustion and 'burnout' occurs. At this stage there is a progressive loss of idealism, energy and purpose and work becomes routine and mechanical. Recovery from burnout is prolonged, taking from months to years, and often requires assistance from trained mental health professionals.

Identifying stress: some of the symptoms associated with stress
Stress symptoms are bodily messages that something is wrong, rather like yellow warning lights in a car. Failing to manage these symptoms is analogous to ignoring the warning lights: eventually it leads to breakdown.

Physical health problems
Headaches, fatigue, insomnia, neck aches, backaches, hypertension, allergies, obesity, weight loss, ulcers, diarrhoea, eczema

Emotional difficulties
Depression, apathy, worry, anxiety, cynicism, outbursts of uncontrolled anger, outburst of uncontrolled crying, withdrawal, isolation, sexual problems

Substandard job performance
Lack of concentration, poor judgement, increased errors, crisis-orientation, indecisiveness, tendency to work longer and harder to stay on top of things

Substance abuse
Over-indulging in alcohol, drugs, caffeine, nicotine, sugar

The outcomes of stress-related problems in practice can be devastating – from communication breakdowns between staff members and complaints from clients, to resignations and high staff turnover. They can also be devastating on a personal basis resulting in collapse of relationships and serious psychological breakdowns.

Why are veterinarians so at risk for stress?

All of the helping professions have unique pressures, anxieties, and conflicts inherent to the work itself and the context in which the work is done. Veterinarians are exposed to clients' (and patients') psychological, social and physical problems and are expected to be both skilled in resolving them and personally involved. In addition, dealing on a daily basis with loss and grief is a known major stressor.

Veterinarians as personalities tend to be 'people-pleasers' even going so far as to display signs of co-dependency, that is an ongoing pattern of thinking, feeling and behaving that stems from an excessive need to please others. Co-dependents always put other's needs before their own and the classic role played is that of 'caretaker'. Caretakers try to meet everyone's needs, to make everyone happy, and to orchestrate positive outcomes for all situations. They regularly give time and effort well beyond their actual abilities and capacities, often sacrificing personal needs to achieve approval from others. Typical behaviours include difficulty saying 'no', constant seeking of approval, never being satisfied with their own achievements, and becoming negatively invested in work, for example through having difficulty letting go of a case. This lack of emotional detachment leads to stress and burnout.

> ### *Work-related stressors for veterinarians in practice*
> - Tendency to be high achievers putting very high expectations on their own performance
> - Lack of feedback regarding job performance
> - Student perceptions of being 'elite' can create a feeling of being different or even alienated
> - Expected to be 'team leaders' for the clinical team when they have little or no training in how to function in, let alone lead, a team
> - Issues of loneliness, isolation and tiredness, especially critical for new graduates working long hours
> - Professional standards in manner, appearance and conduct are not always easy to maintain
> - Expected to be knowledgeable and up to date about the medical and surgical treatment of every type of animal
> - Expected to always be able to correctly diagnose and treat disease, and work miracles for worried owners
> - Deal daily with owners who may neglect or mistreat their animals
> - Need to be competent at dealing with emotional and badly behaved clients

- Expected to be gentle and caring with animals who may be aggressive and dangerous
- Frequently have to cope with work overload, long hours and emergencies
- Have feelings of always needing to be available, and difficulty setting limits to how much they work and delegating responsibilities
- Issues of boredom and frustration as general practice becomes routine
- Constantly facing difficult ethical and moral decisions such as killing healthy unwanted animals
- Frustration over not being able to use medical and surgical skills to treat and heal animals because an owner is unwilling or unable to pay for the treatment
- Dealing with personality conflicts and communication difficulties with other staff members for which they have no training

Of course, stress is not a problem unique to veterinarians. A good manager knows that it is important to be on the watch-out for signs of stress amongst all staff members, and to help resolve them as quickly as possible.

Although the problem of stress leading to burnout and suicide is greatest amongst veterinarians, nurses also experience job-related stressors which may result in them leaving practice. These include:

- not receiving recognition for their role and activities within the practice
- feeling unappreciated by 'ungrateful' and difficult patients for whom they are caring
- feeling unappreciated by animal owners
- not being able to use their nursing skills because the owner decides the animal is not worth it
- not receiving sufficient training for people management if they are put into more managerial roles
- not having the training or resources to manage the emotions of grieving owners, or angry veterinarians.

Managing stress

There are many theories of stress management but nearly all of them build on finding a better balance between the different aspects of your life, i.e. between work, your private and social life, your spiritual life, and your needs for at least a basic level of physical activity and fitness. Maintaining a sense of humour is perhaps the best way to manage stress: laughter is even proven to directly counteract the effects of stress.

A 'giving philosophy' and strong work ethic are the norms in veterinary medicine. It is difficult to uphold a giving philosophy while protecting your own health and well-being – especially when you have not been taught how to do this. However, learning to manage stress is important not only for your own survival and quality of life but also for the success of the business.

You can learn to reduce levels of professional stress by achieving a healthy balance between emotional attachment and emotional detachment – a state known as 'detached concern'. Detached concern is defined as detaching from cases sufficiently to maintain sound medical judgement and equanimity, whilst simultaneously maintaining enough concern for patients and clients to provide them with sensitive and understanding care.

Other ways of counteracting stress include the following:

- Talk to someone you can trust – a non-judgemental listener – about your feelings, especially those emotions that may arise in association with work.
- Spend time enjoying Nature, preferably with a companion animal such as a dog or horse.
- Exercise regularly to maintain physical fitness and flexibility.
- Develop a hobby and allow yourself time to indulge in it.
- Spend time relaxing with family and friends.
- Get enough sleep.
- Practise good eating habits.
- Plan an empty time every month where nothing is booked and you can just 'be'.

Further help

Sometimes, the effect of prolonged stress has gone too far and external help is needed.

In Britain and other countries, the Veterinary Helpline can be a first step. This is a telephone helpline manned by a small cadre of voluntary workers (themselves veterinarians or spouses of veterinarians) who can act as 'befrienders' rather than counsellors to veterinarians with personal or business problems. The next stage may be contact with medical doctors, psychologists or counsellors. What is important is not to 'battle on' alone but to seek and accept help before you reach 'burnout' and face the long road to recovery.

Some last thoughts

Because we live in a society that rewards us for 'overwork', it is difficult to create, and stick with, a stress management plan. If you make a commitment to establish a bond-centred practice, however, it is essential that you also commit to caring for yourself. It is also essential that you allow and encourage your staff to do the same. A rich and replenishing personal life will help you keep this in perspective. We leave you with the words of the renowned grief educator and psychiatrist Elisabeth Kubler-Ross: 'After working with thousands of individuals who were dying, not one ever said, "I wish I could have worked more".'

Lagoni et al., *The Human Animal Bond and Grief*, 1994

8 Developing your practice team

All organisations depend for their success on people.

Veterinary practices compete in two marketplaces: they compete for clients who *provide* the business, and they compete for staff who *are* the business. Systems and strategies *are* present in most veterinary practices to a greater or lesser extent to attract clients, but how many practices think seriously about recruiting the right staff? What are the parameters needed to select the right staff? How can you convert this group of individuals into a team? And how can you motivate your staff to work really effectively? Let's look at some of the answers.

Recruiting staff

Recruiting is about finding the right person for the job. It is a complex and costly process requiring a great deal of skill from those involved. Poor recruitment and selection of inappropriate staff can be even more expensive.

There are a number of stages to the recruiting process. I recommend taking time over each stage, planning carefully, and involving other staff members in your decisions. The method outlined below is not fool-proof, but it should help you find the best people available for your practice.

Define the function and the job

What is the function of the role you want to fill (Table 8.1)? This is actually quite an important question. By defining what the function of the job is, you make it generic and black and white. Colouring, in terms of describing the jobs that need to be performed within the role,

Table 8.1 **Functions of different practice members**

Veterinarian: to generate and sell professional services (including products) to animal owners

Veterinary nurse: to assist and enhance the effectiveness of the veterinarian

Receptionist: to be the human 'gateway' into and out of the practice

Practice manager: to put systems in place to run a healthy business

how the job should be performed and the desirable characteristics of the person fulfilling that role, can then be added.

It may seem pedantic to do this – surely a veterinarian/nurse/receptionist knows what they are expected to do in a practice! The simple answer is – no, they don't as expectations differ from practice to practice. Jobs also evolve over time, so that the job description for a receptionist employed five years ago may have changed considerably when it comes to replacing her. Preparing a role function, job description and list of desirable characteristics in the applicants, in advance, before the job is even advertised, has numerous advantages:

- It clarifies exactly what the practice needs – and can afford.
- It clarifies what the job truly entails for the successful candidate.
- It provides a basis for measurable performance parameters.
- It reduces the potential for misunderstandings.

It is important to clarify expectations, both of what you want from your successful candidate, and of what they expect to receive from the job in the way of salary, further training, continuing education, and so on. Many staff members end up frustrated and disappointed because 'promises' made at the interview never materialise (see 'The importance of matching expectations', Chapter 7, p. 151).

For example, are you seeking a veterinarian with specialist skills in surgery or medicine, or an untrained graduate? If the latter, how much time are you prepared to spend training and helping them to get them up to speed? What sort of personality are you seeking to fit into your practice team and to relate to clients? What are the hours and conditions he/she is expected to work? What proportion of time will be spent on clinical duties? Surgical duties? Farm visits? What is the future for this veterinarian in your practice? (See Table 8.2.)

The specific job description also has to link with the practice policies on, for example, recommending and selling general healthcare products such as pet foods, behaviour towards clients, charging policies and so on.

Table 8.2   **Example of a practice recruitment policy**

Recruitment needs
New post?
Replacement post?
Internal/external candidate?
Job requirements
Written job description
Type of personnel desired
Personal profile and skills profile for job
Advertising
Wording? Size?
Journals? Other outlets such as practice website?
Who receives applications? How – letter? Email?
Selection of candidates
Selection criteria
Number
Interview letters
What information does it contain?
Interviewing
Who does the interviewing?
Where? When? How long for?
Will candidates be shown round practice? By whom?
Selection procedure
Which criteria?
How will final decision be made?
Handling references?
What happens if no one is suitable?
Job offer letter
What information does it contain?
Administration tasks
Who does all the administrative tasks around the recruitment process?

Adapted from: Maggie Shilcock, *Interviewing and Recruiting Veterinary Staff,* 2003.

A basic job description for a veterinary nurse working in the consulting area in a large practice could be:

- assisting the consulting veterinarian(s)
- maintaining a friendly, helpful attitude to clients
- weighing every pet before a consultation
- taking X-rays, blood tests, urine samples, etc. as requested and dealing with them as appropriate
- ensuring clients receive the medicines, healthcare products, etc. that have been prescribed or recommended, and that they understand how to use them
- ensuring clients are properly billed for procedures
- ensuring the consulting area is always clean, that uniforms are clean, etc.
- ensuring the consulting rooms are always properly stocked with drugs and disposables.

What pay and conditions can we offer?

If you pays peanuts, you gets monkeys.

Anon

Many veterinary assistants are, unfortunately, still grossly underpaid. This is a reflection both of the attitude of low self-worth still prevalent within the profession, and of the lack of career structure available. What, for example, should you pay the 'mature, experienced assistant'? To attract high calibre veterinarians, practices should strive to offer significantly better and different salary packages – but link these to the veterinarian achieving defined expectations of productivity.

As the ability of your practice to recruit and pay for the best of employees is a direct function of your profitability, to pay more than the average rate the practice must ensure that sufficient additional revenue is generated. It is important that employees understand their role in generating the income to the practice which, amongst other things, pays their salary.

Many practices hire untrained, unskilled support staff because they are cheap. In most cases this actually proves to be more expensive as the only factor binding them to the job is the wage – if they can earn better elsewhere, they will go elsewhere. In the long run, this wastes more time (and money) seeking and training new staff than is saved by hiring cheap labour.

What personal characteristics do we want?

Your staff are critical to the success of your practice, so it is worth taking time and effort with their selection. What are you seeking from them? Knowledge? Skills? Experience? Attitude? Professional *knowledge* can be codified and easily shared; professional *skills*, such as winning the trust and confidence of animal owners, and making the myriad judgemental decisions as to how each case should be handled, although highly personalised, can be developed with practice. *Attitude*, however, is the method by which these attributes are shared with clients. To create a happy, healthy practice, you need to hire the right attitude.

The primary role of both professional and support staff is to create trust with people, both to ensure a harmonious work relationship with colleagues, and to develop a friendly and productive business relationship with clients. Staff therefore need to be people-oriented – that is, interested in and concerned to help people and their animals. And they need to be good communicators, both within the practice and with clients. They also need to be positive, forward thinking and open to new ideas.

Advertising the position

Advertising is the usual way to seek potential applicants, and advertisements should be short, clear and request a written curriculum vitae/résumé be sent with a letter of application for the position. Good staff may also be found by word of mouth and 'headhunting', that is, identifying someone by their skills and abilities and enticing them to join your practice. However, be careful not to infringe the Equal Opportunity regulations.

Review of applications

Information from the letter and CV sent in by the applicant eliminates many applicants early on. Check the references supplied by applicants you are interested in. An informal phone call to a former employer may give a lot more information about the true value of a candidate than is apparent from their CV, and past performance can give a clear prediction of future performance. (However, this can be a delicate situation as although the present employer may be the best reference, he or she may not yet be aware of the person's application.)

'Headhunted' staff members should still go through all the interview process (see below) to ensure they really are right for the practice. A practice principal I know was delighted when he successfully 'headhunted' the apparently perfect veterinary surgeon; she was medically and surgically very competent, as well as

having an excellent manner with clients. However, within a few months, the story was very different. He was not aware of her chronic physical and mental health problems, which included severe backache and depression, and which had a marked effect on her ability to work. Had this principal investigated her past records more carefully, he might have avoided hiring someone who ultimately turned out to be unable to perform her job satisfactorily and had to have her contract terminated.

Planning for interview

An interview is like a conversation with a purpose, the purpose being to find out how truly suited the applicant is for the job in question. An interview requires careful planning. What do you need to know about the applicant?

Asking open-ended questions will generally give far more information than closed questions that require a yes/no answer. Do this through finding out what the person wants by asking questions such as:

- What is your greatest achievement so far?
- What would you like to do in the future?
- What do you like most about your current job?
- What do you like least about your current job?
- What skills would you like to learn?
- When do you do your best work?
- Who do you enjoy working with the most?
- What is most important about this job for you?
- What would you like to be doing 5 years from now?

An interview is not only to examine an applicant with a view to their suitability, but also to inform the applicant about the practice and present it in a favourable, but truthful, light so that the applicant is attracted to the practice.

Arrange the interview by appointment and make sure the applicant has a contact name and number to ring if he/she has to change the arrangement. Explain the practice policy on providing lunch/paying for travel/overnight accommodation etc.

Conducting the interview

The purpose of the interview is to elicit information from the applicant which will enable his or her experience, qualifications and personal qualities to be measured against the requirements set out in the job specification. Have at least two people involved in the interview to get different impressions of the candidate.

Table 8.3 Dos and don'ts of interviewing
Do:
■ Have a clear description of the job for which the applicant is being interviewed
■ Plan the interview
■ Encourage the applicant to talk
■ Establish an easy and informal relationship
■ Follow the interview plan and cover all that you had planned
■ Probe deeper as necessary
■ Analyse career and interests (both personal and professional) to reveal strengths, weaknesses and patterns of behaviour
■ Maintain control over the direction and time taken by the interview
■ Consider the applicant as a whole – balance the good and the bad in relation to the requirements of the job
Don't:
■ Start the interview unprepared
■ Go too quickly into difficult, demanding questions
■ Ask leading questions
■ Jump to conclusions on inadequate evidence
■ Pay too much attention to particular strengths and weaknesses in isolation
■ Allow the applicant to gloss over important facts
■ Talk too much yourself

When interviewing, set the applicant at ease by being friendly and welcoming and explain how you are going to conduct the interview (Table 8.3). Briefly explain a little about the job and the practice. It is not necessary to spend a long time over this, especially if you are unsure how suitable the applicant is – you can always take time later to fill in the details. Get the applicant to provide a brief autobiographical account of their working life so far by asking about their current job. What are their plans for the future? Try to get an impression of their attitude as well as their abilities; for example ask them about the worst thing they've done – and the best thing. Open, probing questions requiring thoughtful answers are more likely to reveal the applicant's true feelings whereas closed questions generate short, factual answers (Table 8.4).

Table 8.4 **Examples of open and closed questions for interviewing a potential receptionist**

Closed:

■ How many hours per week do you expect to work?

■ When could you start?

Open:

■ How would you handle a client who is rude to you at the reception desk?

■ If you own a pet, what role does it play in your family?

■ What do you feel about pet euthanasia?

It is important to identify strong opinions or attitudes before offering a job to avoid later surprises and frustrations for both parties.

Finally, allow time at the end of the interview for further questions before showing the applicant around the practice and introducing him/her to key members of staff. Ask them their opinions of the applicant afterwards. And be prepared to follow their recommendations.

A veterinary surgeon applied for the position of assistant in the practice I was working in. She arrived for the interview with the practice principal with her hair tied back in a rubber-band, wearing an old skirt and blouse, open-toed sandals which showed a large hole in the toe of her tights, and with dirty fingernails. Needless to say, although she was pleasant to talk to, none of the staff were impressed with her 'professional appearance' and she was not hired.

Evaluate the interview

Does the applicant measure up to the standards you have set? No one will be the 'perfect fit' – they are always 'almost fits', but some people will fit a lot better than others.

Final selection

Decisions about people are time-consuming, but should not be hurried. Don't make too many compromises. It is important to find the right person. Interview potential candidates a second time if necessary. If none of the applicants is really what you want, go back to the beginning and start again. If you don't have a suitable candidate it is probably better to employ a locum or temp to cover the position whilst you advertise again than attempt to work with 'second' best. Review your advertisement – is it attracting the right sort of applicants? Do you need to change it? It may be frustrating to start again, but it will be much more beneficial for everyone in the long run.

Table 8.5   Fifteen essential points in a contract of employment

- The full names of all the parties concerned, i.e. the employer and employee.

- Date of commencement of employment and of continuous employment.

- Method of calculating salary (or scale or rate of remuneration), and when the salary will be paid (e.g. weekly, monthly).

- Terms and conditions that exist relating to hours of work or normal working hours.

- Terms and conditions that exist relating to holiday entitlement such as public holidays and holiday pay. This must be given in sufficient detail to enable calculation of ongoing holiday entitlement and entitlement accruing at termination.

- Terms and conditions relating to sick leave including sick pay provision

- Terms and conditions relating to pensions.

- Length of termination notice required from either side.

- Job description and/or job title.

- The place of work for the employee, or a statement with the employer's address stating that the employee must work at several locations.

- For temporary employment, the period for which the employment will continue; for fixed-term contract, the date when that contract expires.

- Details of the practice's disciplinary procedure, including appeals.

- Details of the practice's grievance procedure including appeals.

- Any collective agreements that directly affect the terms and conditions of employment including, where the employer is not a party, the parties to such agreements.

- (Not usually applicable to general practice) If the employee is required to work outside the UK for more than 1 month, the period of work outside the UK, the currency in which he is to be paid, any additional payments and benefits to be provided, and any terms relating to the employee's return to the UK.

Sending out the contract of employment

There are also certain points that must be included in any contract of employment (Table 8.5).

The first days

There is nothing sadder than starting a new job and feeling you have been abandoned to 'sink or swim'. It takes time for a new employee to learn the practice culture and 'the way we do things around here' and depending on their level of previous experience, this adaptation may be more or less challenging. Help out by ensuring someone is assigned to help the new employee learn the ropes over the first week or so. Depending on what is expected of them in their role, this initiation and learning period may be longer – for a trainee nurse, say – or shorter – for an experienced veterinarian filling a routine position.

Written information about policies and procedures in the practice should be available, as well as an introduction to how the computer functions, where their locker is and other practical information.

Probationary periods and feedback

For most staff there is a 6-month probationary period when they are first employed by a practice. This serves as an assessment time for both the employer and the employee. From the employer's point of view, it is important to make the best use of this time and really find out if they have recruited successfully. If the answer is yes, then all is well – but if it is no, then action needs to be taken promptly. In this situation being kind about someone ('Well, she's probably a bit stressed at the moment') or hopeful that improvements will happen ('She'll probably get better when she feels a bit more settled') can be very destructive. Once someone has been employed for more than 12 months, dismissal procedures become very difficult and complicated.

I heard the story of a receptionist from hell who started off well enough, but after the 3-month probationary period, rapidly went downhill. Initially friendly and pleasant towards clients and other staff members, her true character gradually came out as she became more and more volatile and unpredictable in her behaviour, creating frictions between staff, and deeply upsetting clients. Despite being given every chance, including warnings followed by temporary periods of improvement, the practice owner was eventually forced to sack her. 'It was the best thing I ever did', he told me later. 'I simply hadn't realised how her behaviour had negatively affected us all ... .'

Training and developing your staff

People are perhaps a company's most valuable raw materials, but they do not become assets or sources of organisational capacity until deployed effectively. Human talents exist only as potential until activated by the organisation.

> *Organisational disciplines turn workers with raw talents*
> *into professionals who can be trusted to do the right thing*
> *when empowered to take action not covered by formal rules.*
> Rosabeth Moss Kanter, *Frontiers of Management*, 1997

Not uncommonly in practice, a job is not done, or is not done in a particular way, the effect being to cause anger and disappointment. This situation arises because the *expectations* for the job were not explained clearly enough. It is better to take the risk of seeming pedantic and over-simplistic in your explanation of what you want achieved, and take time over verbal or written instructions, than to err on the side of assumption; that is, assume the person knows and understands what you want of them. Many routine procedures can be documented so that there is a standard reference, for example which laboratory to phone for which analyses, how to identify and deal with a telephone emergency, how to clean, label and sterilise surgical instruments, what the practice advises about neutering, and so on. The problem with having documented methods for procedures in the practice is that someone must be responsible for:

- teaching them to everyone, especially the newcomers
- seeing that they are correctly carried out after the teaching, and errors rectified as appropriate
- updating them as necessary.

Process mapping is a method used in many businesses to analyse and improve the organisation and flow of work within a business, and to lay the foundation for a client-related development of the business. The method provides many benefits including improved quality control of services, easier and quicker identification and management of discrepancies from the recommended procedural behaviour, and a significantly improved effectiveness in how procedures are carried out in the practice, which reduces stress and improves the service to clients. (See Appendix 4 for a more detailed description of the power of process mapping.)

Unsuitable staff

Sometimes despite all precautions, mistakes are made and employees are found to be so unsuitable that it is felt necessary to remove them from the practice. Gross misconduct, such as dishonesty, gross neglect and breach of safety rules, wilful refusal to follow lawful and reasonable instruction, and persistent drunkenness, may justify summary dismissal but usually the reasons for dismissal are not as clear cut as this. To avoid expensive litigation, every employer should be fully aware of the strict regulations governing termination of a contract and should seek legal advice before taking steps to dismiss someone.

Conducting an exit interview

Staff represent an investment of time, money and effort. It can be frustrating and disappointing for a practice if they resign. Exit interviews provide an opportunity for a candid review of the factors that have brought about their resignation and may, sometimes, be a chance to reverse their decision. An exit interview can give valuable insights into problems within the practice – and provide an opportunity to do something about them.

Ideally, the interview should not be conducted by the person's immediate boss or supervisor, and should preferably be performed off the premises or even over the telephone. The aim is to gain information in a relaxed, informal way rather than to interrogate the person. Useful questions to ask include:

- Would you come back?
- What did you learn from working here?
- Was the job description you received accurate?
- If not, why not?
- Do you feel you received adequate training/support/etc. to be able to conduct your job well?
- Were you treated fairly?
- If not, where was the treatment lacking?
- What did you like most about working here?
- What did you like least?
- What would you change about your job?
- What was your relationship like with other practice members/specific practice members (e.g. the boss, the manager, the head nurse)?
- How could the practice – or individuals within the practice – do a better job to help and support your position in future?

If there is time, it may be advisable to ask the person leaving to prepare written answers to these questions so that their answers are more focused, and therefore of more use to you. Thank them for their participation. And use the information they give you!

Creating a practice team

Why create a team?
No one individual has all the necessary skills to provide a complete service for all clients, but by combining all staff skills – veterinarian, nurse and receptionist – the needs of the client, patient and practice are met.

Dennis McCurnin, Veterinary Management Consultant

The staff of veterinary practices traditionally function as a group rather than a team. Groups tend to live day-by-day, completing only those aspects of their jobs that are necessary, and typically suffer from lack of communication and low motivation.

Teams are quite different. A team is defined as: *a highly communicative group of individuals with different background skills and abilities, who have a common purpose, and who work together to achieve clearly defined goals*. They are characterised by:

- purpose
- good relationships based on excellent communication
- high levels of performance from all team members
- flexibility and imagination
- confidence and high morale
- recognition and appreciation of each other.

Figure 8.1 Regular meetings help convert a group to a team.

Converting a group to a team is not easy. Veterinarians, for example, are not taught to be interdependent – they learn to function as independent, critical-thinking individuals. (It is interesting to note, however, that most veterinarians appreciate support from colleagues, which is the major reason for choosing to work in multi-vet practices.) Team members do not have to be all 'jolly hockey-sticks' together. They do not even have to get on particularly well – but they have to be able to accomplish things together.

There are many advantages to learning to think and behave like a team. A good team:

- Collaborates and cooperates to create a symbiotic relationship: the total result is greater than the sum of the parts.
- Works for common goals: staff members are more involved and have better 'ownership' of the practice, which makes them more committed and productive.
- Offers improved medical care for patients: 'The health care system of the future will place more emphasis on the decision-making abilities of a team of individuals working together – a team that should include the client-owner' (I.S. Udvarhelyi, Vice President, Prudential Insurance Co, 1994).
- Offers improved practice productivity and profitability.
- Offers opportunities for improved personal growth and development through receiving feedback and support from other team members.

Working as a team to increase productivity is also important because in veterinary practice the team is made up of people who are essentially knowledge workers, that is, people whose productivity is marked by adding value to information. Business management consultant Peter Drucker points out that such workers' expertise is highly specialised, and that their productivity depends on the efforts being coordinated as part of an organisational team: writers are not publishers; computer programmers are not software distributors; and veterinarians are not business managers. While people have always worked in tandem, notes Drucker, with knowledge work teams become the work unit rather than the individual himself. And that suggests that emotional intelligence, the skills that help people harmonise, should become increasingly valued as a workplace asset in the years to come.

Studies show that in most practices, the most effective unit in terms of clients seen and income generated is one vet working with three or more trained support staff members. The Safari Animal Practice in

Texas, one of the most successful practices in the United States, has a ratio of two vets to 30 staff members (whose roles include nursing, reception, boarding kennels, and boutique)!

So, how do you go about converting your staff-group into a team?

The team leader

Team building is a matter of establishing mutual trust and confidence among the group of people working for you. Your aim, as practice principal and team leader, is to create a feeling of interdependence, a feeling of shared responsibility for getting results.

There are six areas a leader can concentrate on to start the conversion of a group to a team:

- Create the right environment in which to establish a team through having a positive, cheerful working attitude that encourages communication and participation.
- Identify at a very early stage the common purpose of the team. To stimulate and motivate the participants, creating the mission should be a collective decision-making process.
- Encourage participation in agreeing objectives and targets and establish common goals collectively.
- Rotate jobs within the team, where feasible, to get members to identify with the team as a whole rather than just the job.
- Ensure communications flow freely.
- Encourage your staff to act in the way that you want by constantly modelling that behaviour, and rewarding them for responding.

A word of caution: some people just aren't 'team types' – they are better as 'solo performers'. These are people who just don't have the skills to work constructively in teams – and who are unable or unwilling to acquire those skills. There are only three ways to deal with them when teams are formed. One, keep them at a safe distance from the teams so they can do no damage. Two, go ahead and put them on teams under strong leaders and hope for the best. Three, harvest the contributions of these talented people in a way that does not put the team itself at risk.

Faced with this situation in your practice, you will have to decide if a non-team person's abilities are so valuable that the practice needs them at all costs, or whether the team's development would be better off without them.

Stages of team development
Groups become effective teams in stages which can take a variable amount of time.

Stage 1: Orientation
New team members feel eager, have high expectations, some anxiety, and there is a certain amount of jostling for position.

Stage 2: Dissatisfaction
Many groups never progress beyond this highly unproductive stage, which is characterised by feelings of dissatisfaction, frustration, incompetence and confusion. There is often a negative feeling towards the team leader and the group may feel it is not worth progressing. Just knowing that this awkward stage exists and is inevitable can help a good leader guide the team on to the next stage.

Stage 3: Resolution
Harmony, trust, support and respect develop as the polarities and animosities between members start to resolve. Self-esteem and confidence come back. Members use a team language and begin to share responsibility and control.

Stage 4: Production
Team members now collaborate enthusiastically together, feel very positive about team success and perform at a high level.

Good leadership drives the group forward through the different stages by close observation of the way the individual team members function together. This involves looking at how the individuals communicate with each other and how much they participate, the degree of conflict within the group, its ability to make decisions and so on.

Developing key characteristics

Four key characteristics of a team are commitment, cooperation, communication and contribution. These are learned characteristics which enable the team to become creative, imaginative – and more effective.

Commitment comes from participation in decision-making and the feeling that 'my opinion is of value'. But commitment must also be shown by the practice leader. Leaders who are not committed – or not seen to be committed – cannot expect commitment from their staff.

> This apparent lack of commitment from the practice principal is a common reason why teams fail in practice. Principals often throw in ideas, tell the 'team' to get on with them, then take no further interest in them. Another frequent scenario is practice principals who regularly disappear for their game of golf, leaving the 'team' to carry on without them. Although I am not suggesting that principals should have to work 24 hours a day, they have to be able to portray commitment. They have to model the behaviour they want from their staff.
>
> Alternatively, the leader who is over-committed and allows autonomy from no one else is also a severe handicap. The other team members become resigned and passive as their contributory efforts are denied or taken over by the dominating and over-engaged leader.

Cooperation arises from the shared sense of purpose and mutual gain that the practice mission should give. Good communication is vital and can be improved by facing and dealing with controversy, avoiding secrets, and striving to be as open as possible with all team members.

Contribution by all team members to a team is essential. Lack of contribution is demoralising for those who do contribute – they feel they carry the weight of the team and they also can feel undermined by not knowing what the non-contributing team member is thinking and feeling. The effect of non-contribution may also be reflected to the client in higher overheads – someone has to pay for the non-productive team member.

Regular team meetings offer an opportunity for everyone to express new ideas and improve work methods, as well as articulate problems and concerns, and offer solutions. (See Appendix 2.)

Why teams fail

Teams fail for a variety of reasons. The most common are that team members don't know what they are supposed to be doing, they don't agree with what is being suggested, or they don't know and accept the 'rules' of team membership. This lack of clarity leads to people not turning up for meetings or coming late because 'they had more important things to do'; to people sabotaging team efforts by having a negative and critical attitude to all suggestions; or to simply refusing to cooperate.

The effects of insubordination can be very frustrating. For example, it is not uncommon that practice members 'agree' to run a nurse-managed healthcare programme such as an obesity programme. The concept is that nurses work with clients to manage weight loss in obese patients, following a veterinary recommendation. There are clear benefits to all concerned – not least the improved health and life quality of the patient. In practice, the programme often does not work: vets do not make the recommendations, there is little cooperation from the vets with the nurse(s) running the programme, the nurses are not given the extra time needed to manage their patients, and the whole great idea dies out leaving a powerful legacy of 'Well, we tried that and it didn't work'.

When investigated at a deeper level the reasons for failure of such programmes include:

- Veterinarians are trained to solve problems and cure disease, not manage health, and they feel uncomfortable making healthcare recommendations unless there is a problem to solve such as obesity contributing to lameness in an osteoarthritis patient.
- Veterinarians are not natural delegators and feel uncomfortable about handing over responsibility for cases to nurses.
- Vets are not very good as team players as they tend to be individualists.
- Vets associate healthcare programmes with commercialism and product selling rather than animal welfare.
- Nurses do not receive the authority and time from the practice principals to run the programme effectively.
- The nurse loses motivation because she is unsure and unsupported in her role.

Some solutions
- Be clear about practice goals and ambitions.
- Be clear about the purpose and function of team meetings.
- Plan the meetings in advance and use an agenda.
- Draw up the rules of team membership. This includes agreements on what is acceptable behaviour in the group such as coming to meetings on time, behaving respectfully towards other team members, maintaining a positive attitude, and being accountable for results.

The importance of a positive attitude in a practice team cannot be overstressed. A positive team concentrates on the strengths and possibilities in a situation rather than the weaknesses and faults.

A positive attitude can be fostered by teaching team members to present information in a positive manner ('I see *x* as a problem, but think a solution could be ... ') and using effective feedback rather than 'constructive criticism'; that is, attack the problem, not the person. A positive attitude must come from the top, from the boss. It does not mean the practice need constantly exist in a Pollyanna-like state of euphoria ('I'm so *glad* today!'), but it does mean that it becomes open and receptive rather than closed and disillusioned. Encouraging innovation and innovative ideas stimulates a positive attitude; it shows that you recognise that limiting the practice to the current ideas within the profession is not the way forward. Again, *your* behaviour is crucial; modelling a positive attitude is the most important thing you can do to help your team's attitude.

Attitude is a choice – it is not something you are born with so it is possible to learn to have a positive attitude. I, along with my veterinary colleagues, was once bluntly told by our appalled new manager, that if we did not change our, then, very negative attitudes we would be out of our jobs. Shocked to be challenged in this way, we did – and were amazed at how different the world suddenly seemed. It was not a place of gloom and despondency where nothing worked and no one cooperated, but a place of optimism, opportunity and friendly people.

Performance appraisal

> *Employees' two worst fears are losing a job and having a job that goes unnoticed.*

Performance appraisal measures the individual and/or team achievement of goals or tasks defined by the practice. Many practices still do not conduct any sort of formal staff performance appraisal although it is integral to improving the efficacy of practice members and improving job satisfaction.

Formal appraisal systems take time, require clear performance goals and methods of measuring results. To perform an appraisal interview well requires training in communication and coaching techniques, especially focused listening and how to give effective feedback. It is, of course, based on having a genuine interest in helping the person improve their performance.

> *I think it is an immutable law in business that words are words, explanations are explanations, promises are promises – but only performance is reality. Performance alone is the best measure of confidence, competence and courage ... (As a manager) ... just remember that:* Performance is your reality. *Forget everything else. That is why my definition of a manager is what it is: one who turns in the performance. No alibis to others or to oneself will change that.*
>
> Harold Geneen, ex-Chief Executive, ITT

Performance assessment serves two main functions. It not only is a measure of achievement, but it also helps to develop the individual or team. Performance standards can be set for a variety of different parameters from personality attributes to income generated.

In a Canadian practice I visited, the two practice principals reviewed their staff's behavioural and attitudinal performance on a monthly basis – and vice versa! A simple questionnaire for each person was completed separately by the staff member and practice principals. The two sets of answers were then compared and adjustments recommended to the person's performance. The questionnaire concentrated mainly on characteristics such as friendliness, politeness and attitude to colleagues and clients. Each was ranked on a 1–5 scale. Improved performance was rewarded with an end-of-the-month bonus.

The practice principals found it very useful as it meant they could manage not only the desirable behaviour of their staff – but also their own.

To measure performance you need to define the performance you want and agree this with the staff member/team, give suitable training and instruction to enable achievement, agree how and when the performance will be measured and determine what the rewards/penalties are of achievement/non-achievement (Table 8.6). Clearly, the rewards of performance are the motivators you have already identified.

When you decide what the performance is that you seek, you also need to work out a way to measure it. Some performance goals, such as having a pleasant telephone manner, or client satisfaction, can be difficult to measure. Make them as specific as possible; for example, saying please and thank you, and calling the client by name at least twice in a conversation might be specifications for the former, while grading different aspects of 'satisfaction', such as speed of telephone answer, cleanliness of practice, friendliness of staff on a 1–5 scale of requirements may be a way of measuring the latter.

Other goals can be easier to measure; for example, increase in average transaction fee, number of clients seen, number of dentals performed, or

Table 8.6 **Setting performance parameters**
■ Work with the staff member to identify three or four personal and professional goals that are compatible with the practice mission (see SMART goals, Chapter 2)
■ Analyse their ability to achieve these goals
■ Give them suitable training and instruction and ensure the resources – such as time – are available to achieve
■ Agree with the individual how their performance in achieving these goals will be measured
■ Give them suitable training and instruction that will enable them to achieve the goals
■ Monitor their performance at agreed intervals
■ Allow for the learning curve – expect staff members to improve at a pace which matches their own natural aptitude
■ Assess their final level of achievement with them and reward or penalise accordingly

appointment time with clients can be monitored through computer records.

It is very important to be very clear about what is to be appraised; for example, for a veterinarian required to increase his average transaction fee (ATF) the following should be considered: ATF is the sum of all the fees paid divided by the number of transactions. It can be influenced by the number of services supplied per client, and the amount of prescription and other medical and non-medical goods sold. Which of these do you want the veterinarians to concentrate on? Is the increase in ATF to link with a dental focus, for example? It is important to define exactly what the practice is looking for to avoid mistakes – and frustration on both sides.

Frequent and regular performance appraisal stops the person drifting away from their performance goals. Either continuous assessment or at least a review every 3 months is recommended. Continual assessment has the advantage that it provides feedback about a situation *at the time it occurs*, not later – and behaviour responds much more quickly to prompt correction or praise than delayed reaction. Three-month reviews are, perhaps, more formal, but may be easier to plan and organise for the inexperienced reviewer.

The concept of performance appraisal is new for most veterinarians and there is likely to be some resistance to it initially. It takes time for them to understand what is required, the importance of the regular review – and that it is ultimately very beneficial to their own performance.

My advice to principals is to plan carefully: clearly identify the behaviour you want from staff members, and work hard to keep them on track. The results will speak for themselves.

Concentrate on the task and how well it is performed rather than on personality issues. Give guidance, as and when required, on where and how to improve, and get your staff members to agree on any things they need to do to improve. Don't forget to praise the right behaviour. Prompt praising of the right behaviour is the best way to get more of it.

Delegation

What percentage of your professional worktime is spent doing things that a more junior person could do, if we got organized and trained the junior to handle it with quality?
David Maister, Management Consultant

Delegation is a skill veterinarians are notoriously bad at using and yet it is the key to effective management. Delegation means handing the responsibility for a project or situation to a suitably qualified person, to achieve a good outcome. It serves two purposes:

- It helps relieve your own workload – much of which may be neither necessary nor appropriate anyway.
- It encourages people to practise self-management and to take responsibility for their own areas/projects.

Delegation can only really be used on people who are sufficiently-trained and confident to require minimum support and direction. It is not appropriate for a raw recruit or an inexperienced person. There are two primary levels at which delegation usually occurs in veterinary practice:

- from principal to veterinary assistant or practice manager.
- from veterinarian to veterinary nurse.

The first level releases the multi-faceted practice principal for more productive time use. The issues that are delegated could include researching and establishing new preventive healthcare programmes, developing a specialist field, working out staff schedules, administration, marketing programmes, and so on.

The second level serves to release the veterinarian from more mundane procedures, at the same time building up the skills of the nurse (Table 8.7). Many procedures can be performed more profitably by a support staff member than a veterinarian who has a considerably higher

Table 8.7   Reasons for increasing support staff involvement

■ Better service to pet and clients

■ Improved practice efficiency

■ Enhanced practice income

■ More productive use of staff training and experience

■ Clients often talk more readily to support staff than veterinarians

■ Freeing the veterinarians to carry out more procedures better suited to their level of training

■ Increased job satisfaction for staff

■ Developing responsibility and commitment of staff to practice standards

■ Developing staff skills, e.g. in client relations, marketing, minor surgery, etc.

■ Encouraging specialisation by support staff

chargeable hourly rate. In addition, effective delegation to well-trained staff improves the service offered to clients as it reduces the risk of 'burnout' for veterinarians trying to juggle the time needed for delivering quality veterinary care with excellence in client communication.

The myths of delegation

Veterinarians are often afraid to delegate because they believe myths such as:

■ *'I'll delegate myself out of a job!'* – wrong; the veterinarian now has more time to carry out procedures more suited to his or her skills and training.
■ *'It's easier/quicker if I do it myself'* – right; in the short term. But in the long term procedures that can be delegated to, say, support staff are those that are not profitable or particularly satisfying for a veterinarian to perform. They include bandaging, stitch removal, anal gland expression, ear cleaning, general health advice, and so on.
■ *'At least I know it's been done right'* – wrong; it will also be done properly if the person is trained well.
■ *'There is nothing in it for me'* – right; at the moment. There often is no true incentive to delegate, so the feeling is, why waste the time and effort? An incentive scheme for the veterinarians in the practice to encourage and support good veterinary nurse coaching may help solve the problem of reluctance to invest the coaching and supervision time necessary to achieve successful delegation. Establishing a measurable monitoring and reward system for veterinarians within

the practice for their ability to coach junior colleagues and veterinary nurses and achieve performance can encourage them to delegate routine procedures.

The effect of a traditional staffing structure

The more people are together, the more time their sheer interaction will take, the less will be available for them to work, accomplish and get results.

Peter Drucker, Senior Management Consultant

Overstaffing – that is, employing too many people for the real work available – is a common problem. Too many people simply get in each other's way. The exponential increase in the number of possible staff interactions that occurs also increases the potential for time-wasting, boredom and mischief-making. People become an impediment to performance.

In a lean organisation, people have room to move without colliding with one another and can do their work without having to explain it all the time. They may have to work harder, but most people respond to a little 'stretching'.

Understaffing creates work problems too. Constantly being stressed and overworked is as detrimental, in the long run, as boredom. It can be very difficult to get the perfect balance of staff in practice where there are daily, monthly and even yearly variations in the volume of work to be done. Training and motivating existing staff to be more effective, delegating, using part-time staff for peak periods, and hiring specialist or locum help as needed, are all methods of reducing the problems from under- and overstaffing.

The typical staffing structure of a veterinary practice is shown in Figure 8.2. There are a small number of partners or owners, a moderate number of professionals (veterinary surgeons), and a relatively large number of support staff. In Britain, a typical practice may have four veterinarians (of which one or two are principals), and 10 support staff. Does this traditional type of ratio reduce opportunities for delegation?

Leverage is the term used to describe the ratio of junior, middle-level and senior staff in a professional firm's organisation or the ratio of support staff to veterinary assistants and principals in veterinary practice. Leverage in a practice varies depending on the stage of the practice lifecycle (see Chapter 2; illustrated in Fig. 8.3).

By identifying the ideal staffing structure, practices could select and use staff more efficiently. Thus, an 'expert' practice would need a greater proportion of skilled veterinarians than the 'efficiency' practice, who would function best with a high proportion of veterinary nurses.

Figure 8.2 The veterinary practice pyramid.

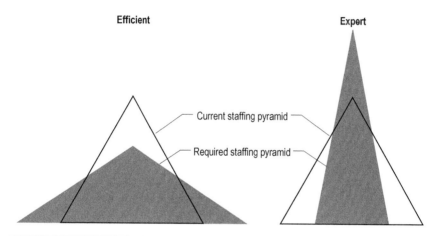

Figure 8.3 The changing staffing requirements of the efficient and expert practice types.

When to delegate?

You should delegate when:

- You cannot find sufficient time for your priority tasks.
- You want to develop other practice members.
- The job can be done adequately by other practice members.
- You have more work than you can effectively carry out yourself.

How to delegate

The only way to develop responsibility in people is to give them responsibility.

Blanchard *et al.*, *The One Minute Manager Meets the Monkey*, 1990

Delegation is a learnt skill. There are basically two approaches:

- Tell the person exactly what you want them to do, how to do it and what results you expect, so that they are left with little or no room for personal intervention.
- Give responsibility for the results to the person. Focus on results, not methods, and rely on the person's commitment and responsibility to get the job done.

The first method is, in essence, an order. People rarely accept orders outside of the Armed Services. The second method takes longer initially, but produces better results and thereby makes you as the manager more effective. Covey (1989) describes five steps to effective delegation:

- *Desired results.* Create a clear mutual understanding of what needs to be accomplished focusing on the *results* not the *methods*; that is, *what* not *how*. Spend time, be patient and clearly visualise the results with the person.
- *Guidelines.* Give minimal guidelines, such as the parameters within which the individual should work, and any known failure paths of the job, so that you are pointing out what *not* to do, but not *what* to do.
- *Resources.* Identify and make available all the necessary resources.
- *Accountability.* Define the standards that will be used in evaluating the performance, and fix dates for the evaluation(s) to occur.
- *Consequences.* State clearly what the consequences are, both good and bad, of the evaluation. This could include new job assignments, financial rewards and so on depending on the nature of the job.

Some people are very difficult to delegate to, however patient and persistent you are with them. By refusing to accept responsibility they are refusing to accept the need to produce the performance the practice requires – and their suitability within the practice should be questioned.

Empowerment

Empowerment is an integral part of delegation. It has been described as *letting go* so that others *get going*; giving people the authority and resources to make better decisions and solve more problems.

Consider the common scenario of a receptionist coping with an appointment system that is half an hour behind schedule. If they are empowered to help clients, they will keep them informed about the delay, give the client the option to rebook their appointment or leave their pet for collection later, and will try to make their wait as pleasant as possible by, perhaps, offering coffee or tea and biscuits; or giving them a pair of free film tickets; or giving them a discount on a pet healthcare product, etc. They are trusted by the practice principal(s) to do all in their power to make this awkward and less than ideal situation pleasant for the client.

Empowering would be inappropriate for a new graduate or employee who is not familiar with the systems and protocols in the practice, because the core ingredient of empowering is *trust*; you have to trust your staff member's capabilities to be able to empower them. But your belief in their abilities can be reinforced by ensuring they are adequately trained to *be* empowered.

Conclusion

Management consultant David Maister writes: 'In the next decade and beyond, the ability to attract, develop, retain and deploy staff will be the single biggest determinant of a professional service firm's competitive success.' What active steps are you taking to attract and develop the staff you want in your practice?

9 Marketing your practice

Organisations typically become aware of marketing when their market undergoes a change.

Kotler and Clarke, Business Management Consultants

The term marketing in relation to veterinary practice often causes a hostile and negative response: 'Professionals don't need to market themselves!' However, marketing should not scream 'hire me', but must gently suggest, 'here are some sound reasons why you might like to get to know us better'. Marketing plays a major role in the management and development of professional service firms such as veterinary practice, and is an integral part of the successful practice.

Why is marketing not done better in veterinary practices? It is partly through lack of knowledge about and awareness of what marketing really entails, but it is primarily because marketing is a *management* issue. Marketing activities represent an *investment* – they require a fair amount of non-money-making time to be spent with uncertain long-term results, and few practices are well organised enough to manage their investment activities. Although *results* may be recognised and rewarded, the value of marketing *efforts* has to be recognised too – and this requires careful management.

Marketing is surrounded by many myths and misconceptions which colour understanding of what marketing is and what it sets out to achieve:

- *Marketing is advertising and selling.* While advertising and selling are both acceptable marketing communications activities, they represent only a very limited section of the whole marketing function.
- *We don't 'do' any marketing!* This concept is linked with the first – that to 'do' marketing you must produce a glossy brochure or have a television advertisement. Marketing is an integral part of having a

business and exists at even the most rudimentary level in the logo on the practice notepaper, the clean white coat, and the friendly pat on the head for the dog. It is part of traditional 'bedside manner'. To be really effective, however, marketing activities have to be more explicit and organised.

■ *Our senior partner/head nurse/etc. 'does' our marketing!* Marketing is a lot more than talking to the kennel club annually. Organised marketing is a managerial decision, but marketing happens in the practice all the time – *all* client contact is marketing. Thus, an indifferent receptionist is bad marketing for the practice, whereas the nurse who goes out of the way to help a client is excellent marketing.

■ *Marketing means meeting client needs at any cost.* This belief is based on the concept that, 'marketing means giving clients exactly what they want – and all they want is top service for pitiful fees, which means we go out of business'. This is *not* what marketing is all about.

So, what is marketing?

Marketing is the analysis, planning, implementation and control of carefully formulated programmes which are designed to encourage and build a productive and profitable relationship between an organisation, such as a veterinary practice, and its target market, a specific group or groups of animal owners.

Marketing is a management skill that matches the practice's personnel, resources and expertise with clients' needs in such a way that the practice achieves its long-term goals and the clients receive continued satisfaction. It is not a haphazard process but a specific managerial task that requires carefully formulated plans designed to achieve certain responses. These plans are most effectively aimed at specific, target markets and should offer what the market wants, not what the practice *thinks* the market wants. To motivate and inform the market well, the practice relies heavily on factors such as effective pricing and good communication (see later).

Marketing is essential to ensure the practice's survival and continual health through serving its markets more effectively. It consists of a blend of the 'marketing mix':

■ design of the services to be offered
■ pricing
■ communication/advertising
■ location of the practice.

In this Chapter I do not attempt to tell you *how* to market, but explain the background to marketing and why it is important, highlight the common pitfalls with marketing veterinary services and present key marketing concepts.

Why do we market?

The services veterinarians think their clients don't want most clients won't want. Why? Because they don't know they are available.

Don Dooley, Veterinary Management Consultant

The purpose of marketing is threefold:

- To ensure that current clients stay with the practice.
- To generate more business from the existing client base.
- To attract new clients to use the practice's services.

Although it is possible to achieve these aims without help, I would suggest hiring experienced marketing consultants who can use their training and experience to develop appropriate marketing systems. They will also help you answer the following key questions:

- What is our business?
- Who is our client?
- What do they buy?
- What is *value* to our clients?

What is our business?

As we established in Chapter 2, veterinary practice is in the business of providing animal healthcare services to the benefit of the animals in our charge and their owners (our clients) and creating a fair profit from the transaction.

Who is our client?

Which clients want *your* business? Which clients are of the most value to the practice? *Which* clients *do you want* to have your business? The majority of your clients will come from your geographical area. However, you may not necessarily want to attract *all* potential animal owners as this may not be how you wish to profile your practice. One of the biggest mistakes practices make is trying to cater to the needs of all clients – from the poorest to the wealthiest, from those who only bring in their pets *in extremis* to those who ring on the slightest pretext, from those wanting basic care at the lowest possible price to those who would give their last penny if it would help their beloved family member. In areas where you are the only practice for a very long way around, you (and the clients!) may have no choice, but, more commonly, not only do clients have a choice of practices to attend, but you have a choice of the type of clients you wish to attract and retain. In a specialist practice such as a feline practice, or one focusing on exotic pets, the type of animal owners needed are obvious (although not all feline/exotic animal owners will automatically choose to go to such practices); but in a broader spectrum practice, identifying the type of clients you wish to have is an important part of the business definition and planning.

The Boston matrix

The Boston matrix can be used to relate the current level of business your clients are generating to the potential level of business they could be generating. By matching this to the services you are offering or thinking of offering, you can most effectively plan the expansion of your business:

Potential business high	*High current* *High potential*	*Low current* *High potential*
Potential business low	*High current* *Low potential*	*Low current* *Low potential*
	Current business high	**Current business low**

High current/high potential clients are in the minority. They are the 20% that provide the 80% of the business. Although their potential for development is low, they are very desirable for their current uptake and loyalty, and care should be taken of them. They are probably the greatest ambassadors of the practice as well.

Low current/high potential clients represent the greatest potential for business expansion. However, it is important to find out why they are *Low current* and, if possible, remedy this. It may simply be that they don't know services and products are available, or it may be there is some underlying dissatisfaction with the practice.

High current/low potential clients should be protected as they are using most or all of your services. However, they should definitely be targeted if new services are developed.

Low current/low potential clients are in this category for a wide variety of reasons – from personal finance problems to lack of interest in and awareness about how they can better care for their animals. Although they would appear to be of least interest they should not be forgotten as their circumstances or needs can change so that they come into one of the other categories.

A practice that was setting up a Senior Health Programme decided, as a method of increasing client numbers, to concentrate their marketing efforts on the owners of older pets who had not been into the practice within the last 18 months. The practice had a zero response and was, needless to say, somewhat disheartened. Unfortunately, they targeted completely the wrong market for their programme – these clients are the ones least likely to be interested in their pets' welfare, least likely to want to spend money on their pets, and most likely to be dissatisfied with the practice. Had the practice concentrated on its 'good' clients who want the best for their pets, bring their pet regularly to the practice and who have a good relationship with the practice, they would have had a very different response.

What do they buy?

A person buying a microwave oven buys the easiest way to cook food; a person buying a car can buy comfort, safety, transport or status (or all four). Your clients are actually buying peace of mind when they come to your practice.

What is value to our clients?

The traditional answer is price – the true answer is actually far more complex and involves the experience of quality, and being listened to and understood. High price in some situations is actually a value to people, for example buying a fur coat (status) or an expensive perfume (luxury).

Market to established or new clients?

Most professional firms say that their existing clients represent the most probable (and often the most profitable) source of new business. However, when one examines their behaviour, one finds that while they have well-established and organized programmes for 'new client' business development, there is little, if any, organized effort to obtain new business from existing clients.

David Maister, Business Management Consultant

Practices can market to established clients or to attract new clients. However, studies have shown that it is less effective, and five times more costly, to market to new clients.

Working with existing and/or new clients requires different approaches. The former is more intimate, more personal and more involved; the latter, being more impersonal, may suit some people better than others. Ideally, practices should aim for a balance between the two. Some of the advantages and disadvantages of marketing to the two different types of clients are highlighted below.

New business from existing clients

- Winning client trust and confidence is a major influence in the sales process of veterinary services, which requires an understanding of the client's concerns and needs. It cannot be stressed enough that these needs are not what the *practice* thinks the client wants but what the *client* really wants – which can only be found out by asking the client. Where a good relationship exists with the client, they are more likely to accept the practice's proposal for further care and treatment if a new problem is discovered than to consider the effort of going to a new practice.
- Marketing costs to win a specific volume of new work from existing clients are much lower than to attract the same volume from new clients.
- Follow-on treatments for existing clients are often more profitable based on their trust and faith in you, than work gleaned from new clients. For example, an established client is more likely to undertake a senior health check for their pet than a new client.
- Profitability can be increased, over time, because more work can be done by non-veterinarians as the client learns to trust and accept younger, less experienced staff in the practice.
- Established clients are more likely to 'give the practice a chance' with something new so that the practice is able to develop and grow its capabilities.

The importance of winning new clients

- New clients are needed to replace natural losses of clients due to patient death, or moving from the area.
- New clients offer new challenges and 'new blood' in the practice.
- They avoid 'overworking' the relationship with established clients.
- New clients are a long-term marketing investment if the practice has well-established systems for developing business with established clients.

Client loyalty

Client loyalty is an area of client relations where there is often confusion. A strong sense of allegiance exists with some clients, who can be devoted to a particular veterinarian or practice. However, loyalty is not simply an emotive attitude but also a behaviour – that of purchasing the same product or service repeatedly. In addition, loyalty is intimately linked with client satisfaction.

> ### *What is client loyalty?*
> French veterinary management consultant Dr Yannick Poubanne has studied client loyalty extensively. 'It is important not to confuse client loyalty with client satisfaction,' he says. 'Consider your own behaviour: you probably have favoured places where you buy products and services with which you are satisfied and to which you would recommend your friends. However, with the choice available today you also use different, similar outlets when it is more convenient, for the novelty experience, because someone has recommended it, because you feel like it, and so on. You would not say you are dissatisfied with the services and products you have purchased before, yet you are not being loyal.'
>
> 'It's the same for clients in veterinary practices. If you ask different veterinarians to define a loyal client, you'll get answers such as "They always come back to us", "They prefer us", "They talk positively about us to their friends", "They come in often and spend a lot", "They will defer treatment and wait for me if I'm away", "They've come to us for years" and so on. Although there is some truth in all these answers, this is not the full story.'
>
> 'By nature, loyalty has two facets', he explains. 'A behavioural one and an affective one. Firstly, a loyal client behaves positively towards

the practice, generating frequent visits and substantial spending relative to his needs. Secondly, a loyal client verbally expresses a positive attitude towards the practice. This latter is however not enough to declare a client as being loyal because habit should not be confused with loyalty.'

'Client satisfaction differs from client loyalty in many ways. First, client satisfaction is a feeling regarding past experiences with the service, whereas loyalty is a feeling and a forecasted behaviour regarding future experiences. Second, satisfaction is generally considered as an antecedent necessary to gain loyalty. Third, satisfaction is not enough to ensure loyalty. There are nowadays an increasing number of satisfied clients who are disloyal. Last but not least, client satisfaction costs money to the practice while client loyalty generates money to the practice.'

'By understanding the nature of client loyalty and its differences to client satisfaction, it is possible to improve client loyalty', he further explains. 'Simple questionnaires that look at the behavioural and emotional aspects of loyalty and plot it against the satisfaction levels can help a practice develop the satisfaction factors that drive loyalty, as well as develop the non-satisfaction drivers of loyalty such as the client's feeling of being important to the practice.'

The problems of marketing services

Veterinary practice is an example of a professional service industry: it sells professional services to clients to create business. A service is defined as: *any activity or benefit that one party can offer to another that is essentially intangible and does not result in the ownership of anything.* Its production may or may not be tied to a physical product. Thus, a practice does not sell purely a vaccine but a vaccination package of healthcare: a clinical examination by a qualified animal healthcare expert, a vaccination which provides protection from serious diseases, and reassurance for the client that they are doing the right thing for their pet (Fig. 9.1).

Features of services

Services have a number of features that distinguish them from products and which make them more challenging to market. These are:

- *Intangibility* – a service cannot be measured, held in the hand, or tried out before purchase; the buyer has to have faith in the service.

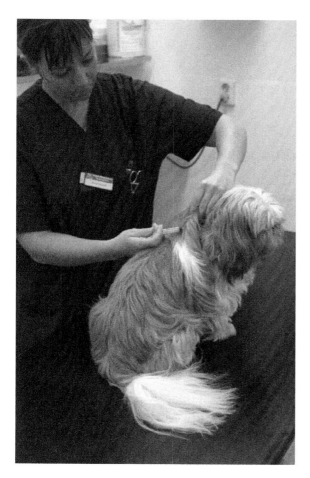

Figure 9.1 Giving a vaccination is an example of a service provided by the practice.

This faith comes partly from trust in the person providing the service, but can also be enhanced by making the service as tangible and concrete as possible through describing the benefits of the service, and using specific, descriptive names for the service. Relating the service to the human equivalent may also help people visualise the service. Thus an Annual Pet Dental Health Check is a clinical examination recommended by the veterinarian for your pet every year, to help your pet maintain healthy teeth and gums.

- *Inseparability* – a service cannot exist separately from its providers whether they are persons or machines; for example, a vaccination health package cannot be given without a veterinarian or nurse to do it.
- *Variability* – a service is not only made up of many different parts, its interpretation will vary according to who provides the service. For example, a senior veterinarian may put less emphasis on the value of preventive nutrition than a keen graduate, even though it has

been agreed that the service is available from the practice. Similarly, the response to a service may vary according to the owner's interpretation, or the pet's reaction.

- *Perishability* – unlike a product, a service cannot be stored. Much of the content of a service is knowledge, and if the service is not used it is wasted.

Other characteristic problems with marketing veterinary services

Marketing veterinary services also has a number of other characteristic problems that differentiate them from products and which should be understood:

- *Third-party accountability*: Veterinary practice is subject to third-party accountability which often involves the opinion of other members of the profession. For example, it is not regarded as acceptable to continue dispensing corticosteroids to a patient without regular examination. Sometimes this third-party accountability may involve ethical and legal aspects of the profession, such as perceived cruelty by a veterinarian, or giving treatment to an animal that is not under the practitioner's care.
- *Client uncertainty*: Clients buying veterinary services are not able to confidently evaluate the services either before or after receiving them, which means they are often uncertain of the *value* of a particular service.
- *Does my pet really need this treatment or is the vet simply trying to make money out of me?*: Client education is an integral and essential part of veterinary services marketing so that clients can evaluate professional services confidently, understand if and when they should seek veterinary advice, and how to employ the veterinarian productively.
- *Experience is essential*: Clients seek veterinarians with prior experience of their animal's particular problem. 'Newness' is not a favourable professional characteristic whereas it is often highly desirable with products, for example new flavour, new consistency, new action. New services in a practice are therefore challenging to market because they may require a whole different way of thinking for both the practice and the client.
- *Limited differentiability*: Differentiating similar services is, unfortunately, not as easy as adding a different sugar coating or flavour to a product. Veterinary services have a limited differentiability from practice to practice – that is, what *is* the difference in having a bitch spayed at practice A compared to practice B? Where a practice is striving to be

Figure 9.2 A clear sign which is easily readable to passers-by, and a clear logo – such as the ship's wheel that gives Wheel House clinic its name – is part of marketing a practice. Acknowledgement Anne-Marie Svendsen.

unique through quality, standards, or the range of services it offers, it needs to market these *differences* very clearly to its clients. This can be done by critically identifying the practice's weaknesses and strengths, then selecting one or two of the strongest characteristics and emphasising these to clients at every opportunity. How to give the practice a unique and individual 'personality', which is of greater value than the competition in the eyes of potential clients, is one of the greatest challenges facing veterinary practice (Fig. 9.2).

What's in a logo?

Artistic representation? Cartoon characters? Child's drawing? Veterinary symbol? Your practice logo is one of the first impressions that clients will receive of your practice, and it will therefore create 'moments of truth' for them about how you are towards animals. It will also help them differentiate between practices as the symbolism conveys a message about 'How we are in this practice' (Fig. 9.3).

Figure 9.3a, b and c Examples of clear use of logos in signage outside the clinic.

■ *Maintaining quality control*: Veterinary practice is a people organisation, run by people for people. As a result, quality control of the services it offers is difficult to standardise because there are so many variables. Not only are there personality and ability differences among the personnel in the practice, but the behaviour of clients and their pets varies too, from the uncooperative owner to the biting dog.

■ *Making doers into sellers*: Most veterinarians are 'doers' – they are trained to do a professional job – they are not sellers. Yet every day clients buy services and products recommended and sold by veterinarians and their support staff. Given the nature of services, clients buy largely on trust, which means that before buying they like to meet and become acquainted with the vets and their staff. To be able to sell their services effectively, vets must learn to 'sell' themselves. Many veterinarians do not have the personal characteristics that make them good at selling, so can benefit from training in sales and

Figure 9.4 Explaining the benefits of using a good quality diet is part of the 'added value' a pet owner gains when buying professional services from a veterinarian. Acknowledgement Anne-Marie Svendsen.

presentation techniques, and from working alongside suitably trained support staff. This training is part of the role of a practice manager. (Fig. 9.4)

- *Allocating professionals time to marketing*: Marketing creates a dilemma – working time for a veterinarian means income generated, but marketing as an activity does not directly generate income (e.g. a talk to the local cat club, or a poster put up in the reception area advertising an obesity clinic). However, it is important that practice marketing involves the veterinarians because they are the key service providers.
- *Pressure to react rather than proact*: It is common in practice to be so time-pressured that all the energy is focused on reacting to clients' demands and there is little or no energy left over for proactively marketing services.
- *Effects of advertising*: The professions have long been bound by strict rules governing the ethics of advertising. Although an increasing number of professional service firms now advertise, there is still a feeling within the profession that it is 'not the done thing'. This attitude limits the scope for advertising and the learning that can come from it.

- *Common mistakes*: There are a number of critical but common mistakes that veterinary practitioners make when they start considering marketing for their practices:
  - They refuse to employ experienced, professional marketing consultants, believing they can 'do it themselves'.
  - They define and limit marketing to 'getting new clients'.
  - They misunderstand or refuse to examine the organisational and attitudinal changes necessary in the practice for effective marketing.
  - They neglect to tie individual marketing efforts into the practical staff appraisal system, so there is no reward or recognition of individuals' efforts in marketing the practice they work in.
  - They rely on 'gut feelings' rather than hard results to measure the effects of marketing efforts.

The dangers of being a marketing 'know it all'

By making themselves self-anointed marketing experts with little or no training or expertise in the area, veterinarians potentially distort, alter, subvert and even kill marketing concepts. John Graham (2003), in his article 'Marketing murder', identifies 13 common ways these 'experts' damage and even destroy beneficial marketing efforts:

- *Basing decisions on personal opinions*: personal opinion is no substitute for research and experience. The veterinarian is not part of the target audience and therefore their opinion is of little worth in this situation.
- *Lack of follow-through*: ideas need to be put into action, and the outcomes measured. A common mistake made by veterinary practices is to judge the effect of a promotion simply on 'gut feelings' and intuition. For example, many practices claim they sell 'loads' of a certain product or product range that they are promoting, when, in actual fact, they have no hard data on the sales figures, and are often shocked to find how little they sell in reality.
- *Failing to do enough*: the talk is bigger than the budget. Successful marketing demands a carefully crafted and expertly executed plan that meets its objectives because the whole is greater than the sum of the parts.
- *Procrastinating*: 'rational obstructionists' always have good reasons for not moving forward. The result? – nothing happens.
- *Refining it for ever*: excessive discussion and analysis kills creativity and initiative and is an effective way to make sure nothing happens.

- *Getting everyone's opinion before doing anything*: keeping everyone informed and involved is important – but getting 'buy in' can be code words for 'What happens if I make a mistake?'.
- *Jumping from one idea to the next*: no plan, no strategy, and no consistency – just hopping from one mail-out to the next newspaper advert. The final comment? Marketing doesn't work.
- *Lack of vision*: without a unique compelling vision of what the practice stands for, why it exists and where it is going, it will end up going nowhere.
- *Short-term results*: marketing is to create customers who believe that doing business with you is prudent; it is not just to get new clients and business on the books.
- *Waiting to see*: instead of acting quickly and decisively when sales sag, many companies take a wait and see attitude, hoping things will turn around by themselves.
- *Risk averse*: marketing requires courage. 'Wimping out' or waiting for a better idea to come along is simply losing opportunities.
- *Turning to marketing only when the bottom falls out:* marketing is often implemented as a desperation move. When it fails to produce emergency results, it is the fault of marketing.
- *Waiting until the last minute*: last minute panicking goes with poor planning, sloppy execution, unnecessary mistakes and cutting corners to get the job out.

So, how should we market?

Effective marketing is about showing selected clients that you can satisfy their needs. It requires careful planning, and the involvement and support of everyone in the practice, especially the practice principal(s). In addition, staff in the practice must understand the *value* and *benefits* of marketing.

What services does the practice offer?

Start by establishing the services the practice has to offer. This includes everything from having well-trained, friendly staff to a good parking area; from ultrasonography facilities to obesity counselling; from a 24-hour emergency service to a vaccination programme. It is not necessary at this stage to increase the range of services, rather concentrate on doing better with the ones you have.

What do our clients want?

The only way to find out what clients want of you is to ask them. Short, focused questionnaires for clients about particular services can be invaluable (see Appendix 7).

 ## What is the competition and how do we differentiate ourselves from it?

Competition is not something to be frightened of: competition, both from other veterinary practices and from pet-related businesses, can have a very positive effect on business. For example, practices selling premium quality pet foods for healthy pets often find their sales are *increased* when another source starts selling the same food locally, because a wider client base see the food, and are not so suspicious of it being a 'vets only' product.

Carefully selected services that differentiate the practice can be very wide-based. For example, they might include:

- convenient location
- long opening times
- hiring friendly, client-centred staff
- small animal/feline/exotic specialisation
- specialist referral component
- total pet healthcare programmes.

Market the benefits: ask the 'So what?' question

Services are sold on the benefits they offer the client and their pet. Understanding features, benefits and the effect they have for the purchaser is crucial to effective marketing of services. This is discussed in more detail in Chapter 11.

Internal marketing to staff

Marketing to every member of the staff is an ongoing and essential component of the whole marketing programme. As with selling to clients, this means explaining to staff why marketing is of value to them and to the practice so that they 'buy into' and accept marketing activities in which they are involved.

A large hospital decided to run a Senior Health Programme for a month and promoted it to clients through advertising in the local papers, which informed about the programme and offered free client education evenings, and verbal and written handout information in the reception area. Those organising the programme were inspired and excited by it. 'Over 50% of our clients are "seniors",' they said. 'Just think what we could do for them!' During the period, it was running I met some of the vets from the hospital in another context and asked them how the programme was going. 'What programme?' they replied, confused. 'Oh, you mean that thing Tim is running. I've no idea.' The programme was, needless to say, not a success.

Attention to detail

Marketing is a specialised form of communication. When you market your practice you are *communicating* it to your clients – you are *communicating* the values, services and professional products you recommend in the practice.

Communication involves all of the senses, especially sight, hearing, smell and touch. Think carefully about how each of these applies to how you market your practice:

For example, the outside of the practice:
  Does it *look* clean and smart?
  Is the flower garden well tended, and the pot plants *cared* for?
  Can they *smell* the practice, or *see* the dog faeces in the car park?

For example, the reception area:
  Does it *look* professional, friendly, and clean?
  Can the client *hear* the staff joking and time-wasting on the telephone whilst waiting for an appointment?
  Is the receptionist's *scent* overpowering?
  Do the magazines *feel* clean?

For example, having a consultation:
  Does the veterinarian *look* professional and competent, and *smell* fresh?
  Can the client *hear* animals crying and howling in another part of the building?
  Does the room *smell* of anal glands from a previous consultation?
  Is the room clean and in good condition, or does everything *feel* grubby and *look* worn?

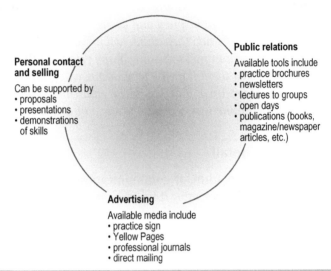

Personal contact and selling

Can be supported by
• proposals
• presentations
• demonstrations
  of skills

Public relations

Available tools include
• practice brochures
• newsletters
• lectures to groups
• open days
• publications (books,
  magazine/newspaper
  articles, etc.)

Advertising

Available media include
• practice sign
• Yellow Pages
• professional journals
• direct mailing

Figure 9.5   Some examples of the communication tools available for marketing a veterinary practice.

Communication tools for marketing a veterinary practice

Figure 9.5 illustrates some of the communication tools available to veterinary practices to market their services. When instigating any of the methods listed it is important to establish a system to measure their effect, such as incorporating a response element in a practice newsletter, or counting the number of referral cases from colleagues that result from advertising in professional journals. Remember, if you can't measure it, you can't manage it: if you don't know the effect of your investments, you can't do anything to improve or refine them.

Advertising

Advertising is a specialised form of communication. Specific examples of 'pure' advertising are Yellow Pages advertisements, the practice website, advertisements in the local newspaper, and the signage outside the practice. In more general terms, a practice constantly advertises itself. The appearance and behaviour of the staff, the appearance of the building, even the appearance and quality of the stationery used by the practice advertise the standards in the practice.

There are still fairly strict restrictions on professional advertising in many countries. There is also discussion about how valuable, for example, Yellow Pages advertising really is as it is a considerable expense for the practice annually and the results are not always easy to measure.

How do clients choose your practice?
Studies show that:

- most clients choose their practice based on geographical convenience (although not necessarily the nearest)
- up to 40% choose based on word-of-mouth recommendation
- around 12% use Yellow Pages
- around 6% respond to external signage (Fig. 9.6).

Figure 9.6 It's easy to see what this practice specialises in!

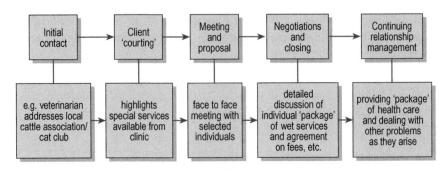

Figure 9.7 The personal selling process.

 Personal selling

Personal selling of services is a powerful and effective communication method used to create business by establishing a personal relationship with a group or organisation such as kennel/cattery owners, breeders, farmers looking for herd health schemes, etc. To attract referral work from colleagues, personal demonstration of skills coupled with lectures and seminars is often the most effective way of communicating the services available. The various stages are shown in Figure 9.7 and are based on attracting the client, and building and maintaining an ongoing relationship with them.

Public relations

Public relations take many forms from sending out a friendly and informative practice newsletter, to being the popular local practice reported by the local newspaper for helping rescue the old lady's cat from a tree. Lectures to interested groups of animal owners can be good public relations, or can seek to create business, for example outlining the benefits of a flock health scheme to a group of sheep farmers.

Marketing and quality

Many practices claim to offer high-quality service based on the fact that they employ technically highly competent staff, and are exceptionally well equipped with all the latest diagnostic and therapeutic gadgets. However, this is only part, and probably the least important part of professional service quality.

Quality, its exact definition, and its control and measurement are discussed in considerable detail in Chapter 12. In simplest terms, *quality* is the difference between a client's *expectations* of a veterinary service, and how the client *perceives* that the particular service lived up to those expectations.

A practice that is serious about its commitment to quality will systematically measure quality perceptions. Quality is the key to differentiation of practices.

Summary

Marketing is the analysis, planning, implementation and control of carefully formulated programmes designed to bring about voluntary exchanges of values with target markets for the purpose of achieving organisational objectives. Simply put, it is effective communication of what the practice can offer its clients. Its purpose is to grow the practice's business through attracting and retaining clients. Marketing involves everybody in the practice, and is constant and ongoing. Marketing in veterinary practice presents particular problems because the 'products' being marketed are services, which are intangible and cannot be owned. To overcome this, it is important to identify the features and market the benefits of these services to clients.

10 Professional retailing in practice

*Any business that wants to succeed must be aware of its customers'
requirements. Failure to do so is a missed opportunity to satisfy client
needs and to maximise profits.*

Geoff Little, Senior Practice Partner

Selling means the promotion of services or products through their
benefits so that a consumer is persuaded to buy. It is something we all
do all the time on both a personal and professional level. We 'sell' our
ideas and beliefs to our friends and by clever argument persuade them
of their value. We 'sell' ourselves to our clients by convincing them,
through our professionalism, of the benefit of employing us to treat
their pet. We 'sell' laboratory tests, courses of antibiotics, and surgical
operations through the benefits they will offer the health of the pet.
Similarly, we are constantly 'buying' based on appreciation of benefits.
We 'buy' our friends' ideas. We choose to buy selected medicinal products, disposable items, and technical equipment for our practices, and
have the practice cars serviced at a particular garage because of the perceived benefits to the practice.

Professional retailing – that is, the organisation and selling of professional goods – is still, for many veterinarians, a controversial issue. They
are not sure how to retail and they associate selling with the old-fashioned image of the pushy salesperson with dubious morals. Retailing is
a skill that involves personnel education, stock management, labour
costs, advertising, administration, employee time, facility management,
insurance, and so on. Veterinarians who learn about retailing profitably
find it is a logical step to then sell not only the services but also the products they are verbally recommending rather than referring owners elsewhere (Fig. 10.1).

(a)   (b)

Figure 10.1a and b Vets increasingly have professional retail areas with product displays in their practices.

Retailing versus selling

Retailing
- Everything that promotes and facilitates the selling process; includes team education, stock management, labour costs, advertising, facility management, etc.

Selling
- The promotion of services or products through their benefits so that a consumer is persuaded to buy
- Five-step process

Veterinarians need to look at pet care from the client's point of view – today's time-pressured clients increasingly seek 'one-stop shopping', and once a sick pet is treated, they want to know when to bath the dog, or how to manage its smelly breath. By not only giving this advice but also selling the appropriate professional healthcare products under the same roof, the practice is giving 'added value' service to the client – an important component of excellent client service.

What is 'added value'?
Using your knowledge, skills and experience to make a recommendation to the client that will help them make an informed decision about what is best for their pet.

Understanding client needs from the client's perspective

Vets perceive problems with animals differently from the animal's owners. Whereas the veterinarian may be presented with a 'challenging case of diarrhoea' or 'interesting case of unexplained weight loss' which they put their efforts into diagnosing and resolving, the owner may simply want their pet to stop messing in the house and waking them up at night, or to eat with its old enthusiasm and get the wag back in its tail (Fig. 10.2). Understanding how people relate to their pets is an important part of effective communication in selling professional goods and services (see Chapter 11).

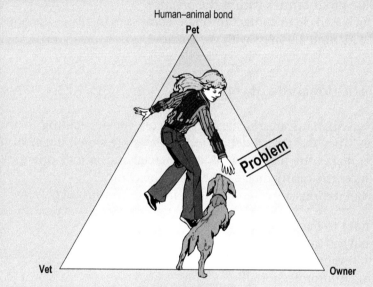

Figure 10.2 Human–animal bond pyramid.

The benefits of retailing

Retailing quality professional products from veterinary practices has many benefits:

- increases practice income
- increases opportunity for building a good relationship with clients through frequent return visits and increased client contact
- can largely be done by trained members of staff
- is better use of trained staff time

- is part of total healthcare service
- provides a welcome service to clients.

Retailing professional goods increases practice income both directly and indirectly. For example:

- Premium quality pet foods for both therapeutic use and feeding healthy animals make a very significant difference to practice income in many practices (10–30% of income can be generated by sale of these products) as well as improving animal health.
- Through more efficient and productive use of time, trained staff can become profit centres within the practice.
- The increased client contact through repeat sales increases the opportunity for more business with the client.

The downside of retailing

Many veterinarians are resistant to the concept of retailing in their practices. They feel that it detracts from the professional image of the practice, makes the practice look commercial and money-orientated, and reduces the caring image fostered in the clinic.

These objections are often based on misconceptions such as:

- 'We have to have a large display!'
- 'We haven't got room for a display!'
- 'I don't want to look like a pet shop!'
- 'Selling is unprofessional!'
- 'It isn't profitable!'
- 'We don't know what to stock!'
- 'I'm a vet – vets don't sell things!'

My responses to these objections are covered in the remainder of the chapter.

But let the figures talk for themselves: an American study investigated the profitability of premium pet food sales in 34 average veterinary hospitals in six states, and found that the profits from food as a percentage of the hospital-wide profits averaged 10.9%. This profit took 3.3 hours per week (equivalent to 8.3% of one full-time equivalent support staff member) and was generated in only 3.3% of the hospital's total area (the 'shop' area), making this the most profitable area in the practice per square metre (data courtesy of Hill's Pet Nutrition, Inc.).

Is retailing professional?

Yes. The reason clients visit vets is that they are seeking a professional – that is, a trained, specialised – opinion. This includes clear recommendations about, for example, which shampoos would be suitable for managing skin conditions, how to prevent and manage dental plaque through regular brushing with special toothpastes and the appropriate use of chew toys, and which pet food is best to fill the pet's current nutritional needs. This professional and thought-through recommendation adds value to veterinary professional retailing for the client.

In addition, many of the products sold in practice form an integral part of preventive healthcare programmes. Selling high-quality healthcare products enhances the bond of trust between the client and the practice – not only is the practice providing reliable, effective products, but the client also returns more often to the practice for further purchases, which allows deeper development of the client–practice bond. The ultimate result is that everyone benefits – the pet is healthier, the client is happy, the practice is more profitable – and it is giving better professional service.

Is retailing ethical?

Selling quality products of benefit to animal health to the correct recipients can only be right. Professional retailing is only unethical if it is done unethically – that is, if products are sold that do not benefit the animal or if they are sold in a way that is unethical.

In the recent AAHA Compliance survey (see Chapter 13 for more details), clients *wanted* the vet to recommend and supply reliable, high-quality healthcare products for their animals. This was felt to be much safer than and preferable to guessing for themselves about what is best at the local supermarket or pet shop.

Planning professional retailing

To be successful, retailing in practice needs careful planning. Ask yourself the following questions:

- *Why do we want to retail?* In what ways, specifically, will it improve our service to our clients?
- *What do we want to retail?* Answers include professional healthcare products such as premium pet foods, flea products, anthelminitics,

(a)   (b)

Figure 10.3   The commercial display in the shop front (a) is very different from the discreet product display in a practice consulting room (b).

behavioural aids, general care products (cat carriers, cat litter, food bowls, nail clippers, etc.).

■ *Who will do the retailing and how?* Do our staff need extra training?
■ *How will we measure the success of our retail business?* Increase in practice profits? Increase in average transaction fee? Increase in client satisfaction?
■ *When will we do the retailing and where?* In the reception area? In the consulting room? (Fig. 10.3)

Make a plan of action that answers these questions and give yourself a timescale to set up a retail system within which to work. Start with a limited range of top-selling products that you are confident about (your distributor should be able to help you identify these) and build up the system.

What are people buying?

David Maister writes, 'The single most important factor in selling professional services is *the ability to understand the purchasing process* (not the sales process) from the clients' perspective. For a professional service firm to achieve a competitive advantage it must have a better understanding of the wants and needs of its clients than does the competition'.

Animal owners buying services and products from veterinary practices are actually buying peace of mind and the knowledge they are doing the right thing for their animal (see 'What do people buy?', below). These are the 'feel good' factors that come with buying a service. Most of the services sold in veterinary practice are high credence. This means that as they contain mostly knowledge they are nebulous and not easily packaged into an understandable form (see Chapter 9, describing the differences between services and products). To convince people to buy them, they need to be described and 'packeted' as clearly and simply as possible. This helps people visualise how good it would feel for them to own the benefits the service offers.

Why do people buy?
People buy things for three reasons:

- To alleviate dissatisfaction.
- To be better off afterwards than before.
- To gain the consequences they expect from owning or using the product or service.

What do people buy?
People buy the imagined benefits or 'feel good factor' that they believe ownership will bring. People make their buying decisions based not – as we might like to believe – on clear logic, but on feelings. For example, if I decide to buy a new dress for a forthcoming party, it is not the ownership of the dress which most stimulates me to buy it (I already have several dresses which would be suitable), but the imagined impact that wearing *this* dress will create at *this* party.

When people buy toys for their pets, they are actually buying the feeling of pleasure which they imagine experiencing when they give that toy and play with it with their pet (Fig. 10.4). In purchasing veterinary services, clients buy a 'feel good' factor from the promise the service offers – the nice smelling breath, the reduced concern for having unwanted kittens and a yowling cat, the feeling that they are doing the right thing for the animal that they care about.

What does this mean in daily veterinary practice?
When buying a professional service, clients enter a relationship with the professional. They need to feel they can trust this person who is going to take care of their beloved animal. As people buy on feelings, then a recommendation from the vet needs to be tuned into those feelings. In most cases, cold, hard scientific fact will not make an owner make a buying decision.

Compare the following:

1. 'Tibbles needs this scientifically formulated renal failure diet which will reduce his blood phosphorus levels and slow down progression of his renal disease.'

Figure 10.4
Pets love playing – and their owners love to buy them toys!

2. 'To prolong Tibbles' life and make him feel as comfy as possible, we recommend this special food which is developed to help cats like him who have kidney disease.'

Although the former statement may appeal to *us* with our scientific training, it is the latter that would most likely touch a pet owner and stimulate him to buy the recommended food.

Communication uses all the senses, especially sight, hearing, smell and touch. To make professional retailing in your practice effective, enhance your selling skills by using these senses.

- *Sight* – product displays, posters, handout information/product brochures.
- *Hearing* – talk to clients about the products, use videos to endorse your message.
- *Smell* – allow clients to smell products such as shampoos and deodorants before purchasing them.
- *Touch* – arrange displays so that clients can handle products before purchase (see below, 'Making an effective product display').

The art of selling

Professional retailing is about helping clients. It is based on identifying a need in your clients and satisfying it with the services and product(s) at your disposal. There are many books written about selling, and several commercial veterinary companies have seminars to teach selling techniques so it is not my intention to describe it in detail here, but the basic steps to successful selling are fivefold:

1. Preparation – know your products and services intimately so that you can make clear and appropriate recommendations.
2. Opening – start by establishing a rapport with the client and use open and closed questions to find out what their needs are.
3. Features and benefits – use features and benefits (see below) to match the products or services characteristics to the client's needs.
4. Objections – deal immediately and courteously with objections. Remember they are usually a sign of interest but an indication that knowledge or understanding is lacking.
5. Close and sale – confirm that the client would like to buy the product or service and complete the sale by asking which bag size they would like or booking a date for the service to be performed.

In addition to these five steps, successful selling depends on:

■ *Proactively working to identify opportunities for sales* – e.g. all your patients have teeth, and many of the smaller patients will have dental problems. Don't wait for the owner to come in with a pet suffering gingivitis and heavy plaque deposits: identify the 'at risk' patients and actively recommend a dental care programme right now.
■ *Supporting and comforting the buying decision* – people always feel vulnerable when they buy something, especially a service that costs a lot and if they are not sure what it entails. Reinforce the benefits of the purchase to the owner and make them feel they are doing the right thing.

Features and benefits: the 'So what?' factor

One of the most powerful – and fun – steps in the selling process is to relate features and benefits of the product to the client's needs in such a way that they are convinced to buy. This is done by presenting a feature, some of the associated benefits and then personalising it for the owner with the phrase 'which means that …'. For example: 'Our opening hours are 7 am to 10 pm *(feature)*. This enables you to leave your pet with us early in the morning and collect him or her late in the evening *(benefits)*, *which means that* you don't have to take time off from work or worry about missing your children's football training.'

A feature is a characteristic of a product or service; a benefit is how it will help the animal and owner. The two are linked by silently asking the 'So what?' question, and then clarified by the 'tag on'. By looking at all the products and services you sell and asking the 'so what?' question you can identify the benefits that you will use to recommend them to clients.

■ *We recommend x-brand flea-spray because it not only kills fleas but the eggs as well* (feature).
  □ *So what?*
  □ *By regular spraying every 3 months, you can keep your home and pets flea-free* (benefit) …
  □ *… Which means that* your pet will stop scratching and you can get a good night's sleep.
■ *Fido is 10 now and we would recommend he starts on y-brand senior food to slow down ageing changes* (feature).
  □ *So what?*
  □ *By giving Fido y-brand senior food, you will help him to a longer, healthier life* (benefit) …
  □ *… Which means that* you not only will have your old friend around for longer but you can also be sure you are doing the right thing for him.
■ *We believe Nogg's nail-clippers are the best available* (feature).
  □ *So what?*
  □ *We recommend them to all cat-owners because they are safe and easy to use* (benefits) …
  □ *… Which means that* you can quickly, painlessly, clip your cat's nails without the risk of bleeding.

This technique of using features and benefits is important in all forms of marketing communication with clients including the practice brochure and website. Remember, it may be clear to you why you have X-ray and ultrasound facilities, a practice laboratory and trained staff – but do your clients not only know about these services, but also understand the potential benefits to them and their animals?

> ### Making staff more effective at selling products
> Even though it may be the support staff who do most of the
> product selling, it is important that both professional and support

staff are involved in professional retailing in the practice. The following are some suggestions for making staff more effective at selling:

- *Sound product knowledge.* Most veterinary product companies are willing to provide training in their products. Product knowledge includes at least a basic knowledge of similar competitor products, the answers to common questions clients may ask, and knowing where to go for further information and references. It goes without saying that if a staff member is unable to answer a client's questions they probably will not sell the product.
- *Knowledge of sales techniques.* Selling is a specialised form of communication with a very clear outcome, and this makes staff more effective in communicating the benefits of the products to the client and successfully completing a sale.
- *Major features and benefits of products.* It is the benefits related to the features that sell products, so work together to make a list of three to five features and associated benefits for all the products you sell and make sure all staff are familiar with them to be able to talk to clients. Remember to consider the features and benefits from the clients' point of view – what do they want from a product?
- *Ensure staff use the products on their own pets.* Personal recommendation is extremely powerful. It makes a nonsense of retailing high-quality pet healthcare products from the practice if practice members *do not* use them on their own pets.
- *Encourage a one-to-one staff–client relationship.* By encouraging nurses in the practice to specialise in certain areas, such as dental care, dietary management, puppy/kitten care and so on, the nurse can be used to establish a one-to-one relationship with clients (Fig. 10.5). This personal contact, whom the client knows by name and can ring for further help and information, builds good relations far more quickly than any other system. Because the client comes to know and trust the nurse, they will buy the products. The dental nurse can then, for example, demonstrate how to brush Fido's teeth to his owner, and explain that the toothbrushes and special veterinary toothpaste are available from the clinic. Similarly, when giving worming advice it can be pointed out that effective anthelmintics are available from the practice.

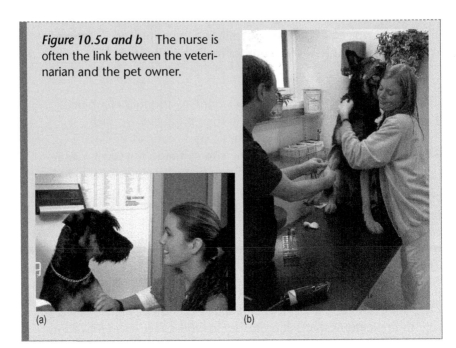

Figure 10.5a and b The nurse is often the link between the veterinarian and the pet owner.

(a)   (b)

Overcoming common objections

Price often appears to be a client's first concern. The skilled staff member can effectively convert *price* to *value* by talking about benefits. Price becomes a secondary consideration when the client understands/appreciates the benefits of the product to themselves or their pets. Sometimes price needs explaining, for example where a pet food appears expensive per sack but the feeding cost per day is less than or comparable with other brands of food.

Objections are based on lack of understanding but at the same time show an interest to know more. It is important to convey to clients that the products they buy from a veterinary practice really do the job they are supposed to – the client is, then, buying peace of mind.

To whom do you sell and when?

Focus your merchandising efforts on the 20% of clients that supply 80% of your business. They are not only the least likely to have image problems related to merchandising in the practice, but are also the most likely to be receptive to your suggestions.

Look for opportunities to recommend products to clients. Vaccination time (worming, flea-control, nutrition), admittance for dental procedures (dental care products, flea control, nutrition), and postoperative care (litter tray and cage for a cat, nutrition, bedding) are all examples of when items can be marketed.

It may not be practical to attempt to discuss, say, nutrition with a harassed mother with a howling babe-in-arms, dog wrapped round her ankles, and a toddler demanding the toilet. However, the old lady with a new kitten and time on her hands is likely to appreciate an explanation of the importance of good nutrition, and worming, and be interested to buy the best products for her pet. Choose your clients but do not discriminate between them – that is, do not assume that they are not interested. Even a simple information leaflet to be read in the peace of their own home can be effective in promoting interest.

Not everyone will buy products, but make it easy for them – make the products and their value as clear as possible using displays and leaflets.

A few words of warning

The profitability of professional retailing in the practice may be measured in several ways but it is neither professional nor, in the long term, profitable to concentrate purely on profit and more or less force every client to purchase something before they leave the practice. This is *not* good professional retailing.

I once spent a long time chatting to an interested client about a particular product that I felt would be of benefit to their pet. Their final comment, albeit light-heartedly said, was, 'All right, I'll buy it. You're a good salesperson!' I was embarrassed – for the client to feel in anyway pressurised into buying was not my intention.

The best way for the veterinarian to retail professionally is to use personal recommendations of the product ('I feed this to my dog/use this on my cat ...', etc.) coupled with a brief reference to the benefits of using the product for the pet in question. Retailing becomes less and less profitable (and more and more like the dreaded pushy salesman) the longer that it is necessary to spend persuading a client to buy the product.

Making an effective product display

The aim of a product display is to catch the attention of people and, through projecting a favourable image, influence them to buy. There is a whole art and science behind what makes an effective display, from the discreet display in the corner of a consulting room through to the massive displays in multimillion-pound turnover supermarkets. In making your display, remember all the senses are used in buying: exploit this to the full!

For example, to maximise your purchases in a supermarket:

■ People automatically look left on entering a building, so fresh product displays are sited to the left of the entrance. This also promotes the concept of health, and natural products.
■ The smell of fresh-baked bread or newly roasted coffee is wafted to the front of the supermarket to tickle the taste buds.
■ Basic essential items (bread, flour, butter, milk, washing powder, etc.) are scattered all over the shop so that you have to pass many displays of other products to find them. Every so often, these essential items are rearranged so that you are forced to re-explore the shop.
■ Canned music is played at different speeds at different times of the day to control the speed you pass through the shop – special offer announcements are made over the loudspeakers to stimulate interest.
■ Shelves are always heavily stocked as customers are reluctant to buy from poorly stocked displays.

Without having to resort to such sophisticated tactics, it is possible to make your displays very effective. Consider the following basic points:

■ location
■ size
■ product range
■ lighting and cleanliness
■ enhancing your display.

Location of displays

People read from left to right, and look from left to right in a new situation, so your display should be placed to the left of the door as they enter the reception area. To attract interest, it should also be regularly updated for maximum impact (how would you react to a dusty and ancient display of products at your local supermarket?). If possible, locate it in a high traffic area to ensure people see it. One of the best places to have a reception display is near the reception desk. There are several reasons for this:

■ Trained staff are immediately on hand to talk to clients and to answer questions.

- Clients may have to wait several minutes to register or to pay, which gives them a chance to look at the products.
- Most purchases are made at the time of final payment when the client is leaving.

Product displays can also be located in the consulting room where their main function is to remind personnel to recommend them. However, although they do not need to be large or heavily stocked, some veterinarians feel it puts pressure on a client who is already in a low comfort zone.

Point of sale displays (i.e. products sold from, say, the receptionist's desk at time of final payment) serve to increase sales through impulse purchase. If this technique is used, the goods must be carefully selected to maintain professionalism. There are many items which can be used at point of sale such as rawhide chews, packaged food samples, and bandages, but potentially therapeutic preparations such as vitamin supplements that need explanation to use them properly, or gimmicky toys that detract from the professional image, should be avoided.

> Another aspect of image is what the client perceives – several Nordic practices I have visited sell dried pig's ears as chews for dogs. Although dogs love them, how acceptable is this to the caring image of the practice?

Displays are no use where clients cannot see them. Similarly, they are far less effective where clients cannot pick up and examine the products. Displays behind the reception desk or in glass cabinets are known as museum displays and are not user-friendly.

Practices are increasingly designing separate retail areas off the reception area. As long as they are still readily accessible to the trained reception staff, this has several advantages:

- It helps retain the more clinical and less commercial feel of the reception area.
- It focuses all the products in one area so that they are easier to see.

The problem is people will often not go into these retail areas unless they are specifically looking for something – they are not high traffic areas, which may reduce their profitability.

Size of display and quantity to stock

The main purpose of a display is to raise client awareness of the products you recommend, so displays do not *have* to be big to increase sales significantly. However, the bigger they are, the more powerful they tend to be.

A guide to the quantity to stock can be obtained from your wholesaler, who should know your potential sales ability. You should be able to order fast-moving items such as foods for healthy pets so that you need to maintain minimum stock (see below, 'Stock turnover').

Choice of products and product range

There is clear guidance for veterinarians about which medicinal products can and cannot be sold from veterinary practices.

Your veterinary wholesaler should be able to advise you about which are the top-selling brands in any range, and the quantity of each to stock. I do not recommend stocking a wide range of similar products as it confuses clients, and shows that the practice does not have a clear idea about the value of each product.

For example, in one practice I visited I counted seven different types of wormers on their display. Even though they were an equine and small animal practice, they were able to reduce this to two they could confidently recommend.

Select only those products that you feel confident to use and recommend. Show clients your sincerity by using the products for your own animals.

Talk to colleagues about what they retail in their practices. You don't have to retail different things from your competitors to have good sales – in fact, often sales of a product increase when clients see it in several different outlets.

Listen to what clients are asking for and respond to their needs with top-quality products.

How to display products on shelves

The following are tips to improve the way you arrange products on your display:

- Shelves should always be full of well-organised, clean products.
- 'Eye level is buy level' and the middle sizes of a product with a range of sizes should be placed at this level.
- Smaller sizes of a product go higher, larger sizes lower on the shelves.
- Don't display damaged or out-of-date products.
- Avoid artistic arrangements of products – they deter purchasers.
- Place life-cycle products from left to right, starting with the young animal on the left.

- Block merchandise vertically as people tend to scan horizontally and this increases the range of products they see.
- Do not use price tags on products, but place them to the right of the product on the shelf. In this way the client sees the product before the price and so is able to appraise the product before finding out how much it costs.
- Displays should always be well stocked: more purchases are made from full shelves than half-empty ones.

Where the traffic flow is from left to right past a particular display unit, the potential 'off-take' of product along the shelves both horizontally and vertically will be in the following proportions (Little, 1992a):

4.5%	2.6%	2.6%	5.2%
12.0%	7.0%	7.0%	14.0%
10.5%	6.0%	6.0%	12.3%
3.0%	1.75%	1.75%	3.5%

In addition, the horizontal bands contribute the following potential 'off-take':

Reach level	15%
Sight level	40%
Take level	35%
Stoop level	10%

This shows that the first and last vertical columns, and two central horizontal columns are the most effective for location of products. Thus, almost 50% of the selling power is contained in only 25% of the space at sight and take level at either end of the display.

Finally, men tend to select from shoulder height, women from waist height. As most clients to a veterinary practice are women you can position a very powerful display.

Creating an attractive display

Spot lights or imaginative lighting focus attention on a display and make it more attractive. Careful choice of colour for the shelves and display units makes them more inviting. Make sure the shelves are well stocked with products arranged in neat lines, and that the display is

Figure 10.6 A well-organised display should be attractive and appealing to the client. However, remember that a professional display only becomes effective when there is a clear recommendation from the vet to guide the client's choice of products.

clean (Fig. 10.6). No one wants to buy from a grubby display in a dark corner of a room.

A shelf or unit product display can be enhanced by using posters and pictures of normal and unhealthy animals. Posters and models can also be used to create a product focus that links a product with a service; for example, illustrations of fat dogs before and after slimming could enhance the value of a slimming diet.

Making the display really effective

People use all their senses when they are buying. Make sure your clients are able to do this with your display:

- *Sight*. Make the display visually appealing and clean. Make sure the product name and instructions for use are not obscured by labels.
- *Hearing*. Is this product a spray? A powder? A full can? Damaged?
- *Smell*. How does this product smell?
- *Touch*. What is the weight and texture of this product? What does it feel like?

Displays should be accessible to clients so that they can pick up and handle products. Change them at least every 2 months to create interest in the products. Cross-merchandise products to create a 'package': for example a 'Complete kitten kit' could include a cat basket, starter pack of kitten growth food, basic grooming tools, and a food and water bowl.

Answer the buying questions

Potential purchasers seek the answers to five questions:

- What is it?
- Why should I buy it?

- How much does it cost?
- Of what use/value is it to me/my pet?
- Should I buy it now?

Answer these using 'shelf-talkers'. These are signs that attach to the front of the shelf and which can increase sales by as much as 300%. Make them easy to read and professional in appearance.

For example, a shelf-talker for the kitten kit above could be:

Complete Kitten Kit.
Give your kitten the best start.
Get all the things your kitten needs for only £xxx.
Offer applies to the end of the month.

For example, for a premium growth diet for puppies could be:

X-brand puppy growth food.
Veterinary recommended.
Costs yy p/day to feed.
Gives your puppy a healthy start.
Choose from 2 kg, 5 kg, 10 kg and 20 kg.

Using support literature

Product literature and information can be located on or near displays. It is not effective to merely place them in a pile on the display – they should have a proper display box that fits onto the display unit. Leaflets should also be available behind reception for the receptionists to use to support verbal recommendations.

Calculating the profit from retailing

To calculate mark-up in per cent

$$\text{Make-up \%} = \frac{(\text{selling price} - \text{purchase price})}{\text{purchase price}} \times 100\%$$

e.g. a shampoo bought for 50p and sold for 75p has a mark-up of:

$$\frac{(75 - 50)}{50} \times 100\% = 50\%$$

To calculate profit margin in per cent

$$\text{Profit margin \%} = \frac{\text{(selling price} - \text{purchase price)}}{\text{selling price}} \times 100\%$$

e.g. the same shampoo has a profit margin of:

$$\frac{(75 - 50)}{75} \times 100\% = 33.3\%$$

Pricing and profit margins

The net profit from retailing is calculated by subtracting the costs of staff training, staff time, capital in stock and so on from the income generated by sales of the products. If the income from retailing accounts for less than 15% of the gross income then probably no extra costs are incurred from staff.

If the income from retailing in the practice is more than 15% of the gross then it is better to run the retail business as its own profit centre.

Pricing for profit

It is recommended to work on *at least* a 33% mark-up to ensure rapid turnover of stock, and keep the practice competitive (compare with a mark-up of a minimum 100% for prescription medicines). Although this may not seem to be a large profit margin, on fast-moving items such as pet foods the profit comes from the repeat sales. Profit margins may be significantly increased where wholesale discounts are obtained.

Effect of discounting

Underpricing or discounting is risky and unprofitable:

Price	Mark-up	Units	Profit	Change	Units	Profit
£1	33%	100	£33			
				−10%	143	£33
				+10%	77	£33

As the example above shows, 43% more product has to be sold to generate the same profit if an item is discounted by 10%. Of course, sometimes it is worth a brief period of discounting as part of a mini-promotion to move or clear out stock, but discounting is often seen as a sign of lack of confidence in a product, and its effect can be to make the practice look like a bargain-basement store.

It is important to remember that in veterinary practice, you are promoting products you believe in and trust, and you are selling them based on their value to the pet, not the price. Clients *want* products they can trust and are prepared to pay for them, so don't be frightened to price profitably.

Stealing

In some practices, stealing from displays is felt to be a problem. This can be alleviated by using closed displays, or dummy packs (available in some cases from distributors), but these displays also serve to reduce sales effectiveness.

Not infrequently, it is staff who steal either by taking products for personal use directly from stores or displays, or by charging up a false transaction on the cash register. Where this is not part of a staff agreement this can significantly affect profits. It can be controlled by strict stock control and making sure staff order and pay for the items they require.

Stock turnover

Stock represents capital, and unnecessarily high stocking-levels tie up money and reduce profits. While it is necessary to have adequate stock to supply clients' needs, it is wasteful to overstock, especially if it goes over the product expiry date. Total stock should turn over at least 10 times per year in small animal practice, and at least 6 times per year in large animal practice. Fast-moving retail items such as pet food may turn over far more often than this.

Stock can also take up a lot of space in a practice, especially in those designed before bulky pet foods were so popular. Where space really is a problem, good-sized retail displays can serve as primary storage space.

Conclusion

Professional retailing offers huge scope for increasing practice revenue. It is estimated that 85% of pet healthcare purchases are made outside of veterinary practices, which means there is tremendous opportunity for the profession to improve their service to their clients. A sale starts with a clear recommendation from the vet.

Ultimately, it is your personal choice whether you want to retail in your practice or not, but as long as you only retail those products which you feel confident recommending and as long as you retail them in a suitably professional manner then they can only benefit the practice.

11 Understanding your clients

We depend on our clients, they do not necessarily depend on us.

Veterinary practice is a service industry committed to serving the needs of clients (animal owners and their animals). Practices cannot exist without their clients, and yet increasing competition means clients have more choice than ever before about where to take their animals. Clients seek good service and often use service standards to differentiate between practices. Good client service is based on trust, which comes from good communication, both externally towards the clients and internally between staff members. The more trust that is developed between staff and clients, the more cooperation and success the clinic will experience.

Understanding clients

> *The diagnosis and treatment of animal health problems is only one side of modern veterinary practice. The primary difference between a good veterinary practitioner and a merely adequate one lies in the former's ability to gauge and understand client–patient relationships. Without this empathetic dimension, the veterinarian is not substantially different from a car mechanic or a TV repair man.*
>
> Professor James Serpell, University of Pennsylvania

You have more in common with your clients than you may realise. In your professional role it is easy to become detached from the fact that your clients are people with feelings, emotions, concerns, issues and a whole other life out there – just like you. They are not always logical, sensible and rational in their decisions and behaviours – just like you. They can be rude and difficult to deal with – just like you. They can also be charming, heart-warming and an absolute pleasure – just like you.

When clients make contact with your practice they generally have a problem that needs your help to solve. As you know when you have sought help from other professionals such as doctors, lawyers, or tax accountants, buying professional services is rarely a comfortable experience. Your clients care about their animals and when they seek your help they are usually feeling a mixture of:

- concerned (What is wrong? Can the vet fix it?)
- worried (What if it's cancer? How much will it cost?)
- vulnerable (I'm dependent on this person and trusting they will give me good advice)
- threatened (My animal is my responsibility, and even though intellectually I know I need outside expertise, emotionally it's not comfortable to put decisions about the care of my animal into the hands of others)
- afraid (What if I've done something wrong? They criticise me? My animal can't be cured?)
- impatient (How long will I have to wait? When will my animal be better again?)
- and suspicious (Will they try to sell me something I don't need? How will I know they are telling the truth?)

If you, the professional, can understand this mixture of emotions and concerns – which is just the same as your own in a similar situation – it will be easier for you to do and say the right things to create the necessary bond of trust with the owner to be able to care for their animal.

Client perception

Although their feelings may be inherently similar, the client's *perception* of veterinary practice, and the professional services and products offered, are very different from your own. The client's perception is based on a mixture of personal experience, word-of-mouth information, what they've seen on the TV, a bad experience 5 years ago in another practice, and, perhaps, a competitor's recent small act of courtesy. You, on the other hand, are working in a familiar environment where you are the professional, where you can exercise your skills to the highest level, and where you have your friends and workmates around you.

In addition, clients speak a different 'language' from veterinarians and veterinary nurses – just as you speak a different 'language' from your banker, lawyer or tax accountant. This means that you need to be extra careful about what you say and express it in terms that non-vet clients can understand.

As we have already seen, clients visit practices with their animals because they have to – they have a problem which requires your help. It is therefore important to make them feel welcome and wanted. Imagine your last visit to another professional – how did they make you feel welcome (or not)? Clients respond very positively to practice members who:

- are friendly and who greet them and their pet by name
- make the client feel like a friend rather than a number by establishing personal contact with them
- are polite and courteous in their manner
- look and behave like professionals
- respect that the client's time is valuable too by being on time for appointments
- show interest in and enthusiasm for them, their pets and their children
- show affection to the pet
- handle the pet kindly and do not use unnecessary restraint
- give an accurate estimate of the fees
- accept phone calls from clients requesting information as often as possible.

Understanding the human–animal bond

Part of being a human being is to live together with animals. Interest in animals exists in our genes.

Professor Per Jensen, Linköping

Humans have enjoyed the company of animals since prehistoric times. Once seen only as a source of food or clothing, animals eventually emerged as members of the human social community as fellow hunters, guardians, companions and confidants. Our behaviour towards animals parallels the way we behave towards each other. As Mahatma Gandhi has said: 'The moral standards of a nation are reflected in the way we care for our animals.'

Humans are social animals, not naturally adapted to a solitary lifestyle, and are most comfortable being part of a social group. In order to feel, fulfilled, happy and safe, we all have a basic need for interaction with others, and the interactions need not always be with our own species. Animals bring us back in contact with Nature and our own animal origins, roots that are lost in the modern, industrialised societies in which we live. In addition, close contact with animals, especially those we keep as pets, has proven therapeutic value (Fig 11.1).

Figure 11.1 Sometimes the world can feel like lonely place. A pet provides unconditional love and someone to hug can make all the difference.

Pet owners are known to differ from non-owners in terms of social, life-stage and psychological characteristics. They may also exhibit different social attitudes and personalities. When companion animals live in close association with their owners, interaction with them can have at least three separate functions for their owners:

- self-image
- social facilitation
- companionship.

Self-image

> *A person publicly identified with a companion animal makes a symbolic statement of his/her personality and self-image.*

Whether or not this process is intentional, the presence of a pet and the way it is treated can become factors that influence the image others form about us as well as affecting the way we see ourselves. The kind of pet we select, like the kind of car we drive or the style of clothes we wear, is a way of expressing our personality. Selecting a macho dog may be a way of projecting a macho image, whereas selecting a Persian kitten may be an attempt to project cute and defenceless feminine dependency.

Barrie Gunter, *Pets and People*, 1999

Throughout history, animals have been selected as status symbols. Kings kept tame lions and rode magnificent Iberian horses: today's celebrities keep pet ocelots and carry chihuahuas as 'must have' fashion accessories.

Pets in modern society not only live with their owners, but also do so at the same standard of living. Indulging one's pet is indulging oneself. Pets have become humanised to the point that just about anything that is available to their owner is available to the pet. Beauty parlours, aromatherapy, custom-made clothes, day care, summer camp, specialised hotel facilities and restaurant catering are just a few examples of the 'petishism'

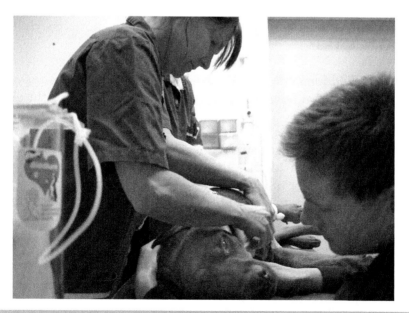

Figure 11.2 Many practices now offer a blood bank where donor dogs and cats regularly give blood which will be used to help acutely ill patients.

Figure 11.3 For children with physical and mental handicaps contact with affectionate animals reaps many rewards.

that exists in modern society. This also extends to the level of veterinary medical care available: for example, pets can receive organ transplants, new joints, and radical cancer therapy including hospice-style care (Figs 11.2 & 11.3).

Social facilitation

Pets have a distinct function as 'social lubricators', increasing the quality and quantity of social interactions. For some owners, loss of a pet can represent a huge loss of social contact. As one elderly client once sadly said to me after we had put down her old dog, 'Charlie was really popular in the park with the other dog owners where we used to walk together. But who's going to recognise me now he's gone?'

Pets attract attention, generally in a positive way, and provide openings for contact with like-minded and interested people. They can be social ice-breakers, sources of entertainment, or indicate interest in and knowledge about specific breeds. This latter is of particular relevance in the showing and breeding world.

Pets as alternative companions

Most people keep pets as companions. They provide friendship and stave off loneliness for those living on their own; are a playmate and comforter for children; a motivated exercise companion for the more

Figure 11.4   Working animals also play a vital role in society. Regular swim training at the dedicated pool at Helsingborg Animal Hospital helps keep this police dog in top trim. Acknowledgement: Susanne Max, Regiondjursjukhuset Helsingborg

active; an interest or hobby, a surrogate partner, parent or child and many more roles besides. (Fig. 11.4)

Almost all interaction with pets involves some anthropomorphism, which means they are, at least to some extent, a substitute for human relations. Thus one of the most significant factors in our relationships with our pets is the degree to which they are treated as humans, and are used to replace them. This is partly reflected in the names we give pets. Human names such as 'Sid' or 'Lucy' imply that the pet is perceived more like a human than those with names such as 'Scruffy' or 'Tibbles'. Comic names such as 'Killer' (for a chihuahua) or 'Tiny' (for a Great Dane) imply a more light-hearted and humorous relationship.

In our family, for example, we have a Staffordshire bull terrier, called Bert, and two rescue cats, called Charlie and Frodo. I also own a beautiful Lusitano horse called Shadow whom I spend many enjoyable hours riding and training in the woods near our home.

Our animals are very much part of our family and everyone is concerned if one strays or is off colour. Bert, for example, plays football and other rough and tumble games with my teenage sons and their friends, and also sleeps on their beds. They affectionately call him 'their little brother'. His enthusiastic paw cleaning, and snoring amuses family and friends alike, whereas his 'tough' appearance is a source of fascination modulated with fear for strangers, and belies his gentle, loving nature. He comes out riding with me, and is always ready to follow my husband out jogging. He begs (and receives) table scraps despite being fed on a prime quality commercial food. He is always glad to see us when we come home – whatever time of night or day, and never judges us for how we are feeling or how we look. At Christmas and on his birthday he always receives presents from us – perhaps a new collar, a chew toy and some treats.

People talk to their pets using language and voice modulation in the same way as talking to a child. They enjoy physical contact with their pet and a variety of studies have shown the endorphin-releasing calming effects of petting and having near contact with another living creature. A frail elderly lady with a Yorkshire terrier once explained to me about her little dog: 'He's just the right size and weight to be able to lie on me at night. He keeps me warm, like a little hot water bottle, and it feels so nice and safe to have him there.'

What all this means is that the relationship people have with their animals – especially their pets – is complex. It is also dependent on that relationship working, i.e. that the animal is behaving in the way it is expected to behave, and doing what it usually does. This includes the little routines and habits that owners can tell you about – the dog rushing to greet the owner when they get home, the cat sitting and purring on the owner's lap, the dog bringing his favourite toy to play with, the horse who always tucks into his hay with enthusiasm. When this behaviour changes, for whatever reason, the relationship is put under strain: it is no longer working. It is then that most owners contact the veterinarian.

The better we can understand the relationship a particular owner has with their pet, the more likely we are to be able to influence that owner to give that animal the best and most appropriate care. However, when there is a breakdown in the relationship – the dog is miserable and does not run to greet the owner, or has difficulty rising due to old age, or the cat withdraws from contact and does not purr – owners are concerned and worried. In this state of mind, the chances of communication breakdowns and dissatisfaction with the service received are more likely to arise.

Managing the dissatisfied client

You can please some of the people all of the time and all of the people some of the time, but you cannot please all of the people all of the time.

Working in practice, you are required to be much more than just 'good with animals'; you need to create and maintain a high level of goodwill with both your colleagues and clients. Focusing on the latter group, you deal with a cross-section of the community daily, and it is inevitable that some clients will not be satisfied with the job you have done. Almost invariably this is due to *misunderstandings* about what you have actually said, how you behaved, or what you expressed as a prognosis.

Dissatisfied clients are less likely to return to the practice and more likely to complain about you to friends, so dissatisfied clients are to be taken seriously. The problem is – to identify them! It is generally only the *highly* dissatisfied clients who will actually complain to the practice in such a way that you can respond and do something about their complaint. This type of complaint, although sometimes very uncomfortable, may actually be a golden opportunity to improve service and communication levels in the practice. Studies show that 70% of clients with grievances will stay with the practice if efforts are made to remedy their complaint; 95% will stay if their complaint is rectified on the spot.

(Those clients who are not really satisfied but who don't complain either do not return to the practice, or feel a very low level of loyalty towards the practice. They can be very difficult to identify and it is important not to feel paranoid about them. However, many of the roughnesses in communication and service that may create these clients can be identified through well-planned client questionnaires that look specifically at these two areas. It is important to then act on the findings!)

The main sources of irritation to already worried clients are being kept waiting, not receiving an accurate estimate of the bill, or that the vet/staff handled the pet roughly, especially in association with a euthanasia. Sometimes there is a genuine error on the part of the practice – a promised phone call to a worried client was not made at the agreed time, or a client was not informed beforehand about increased costs of a treatment due to unexpected complications. However, in most cases, client complaints are a result of a communication breakdown – something has been misunderstood or misinterpreted so that client expectations were not fulfilled.

It is important to note that *what* the client complains about may not *actually* be the problem. Often there are unexpressed *feelings* behind the complaint. For example, a client may complain about the *costs* involved in treating a case when they are actually upset that the pet has not got better as expected (*and* it doesn't eat its new diet food *and* they can't get the pills into it). However, it is easier to complain about something concrete like money than to talk about something nebulous such as feelings.

People express their frustration in different ways and can sometimes be extremely unpleasant. They may write a scalding letter of complaint to the practice principal, make an official complaint to the veterinary governing bodies, threaten litigation, or phone or visit the practice and berate the nearest practice member – often the receptionist or nurse. This experience can be particularly upsetting and unpleasant for younger staff members so it is important that systems are in place in the practice to manage these complaints efficiently and promptly when they arise.

One of the most important aspects in managing complaints and dissatisfied customers is ensuring staff receive appropriate training in client complaint technique (see the 'Managing the dissatisfied client' box below) and are empowered to resolve problems, which includes knowing when to pass them on to more senior staff members – such as the practice manager.

Managing the dissatisfied client

The AAA method is a simple but powerful way to manage upset, angry and dissatisfied clients. It is based on effective listening. Practise this method through role-play with all staff members so that they feel confident to use the technique when needed.

Firstly, remove the angry client from the waiting room to a quiet room, or transfer the call to a telephone where other clients will not overhear you and where you can focus on what the client is saying.

Acknowledge: Let the client describe the problem in full detail. Listen empathetically and be sure that you understand it by paraphrasing it back to them. ('If I understand you correctly, what you say is ...) Then acknowledge that the problem exists ('Yes, I can see that this is a problem/unpleasant situation/that it has made you very upset ... '). It is important not to become defensive as the client tells their story; however, it may be appropriate to set clear boundaries for acceptable behaviour, especially if a client is very aggressive.

Apologise that this situation has arisen and thank the owner for bringing it to the practice's attention. Note that an apology ('I'm sorry that this has happened to you/that this misunderstanding has arisen ... ') is not the same as taking responsibility for the problem.

Action: Take the necessary time to check the facts of the case, for example by talking to the staff member concerned, or reading the case history notes. Ask the owner how they would best like to resolve the situation. The most common reason for complaints is misunder-standing, so ensure the owner gets the opportunity to have a full and complete explanation. Note that it is seldom appropriate to give money back (unless there has genuinely been a charging error).

Finally, discuss the case with the appropriate staff members and decide if changes need to be made within the practice – for example, an out-dated routine may need revising, or perhaps a veterinarian with a series of client complaints needs help with communication skills. In most cases, listening to the dissatisfied client with a genuine desire to satisfac-torily resolve their complaint will produce good results for both the client and the practice. An angry client will often apologise for their abusive behaviour, and may become very loyal to the practice. However some clients are chronically dissatisfied, or consistently unpleasant with staff: how can these people be best managed?

The genuinely 'difficult client'

Although anyone can have an 'off day' and behave uncharacteristically unpleasantly, a few individuals (and it really is only a very few!) seem to completely lack the social graces and are consistently nasty in their man-ner. These clients can be very demanding and wearing to deal with, sap-ping energy, self-confidence and joy from staff members in anticipation of and in the aftermath of their visits to the practice. In some cases, these people seem genuinely unaware of their unattractive attitude and a clear request for a change in behaviour from a respected senior staff member may reduce the problem to manageable proportions. In other cases, however, it is simply better that a senior staff member request the difficult client to leave the practice. Although this may seem like a difficult request to make, with a fear that the client will be very unpleasant in return, in the long term it pays huge dividends to staff enjoyment of their job.

The grieving client

It is important that veterinarians and all their clinical staff are familiar with the manifestations of anticipatory grief, as well as bereavement following death, in order to be prepared,

> *to understand and to be able to provide appropriate support*
> *for clients, whatever their reactions might be.*
> Mary F. Stewart, *Companion Animal Death*, 2003

Euthanasia of an animal, especially a much loved pet, is probably the most emotionally loaded and stressful procedure a veterinarian performs. It is also, in the client's eyes, more memorable for being performed well – or badly – than all the heroic surgery or medical procedures their pet may have undergone.

Grief is a natural emotional and behavioural reaction to the loss of someone or something of value. Mourning is the process through which the bereaved person copes with loss and is a necessary part of the adaptation to loss. The level of feelings experienced and behavioural changes displayed depend on the strength of the relationship with or attachment to the deceased being or lost thing, and on the individual person.

Grieving clients can be a disturbing and traumatic category of people to deal with, not only because of the level of sorrow they may show themselves, but also because of the feelings they may awake in you. The feelings bereaved owners have over the loss of a pet may be further complicated by feelings of guilt that they could have done more for the animal, or previous associations coupled to the animal (see below), or that the loss of the animal represents loss of a whole lifestyle.

Examples of complicated grief

Previous associations

An elderly lady agreed to euthanasia of her old and ill Labrador a week before Christmas. She broke down in floods of tears, and explained to me between sobs and unwarranted apologies for the outbreak of grief, that her husband had died a year ago, her beloved son-in-law six months later, and now her only remaining link to them was dead too. And *only* now could she grieve: before she'd had to concentrate hard on keeping a 'stiff upper lip', being in control and not 'breaking down' in front of family and friends.

Change of lifestyle

A friend recently made the difficult decision to euthanise her much loved but profoundly lame horse. Although she knew it was the right and humane decision for the horse, she grieved deeply not only for

> his death but also for the loss of her lifestyle: the routine of the daily visits to the stables and mucking out, the pleasure of relaxing and riding out in Nature, and the warm and undemanding contact of a beautiful and powerful living creature.

It is important to know about and understand the grief process to be able not only to offer compassionate, sensitive understanding at the time, but also to recognise abnormal or pathological grieving and recommend appropriate counselling by trained therapists.

An elderly male client, grieving the sudden loss of his beloved pug dog due to an acute illness, explained to me that the dog had been like a child to his wife and himself, and that they were both experiencing deep sadness at their loss. The problem was that if the dog had been a child this grief would have been accepted and understood by sympathetic friends and work colleagues, whereas because he was 'only a dog' the owner felt guilty even taking time off work to mourn.

The purpose of grief management is fourfold: to accept the reality of the loss, to experience the pain of grief, to adjust to the changed environment, and to withdraw emotional energy from the deceased and reinvest in a new relationship. Immediately following a death, these phases are characterised by behaviours and feelings such as numbness, yearning, disorganisation and despair, and eventually reorganised behaviour with a calmness and acceptance of the situation. These phases occur over a period of time, which can vary from hours to months (even years in the case of a close human), and which is primarily influenced by how close the owner felt to their pet.

For an in-depth explanation and discussion of the grief process and how to manage it, I would refer you to the excellent work done at Colorado State University and published as *The Human Animal Bond and Grief* (Lagoni *et al.*, 1994).

Children and grief

Concerned parents of dying pets often ask questions such as, 'What shall I say to the children?' and 'Should they see the animal dead?'. Honesty about the situation, accompanied by clear, appropriately simple explanations, is usually the best policy in explaining death and the necessity of euthanasia to children. Where it is the child's pet, it is necessary to let them be involved in the decision to euthanise as this helps them understand their responsibility in caring for a sick or elderly pet. Showing them the body of the dead pet afterwards can help satisfy curiosity about death and what it looks like, as well as providing a completion for the child.

Veterinarian Dr Robin Downing writes in her book, *Pets Living with Cancer*: 'Creation of a memorial ceremony or short ritual may be the best way to help a child say good-bye in a healthy fashion. They may want to read a poem or say a prayer for the pet. They may want to cut some hair from the pet's body to save as a memento. Flexibility is important as we help children live with the loss of a best friend.'

Managing a euthanasia in practice

A well-managed euthanasia is often the most appreciated service you will ever perform in practice, so it is vital it is well planned. Steps in the process include:

- Prepare the owner beforehand by explaining what is involved with a voluntary euthanasia.
- Discuss management of the body and take payment beforehand so that the owner does not need to deal with these practicalities when they are most upset.
- Use a quiet, pleasant room with a separate exit where clients can mourn privately and leave when they are ready without the need to go through a busy waiting area on their way out.
- Take time over the procedure, and be prepared that either you or a capable nurse can talk to the client afterwards if they so desire.
- Phone or send a handwritten card a few days later expressing your condolences.
- Home euthanasia as an option is often very welcome, reducing the stress for the pet and owner alike.

Improving the care you offer grieving clients

Dr Robin Downing, of Windsor Veterinary Clinic, Windsor, Colorado has a 'Comfort room' in her practice. This room is specially designed to create a relaxed, friendly, homey feeling for owners visiting hospitalised pets, for talking through difficult issues regarding their pets, and for euthanasias. A comfortable sofa, mats on the floor, book-lined walls, framed animal pictures, a box of tissues, and a large comfortable pet bed are some of the features of this very non-clinical room. Variations I have seen in other practices include candles, a book of memories (cards and pet photos sent in by satisfied owners), tea and coffee facilities, and fresh flowers.

At the Safari Animal Care Center in Texas, Dr Steve Garner and his team offer an unusually caring service after the death of any former patient. At once weekly staff training sessions, everyone personally signs a condolence card to the pet owner which is sent with a little model pet angel of the appropriate breed or species of pet. This carefully selected token in addition to the personally written card is enormously appreciated – and has created many bonded owners who subsequently gladly return to the clinic with their new pet.

Coping with your own feelings

It is a recurrent problem for those in the 'helping professions' that in order to function effectively, to enjoy being a good doctor, nurse (or vet) they must allow themselves to approach, and to a degree, share the distress of those they are attempting to help.

Colin Murray Parkes, OBE, MD, FRCPsych

As veterinarians or nurses involved with the emotions of upset and worried clients you may find yourself being drawn into situations for which you have neither the time nor the necessary skills. You may be left reeling after a furious outburst from an angry client, or sad because of the grief expressed by the euthanasia of a beloved family pet – and still be expected to get on with work as normal. The long-term effect of 'swallowing' your emotions is energy draining, and contributes to stress and burnout.

Talk to others in the practice about your feelings, and learn to establish boundaries for your and others' emotions. Professional boundaries are defined by your job and responsibilities. Professionalism implies a pride in your work, a commitment to quality, a dedication to the client, and a sincere desire to help. Practically, in the situation of a voluntary euthanasia, this means the animal is gently and humanely euthanised and that the owner is respectfully and empathetically cared for by you and your staff. It does not mean becoming a psychotherapeutic crutch for the owner.

Personal boundaries depend to a large extent on what you feel comfortable with, which is influenced by your own emotional maturity and experience. For example, showing your personal empathy by having tears in your eyes at the client's grief is often much appreciated by caring pet owners, whereas recent major losses in your life may affect your ability to deal with the grief of others.

Summary

The clients' relationships with their pets are complex and range from friend and companion to child substitute and hobby. Understanding the emotions involved in this relationship enables clearer communication with the owner when the pet is ill or requires euthanasia. Taking care of your own emotional well-being is part of being able to offer a good professional service to clients.

12 Achieving excellence in client service

Quality will be judged by its user, not announced by its maker.

Lockheed Industries

The importance of client service, that is serving the needs of clients, is appreciated by most professionals and most professional firms. Banks, legal firms, publishing houses, fast-food firms, travel agencies, hairdressers, hospitals, dental practices, and so on are examples of businesses that exist only to perform services to their customers or clients. Veterinary practice is also a professional service firm. Animal owners cannot easily judge the level of medical and surgical care you give, but they can and do judge the level of service they receive. As this may be, in the client's eyes, the only major factor that distinguishes you and makes you unique from other practices, striving for excellence in client service is essential.

What is client service?

Client service is the ability to meet client requirements. Client requirements are identified by being attentive to what clients say and do. Client service is not about following slick formulas such as 'answer the phone within three rings', 'a toothpaste smile for every client', and saying 'Have a nice day', but is a genuine commitment to caring for the client (in our case, the animal owner and their animal).

Valuing the client

Clients don't care how much you know until they know how much you care.

Table 12.1	Code of attitude to clients

- Our clients are the most important people in this practice
- We depend on our clients, they do not necessarily depend on us
- Our clients are not an interruption of our work, but the purpose of it
- Our clients do us a favour by contacting us
- Our clients are part of our practice
- Our clients are not simply cold statistics, but flesh and blood human beings with feelings and emotions like our own
- Our clients are not for us to argue or match wits with
- Our clients bring us specific needs – it is our job to satisfy them
- Our clients deserve the most courteous and attentive treatment we can give
- Our clients are the lifeblood of this practice

Adapted from *Receptionists Rule OK* (1992).

Client service can only begin when the practice accepts that it is a *client-driven* business; that clients, and their animals, are essential to its survival. Veterinarians, however, are often more interested in developing the intellectual and technical aspects of their craft than in being responsive to clients. All too often clients are regarded as rather annoying – and ignorant – interruptions to the day.

Table 12.1 summarises a 10-point code of attitude to clients. It highlights the importance of the client in the practice – that without clients (and their animals) there is no practice.

Planning for excellence in client service

Excellent client service doesn't just happen. It needs to be planned, reviewed and updated all the time. As part of the planning, some of the factors to be considered include:

1. Commitment by practice leaders/principals/managers.
2. Internal evaluation of the practice strengths and weaknesses.
3. Identifying client needs.
4. Staff motivation.
5. Setting goals and performance measures.
6. Assessing client feedback.

1. Commitment by practice leaders/principals/ managers

Focusing on clients is not simply a case of declaring a new policy. It involves change and commitment in the practice's *whole attitude* starting with that of the practice leaders. They are responsible for setting standards, modelling behaviour, committing resources, and communicating their full support and commitment to everyone. And they always have to stay involved.

It is essential for practice leaders to 'walk what you talk'; that is, to lead by example. Telling your staff that you are committed to your clients whereas in reality you ignore them and are rude about them behind their backs gives a dishonest message, and will encourage your staff to behave in the same way. On the other hand, answering the phone yourself, helping an older client to the car, or wiping down a dirty wall when your staff are busy, and praising your staff when you see them doing a good job, encourages your staff to follow your example of commitment to service.

 ## 2. Internal evaluation of practice strengths and weaknesses

By identifying what you are (or are not) doing currently for your clients you know where you are starting from in striving to improve service to your clients. To do things right means:

- Defining your clients' requirements.
- Turning those requirements into specifications.
- Identifying key indicators that you can track to learn which requirements are met and which are not. For example, a key requirement for clients might be a maximum 5 minutes waiting time. Does your current system achieve this? If not, how can you modify it to reduce waiting time to an acceptable level?

3. Identifying client needs

Reality to your clients is the way *they* see things. To get a clear picture of this, ask them:

- Why they come to you for their animal's care?
- What do they value about the services and products in your practice?
- What they like and dislike about the practice?
- How you compare to your competitors?
- What you do that pleases or annoys them?

(See Appendix 7 for research techniques for client feedback.)

Studies in the USA have shown that today's veterinary clients want:

- full service care for their pets
- quality service
- easy access to the veterinarian (which may mean offering more flexible hours in the clinic)
- behaviour services (behaviour problems are the primary cause of euthanasia in young animals)
- diagnostic services
- dental services (including preventive care advice)
- clear recommendations about what services or products are best for their animal.

How many of these are you providing in your practice? Do your clients know about them?

4. Staff motivation

Client relations mirror employee relations. It is important that staff consistently give the caring image you would like them to. When a client meets a practice member, that person *is* the practice for the client. Sharing practice information with staff, such as monthly income, food sales targets, and progress towards goals helps keep them involved and interested. By making them feel an important part of the practice they will be more motivated to help clients.

Staff need training and empowering to do the best for clients. This means they should have the right to make their own decisions to help clients. For example, although it may be a practice policy to have a strict cash-only payment system for clients, the staff member should have the power to waive this for old, established clients who may have forgotten their wallet.

It is also important to have a reward system for good client service. Examples I have seen in practices include recognition and praise at the monthly staff meeting, being given a special lapel pin, or receiving a practical gift such as extra time off, or dinner vouchers for a meal out.

In one of the practices using a lapel pin, the pin was actually shaped in the form of little banana. The story was that the practice principal had wanted to reward a staff member on the spot and the only thing she had to hand was a banana. This became a practice tradition in recognition of work well done.

5. Setting goals and performance measures

Having done an internal assessment of the current status of the practice, and an external assessment of the clients' needs, the results must be integrated to develop the goals and performance measures for client service in the practice. Goals should be clear, simple and easy to measure; they should also be prominently placed in the practice for all to see including, where appropriate, your clients. For example, if you are working to improve your telephone service *tell* your clients. If you introduce a new service such as better laboratory facilities, *tell* your clients. Help them see and understand you are constantly striving to improve your overall service to them; show them that they matter to you.

One of the most important performance measures is client satisfaction. This is discussed in some detail below.

6.   Assessing client feedback

Face-to-face interviews, random phone calls and mailed questionnaires are three easy methods to ascertain your current level of client service right from the horse's mouth – the clients themselves.

Negative comments and criticisms are nothing to fear: they provide specific opportunities for you to improve your service. For example, they may include things like the pet being returned smelly after a day in hospital, being kept waiting a long time for an appointment, difficulty contacting the practice by phone, difficult access for disabled people – and often clients are too polite to say them directly to you. Many of these problems can be resolved quickly. But what about complaints about 'staff attitude', 'tone of voice on the telephone', being 'unhelpful', and so on? These grey areas can be more difficult to measure and correct – but it is possible and it is *very* important.

The process of assessing client satisfaction should be repeated regularly. By keeping constantly in touch with the clients' level of satisfaction you can nip problems in the bud and give prompt feedback to your staff.

Achieving excellence in client service

Excellent client service is measured in terms of client satisfaction. Satisfied clients are more likely to come back again and to recommend you to others. Client recommendations are very powerful; whereas satisfied clients will recommend you to four or five other people, dissatisfied clients tell nine to ten people. Studies have shown that for every dissatisfied client that does complain, twenty say nothing – they just don't return. Regularly measuring levels of client satisfaction in your practice not only helps you fine-tune your level of service but also helps your practice reduce those 'silent' losses, and maintain a more stable, satisfied client base.

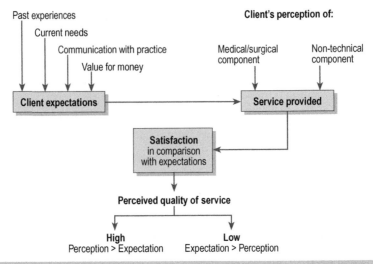

Figure 12.1 Factors influencing satisfaction as a measure of quality.

The following equation powerfully describes where satisfaction comes from:

$$\text{Satisfaction} = \text{Perception} - \text{Expectation}$$

If the client perceives better than expected service then satisfaction is high; but if the service received did not meet expectations then satisfaction is low (Fig. 12.1).

Satisfaction also includes a perception of quality. The highly satisfied client will feel they have received a high-quality service, whereas the dissatisfied client will be disappointed by the quality of service.

Understanding quality

Quality is more a journey than a destination.

Anon

Quality is about caring. To do quality work, provide quality service, or produce a quality product requires caring, which comes from enthusiasm, engagement and personal motivation to do an even better job. It also requires meticulous follow-ups.

Quality is complex because it is:

■ *situational* – different situations require different standards of quality

Standards of quality: do they exist?
'High' or 'low' quality does not really exist – either the service meets the client's requirements or it does not. Compare a French restaurant with a McDonald's; the French restaurant does not have 'higher' quality than McDonald's because its customers have different needs. Diners in the French restaurant want gourmet food and elegant service; McDonald's customers want predictable food, cheaply, in a hurry. The customer's requirements, and therefore perception of quality, are either fulfilled or not.

- *relative* – what one person perceives as quality may not be as important to another
- *made of symbols* such as the friendly smile, the spotless white coat, the pet sent home washed and dried after surgery
- and *dynamic* requiring constant reassessment and change. What was accepted as quality 10 years ago may no longer be acceptable now.

An example of this is the demand for low cost air travel. In the 1990s, Scandinavian Airlines were a shining and oft-quoted example of excellence in customer service (at a price). Since the millennium shift they have been on their knees trying desperately to recover the market they have lost. Customers who once defined service in terms of a helpful booking agent and a smiling air hostess (and sometimes dubious cuisine) now define service as the ability to easily book their own flexi-tickets over the internet, and fly as cheaply as possible (and take their own sandwiches if needed).

How quality of service influences consumer purchases

When consumers purchase *goods* three main deciding factors are involved:

- price
- product quality
- service quality.

Where the products appear the same, price is the deciding factor. If price is broadly similar then product quality becomes the deciding factor, and if price and product quality are pretty much the same then the quality of service associated with the product is used to select it (Table 12.2 and Fig. 12.2).

The *generic product* is what the client needs: they need milk, or a new car, or a notebook.

The *enhanced product* is the benefits the product will bring: skimmed milk may taste better than whole milk; a four-door saloon car may be more convenient than a two-door; a hard-backed notebook is more durable than a soft-backed one.

The *integrated product* is how the product is 'packeted' to be sold including service, word-of-mouth references, convenience of locality for purchase, the market image of the product, and so on.

Around 20% of people make their buying decision based on price only. The remaining 80% consider the value and benefits of the purchase as well as the price. In today's competitive market service quality is becoming more and more the deciding factor in purchasing goods. It is also becoming very significant in the purchase of services.

Table 12.2   **Improving the product**

Product	Generic	Enhanced	Integrated
Milk	Price	Taste	Delivery Packaging Friend's recommendations
Pet food	Price	Dog? cat?	Pet health management
		Palatability	Professional recommendation TV advertising

Figure 12.2   What sells a product.

How do clients define quality when purchasing veterinary services?

The measurement of satisfaction/quality in veterinary practice is still in a primitive state because there is no standard formula that precisely matches all individual client requirements. In addition, quality is affected by many variables, from individual veterinarian's interpretation of the service to client compliance with instructions.

Research in the USA has produced a widely accepted set of 10 client quality evaluation criteria. Although they are for non-professional services, they still help to highlight the importance of identifying quality criteria issues that are *actually* important to clients and that clients really *do* use which are often different from the criteria professionals such as veterinarians *think* are important to clients, and which *they* use to evaluate quality.

- *Reliability*, which involves being consistent, dependable and keeping promises.
- *Responsiveness*, meaning how quickly and willingly the service is provided.
- *Competence* shown by the contact staff.
- *Accessibility* in terms of both physical accessibility to the service provider, and the friendliness and ease of contact on a personal confrontation basis.
- *Courtesy*, including the consideration, politeness and friendliness of the contact staff.
- *Communication* both through making contact with clients and taking time to explain things to them; and through being a good listener to their particular problems.
- *Credibility*, which involves honesty, integrity, trustworthiness and reputation.
- *Security*, meaning freedom from risk, doubt and even danger.
- *Knowing/understanding the client*: the level of effort made to fully satisfy the individual's needs.
- *Tangibles*: quality is also reflected in tangible elements such as the physical facilities and equipment, personal appearance and attitude of contact staff, and level of fee set.

How can these criteria be incorporated into service delivery in practice? Just as with products, client service can also be expressed in terms of the generic, enhanced and augmented product. These are circles of service (Fig. 12.3). The innermost circle represents the generic or core

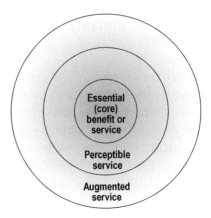

Figure 12.3 Circles of service.

expectations or needs of the client, the next circle is the enhanced or perceptible level of service, and the outer circle represents the augmented or excellent client service. It is this outer level that differentiates practices.

For most people, coming to the 'vet's' is a necessity, not a pleasure. The purpose of striving for the outer or augmented level of service is to make the visit a highly satisfactory experience; the client's perceptions of the service received should be greater than their expectations.

Core level: what is the client really seeking for their pet?

In coming to a veterinary practice clients seek:

- freedom from worry about their pet's health
- reassurance that they are doing the right thing for their pet
- to have access to experts in animal healthcare.

Every practice provides this generic core.

Perceptible level of service

This is the standard of client service offered by the majority of practices.

Augmented service

An increasing number of veterinary practices compete at the augmented service level. It is an opportunity for practice members to really use their imagination to create exceptional service for clients.

Practices functioning at the augmented level are taking veterinary practice out of the basic commodity level and moving it towards a specialised or branded level. In product terms, it is like comparing

Table 12.3 Improving the service in veterinary practice

Service	Generic	Enhanced	Augmented
Vaccination	Price	Health protection	Total healthcare
			Peace of mind
Euthanasia	Price	Body disposal choices	Care and compassion from staff
			Client recommendations

generic-label products with brand-name products. Some people will seek the generic-label product, others will seek the brand-name product because of its association with quality and value. The more the practice can differentiate itself through quality of service, the more control it has over its own development and progress (Table 12.3).

Striving for augmented service

How can you make a client's visit to your practice memorably pleasant? Even if *you* feel your service is better or more sophisticated than your rival practices, if clients *don't see* the difference, they will go back to their basic criteria of evaluation and compare you on a fee basis – and the cheapest fees usually win.

Myths about quality

The term quality was first used in the business sense in relation to products. Systems such as total quality management, which ensured consistent product quality, were very popular in the 1980s and 1990s. As the concept spread to the provision of quality services, a number of myths about quality arose. These included:

Myth 1: Quality in a product or service is what the supplier puts in. No, it is not, argues management guru, Peter Drucker. 'Quality is what the customer gets out and is willing to pay for. A product is not "quality" because it is hard to make and costs lot of money, as manufacturers typically believe. That is incompetence. Customers pay only for what is of use to them and gives them value. Nothing else constitutes quality.'

Myth 2: Quality is an optional extra in the delivery of services. No, quality is actually integral to any service, because quality is how the client perceives the service. Their perception then affects their choice to do business with that company again, to recommend that business to others, and so on.

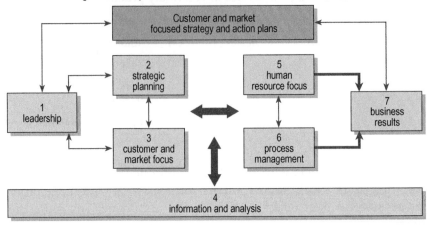

Figure 12.4 Relationship between the main systems in a service management system.

Myth 3: Quality can be one of the core values of a business. No – the core value is caring: the effect is quality. What caring creates is a culture that is innovative, productive and self-driving, that is, people committed to 'going the extra mile' to serve customers and to find new and better ways of doing old things. Lack of quality – of caring – is deadly to development, both at an individual level and also at a business level. The quickest way to kill the human spirit is to ask someone to perform mediocre work.

Myth 4: 'We always provide quality service.' Actually, you probably don't. To consistently provide a quality experience for your clients requires an extraordinary commitment to managing detail, and the systems in place to do this. Provision of quality in a service firm is not the job of one individual but an integral concept driven by management. This is illustrated in Figure 12.4.

Myth 5: Quality is a reason for buying something. No it is not. As we saw earlier, quality is only one of several factors that go into the buying decision. And because of enhanced consumer awareness of product and service availability, combined with the extreme competitiveness of today's marketplace, quality is a basic minimum for being in the market in the first place. It is a hygiene factor. Your customer assumes that your product or service has a minimum level of quality or you wouldn't even be in business. As master seller Brian Tracey writes: 'Quality, service, value and price are all hygiene factors. Their existence does not increase the desirability of your product or service, but their absence certainly decreases the attractiveness of your offering.'

Barriers to excellence

There are six major difficulties many practices face when trying to provide the best service to their clients:

- *Disagreement amongst the practice principals* about the importance and value of quality client service and what it is in this practice.
- *General undervaluing of the client.*
- *Failure to listen to clients.* Too many veterinarians believe they know what their clients want without asking the client.
- *Indifferent, unmotivated employees.* Where there is little training, empowerment or motivation for delivering service quality excellence, staff do not see the value of the extra effort involved. If staff feel they are not valued they see little reason to value the client.
- *Frontline contact staff are powerless to solve most clients' problems.* Most clients will stay with the practice if their problem can be resolved immediately. By training and empowering frontline staff to deal with problems – and potential problems – client satisfaction will be much greater.
- *Practice dishonesty.* There are many practices which claim to give good client service but really don't. Quality client service requires vigorous attention to detail. If the practice sets itself up to be the best practice in town it has to be the best practice in town – at everything. It has to be the cleanest, smartest and most efficient practice, have the best staff, the best facilities, and so on. Clients soon notice if the fees charged are not, in their view, compatible with the service they receive – and they will go elsewhere.

For example, I visited a companion animal practice that claimed to offer the best service in town – it certainly charged the highest fees. On entering the practice I noticed it was grubby – the floors and walls had not been properly cleaned, and there was fur and dirt around the edges of the floor. The commercial displays were dusty and poorly stocked – and dogs had urinated on the lowest level. In the consulting room the wall paint was scuffed and worn and the rubber mat on the consulting table was badly scratched and damaged. Leaflet displays were half-stocked. The vet's writing table was piled high with a jumble of papers, an old coffee cup and a half-eaten sandwich. This practice did not say 'quality' to me and I'm sure it did not to clients either – and they were voting with their feet.

Managing client expectations

As we have seen, client service is about attention to detail and being consistent, but it is also about getting things right first time and about creating trust with the client. Where details are ignored (or the systems are not in place to ensure details are well managed), or where trust is broken, the result is dissatisfaction, annoyance and even a feeling of being cheated. Unfortunately, such negative service experiences are not uncommon. Consider the two true-life examples in the box below on mismanagement of client expectations.

Mismanagement of client expectations

Hotel 1: 'We really care'

I stayed recently in a hotel, one of a standard chain in the UK, claiming in its brochures to 'really care' and to offer 'excellence in client service'. It was certainly very clean, with pleasant, standardly equipped rooms, and a convenient city centre location. However, on arrival, rooms that had been specially promised would be ready for mid-morning access were not – and the reception staff not only denied all knowledge of the request, but also had trouble overriding the computer system to, in fact, find prepared rooms. Later, I rang the front desk to ask for more milk and was promised it 'straight away' – and was still waiting for it when I checked out the following day. We ordered a taxi at the front desk which was promised to come 'shortly'. After 20 minutes of waiting I asked the two receptionists (who, at that time, were not busy) to find out if and when the taxi was coming as we had a reception to get to. The receptionist phoned again and told us 'it'll be here in 2 minutes'. Fifteen minutes later we left, taking our own car and nearly arriving late to the reception. The outcome? I would not use or recommend this hotel to anyone on the basis of its service.

Hotel 2: 'We stand for quality'

The entrance to this international high-quality conference hotel was imposing. As I walked across the vast floor towards the reception desk I admired the fountain in the middle, and the fine flower bouquet on the desk – until I got nearer and saw that the flowers were dead. Warning bells started to ring in my head. An indifferent receptionist checked me in and I took the lift to my room. As I freshened up in the lavishly tiled bathroom I noticed smears of dirt on the walls (not smears of cleaning materials but actual dirt). The bells rang louder. Going back into my room, which was large with a panoramic view over Copenhagen, I noticed dust balls around the edges of the carpet, and a thick layer of dust on one of the lamps. One of the bedside lamps did not work. From then on, the 'quality' simply degenerated: everywhere I looked around the hotel there was poor hygiene, and sloppy indifferent service. Another disappointing service experience.

Quality control in practice: service cycles

Services are *experienced*, and the veterinarian's duty, as the service provider, is as much in managing the client's *experience* as in providing technical expertise.

To manage the service experience and apply quality control in your practice, service cycles are a practical and easy-to-work-with method to which everyone in the practice can contribute (Figs 12.5–12.7). The method is simple: identify a service and write, in step-wise fashion, what should happen ideally. This is the inner ring of the cycle. Then, for every step, identify all the things that could go wrong. This is the

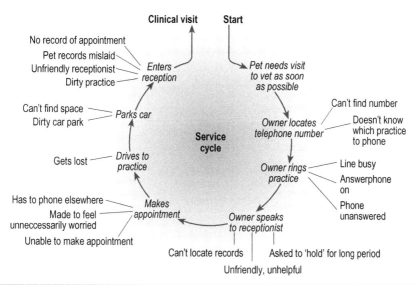

Figure 12.5 The service cycle for a client trying to make a same-day appointment. The main circle represents the 'ideal'; the outer comments are the things that could go wrong.

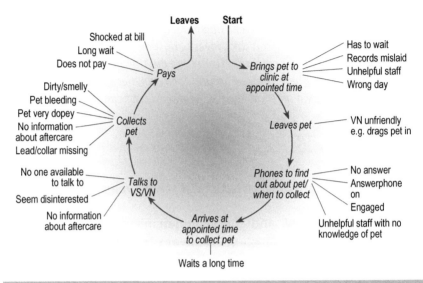

Figure 12.6 The service cycle for a client leaving a pet for elective surgery.

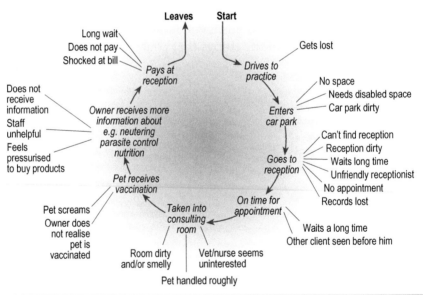

Figure 12.7 The service cycle for a client bringing a pet for vaccination.

outer ring. Finally, decide what steps you need to take or systems you need to have in place to ensure that potential problems are controlled and prevented before they happen. You are, thus, controlling the quality of service that you give.

And quality of healthcare?

Healthcare is not a product or a simple service that can be standardized, packaged, marketed, or adequately judged by consumers according to quality and price.

A. Relman, Professor of Medicine and of
Social Medicine, Harvard Medical School

Although quality and quality service have been dealt with fairly extensively in this chapter, it is important not to lose sight of the fact that a veterinarian's prime role is, and always will be, in treating animals as well and as humanely as possible. The art of veterinary care is a highly personal and individualised service, the true value and success of which can be fully appreciated only by individuals in their individual circumstances. As Professor Relman writes further:

Business managers don't understand why they shouldn't be able to get reliable information about quality of care, which they can weigh against the prices charged. The fact is that the measurement of quality is in a primitive state and is likely to remain so for the foreseeable future. Here is the best definition of high-quality medical care that I can come up with: it is the care given to a particular patient under particular circumstances by a compassionate and competent physician who has access to consultants and the best current information, who is not influenced by economic incentives to do more or less than is medically appropriate, and who is committed to serve the patient's best interests guided by the latter's wishes and medical needs. This definition emphasizes the physician's key role in allocating medical resources and preserving standards of quality.

Conclusion

Achieving excellence in client service is like people's desire to stop smoking, or to lose weight. They know and want the goal, they know how to do it, and they know it's worth doing – *but* they don't like putting up with the temporary discomfort to achieve a long-term goal. Client service is not a 'frill', nor is it merely problem-solving, so education and training of staff alone is not adequate. Helping people achieve the aim of excellence in client service means helping them find the self-discipline they need – which means a well-thought-out programme or system is necessary. Developing a monitoring system in your practice may create short-term discomfort, and will certainly require disciplined changes in daily lifestyle, but it will encourage practice members to live up to the goals to which they have agreed, and give excellent client service.

13 Compliance: the art of making effective recommendations

In 2003, the American Animal Hospital Association (AAHA) supported by Hill's Pet Nutrition conducted a comprehensive survey into the importance of compliance for the veterinary profession. Over 1400 patient records from over 240 veterinary hospitals were audited, hundreds of veterinarians and practice managers were interviewed, and over 1600 clients were surveyed to determine their feelings and perceptions about compliance issues for their pets. The result was the groundbreaking publication *The Path to High Quality Care – Practical Tips for Improving Compliance*. This chapter explores the phenomenon of compliance, and its relevance to practising excellence in veterinary medicine.

The importance of compliance

Virtually all practice teams are capable of delivering high-quality care to pets. Most likely, you and your team believe you provide the best care possible for your patients. But a comprehensive, in-depth study by AAHA shows that millions of dogs and cats are not in compliance with what we all believe is the best wellness care and treatment of medical problems. (And we studied just the dogs and cats that visit a veterinarian at least once a year!).

Introduction to *The Path to High Quality Care – Practical Tips for Improving Compliance* (AAHA, 2003)

Compliance in veterinary practice is defined as: *the animals in your practice receiving the care that you believe is best for them.* It is a team result: the team of veterinarian, nurse and owner working together to provide the best care for the animal. Where compliance is high, the animal receives the best possible care: owners are satisfied, practice members know they are doing a good job, and practice profits are healthy. However, as the AAHA survey shows, surprisingly often clients do not follow vets' recommendations for treatments, for dietary management or for long-term care. (Sometimes, of course, the culprit is the pet itself who hides medication, licks out stitches, or tears off bandages.) The outcome is the pet's health and recovery is compromised, clients are dissatisfied, staff members are disappointed and frustrated, and ultimately practice profits are negatively affected.

Compliance – or, rather, a lack of it – is an age-old, well-documented problem in the human medical world. Despite the potential for modern medicines to prevent, relieve and cure many forms of ill-health, people often do not take them as prescribed. In developed countries, compliance amongst patients suffering from chronic diseases such as asthma, advanced renal disease, diabetes mellitus and cancer averages only 50%. This has enormous repercussions not only in terms of human suffering, but also in creating feelings of resignation and cynicism amongst medical staff, and financial costs measured in billions of dollars for the medical profession (and taxpayer) who now have to treat the complications as well.

Compliance versus adherence

The term 'compliance' suggests a patient acquiesce, yield to or obey a physician's instructions and implies a submissive patient obeying an authoritative practitioner. A non-compliant patient is therefore perceived in a negative fashion by the practitioner, which hampers communication and issue resolution.

These negative connotations have meant the medical world has largely moved away from the term compliance, replacing it with the term 'adherence'. Adherence is felt to capture the increasing complexity of medical care by recognising patients as independent, intelligent and autonomous people who take active and voluntary roles in defining and pursuing goals for their medical treatment. The question of why patients may or may not adhere to medical regimes necessarily implies a broader social and personal range of issues than just the medical goals implied by 'compliance'.

> **Who official definition of adherence**
> The extent to which a person's behaviour – taking medication, following a diet, and/or executing lifestyle changes – corresponds with agreed recommendations from a health care provider. (WHO, 2003)

Adherence problems are observed in all situations where self-administration of medication or treatment is required, regardless of the type or severity of the disease and accessibility to health resources. Non-adherence is a complex and multifactorial problem often with profound negative consequences for the patient.

The World Health Organization (WHO) identifies five major groups of factors that affect adherence amongst human patients:

1. Social and economic factors:
   - poverty, illiteracy (in Britain illiteracy rates can be as high as 40% in some parts of the country, so written recommendations have limited effect), cultural factors, family dysfunction.
2. Whereas a good patient–provider relationship improves adherence, healthcare team and system-related factors can negatively affect patient adherence through:
   - management systems that may directly influence patient behaviour by directing appointment length, determining fee structure, allocating resources in such a way that personnel are stressed and unable to perform well, and that do not provide training in effective communication
   - poor management of patient education and follow-up
   - lack of knowledge about adherence and the effective interventions required to improve it.
3. Disease-related factors such as severity and rate of progression of symptoms which may affect the patient's ability to take medication or make lifestyle changes.
4. Therapy-related factors including complexity of medical regime, duration of treatments, immediacy of beneficial effects and severity of side effects.
5. Patient-related factors including:
   - knowledge and beliefs about illness
   - knowledge and beliefs about recommended medicines and treatment protocols
   - motivation to manage the disease
   - confidence (self-efficacy) in their ability to engage in illness-management behaviour

- expectations regarding the outcome of treatment and the consequences of poor adherence.

The basic issue with adherence is that healthcare providers and patients perceive disease from very different viewpoints. Doctors refer to facts and technical knowledge, restrict themselves to biomechanical issues and tend to avoid psychosocial issues. Patient studies show that knowledge alone is inadequate for high adherence. This is typically illustrated in weight management programmes where clients *know* that to lose weight they must eat fewer calories and exercise more, but, as this requires an (uncomfortable) lifestyle change, they are often not sufficiently motivated on their own to take the necessary actions, and continue to live with all the negative effects of being overweight.

In Western or conventional medicine, disease management focuses on managing symptoms rather than identifying and treating the cause. This means that even if patients follow medication regimes they may relapse at the end of treatment as the underlying cause of the problem has not been resolved.

Doctors tend to over-control patient interviews, on average interrupting patients after only 18 seconds although the patient problem description typically lasts more than a minute. Open-ended questions are rarely used, which means doctors frequently obtain less than half of the information available. In addition, doctors feel uncomfortable and poorly trained at patient education and typically underestimate the amount of information a patient wants. They rarely check to see if information has been understood as intended – which is critical, as at least 50% of patients do not recall information accurately. In addition, use of medical jargon and unfamiliar words reduces understanding. Doctors also seldom follow up on adherence levels, although adherence has been shown to improve when they do.

Most patients want to be involved in their choice of medication and treatment regime. They need support to follow a regime, and do not want to be made to feel guilty for 'failing', or 'not doing as they were told'. Identifying practical ways in which following a regime can fit more easily into their daily lives helps adherence. These include regular nurse phone contact, integrating medication times with daily habits, and using dosettes to simplify medication intake.

Motivation and patient adherence

Patient motivation has long been believed to be one of the most important driving factors of treatment success. Motivation includes the value the patient places on following the recommended treatment, and the degree of confidence with which they feel they can achieve the desired outcome. However, recent research in the behavioural sciences shows that patient level of readiness to follow health recommendations is even more important. A lack of match between this level of readiness and the practitioner's attempts at intervention will result in poor adherence.

Making effective recommendations

The best levels of adherence are achieved by the interactions of a motivated multidisciplinary healthcare team with the patient and their family, where the patient feels the team actively cares about whether or not they stick to the plan. Medical recommendations have typically focused on providing education to increase knowledge. However, the available evidence shows that *knowledge is not enough*. To be effective, a practitioner's interventions must additionally include psychological (assessment of the motivational status of the patient) and behavioural (reinforcement of motivational and adherence) components. The doctor and his or her team must be perceived by the patient to feel *concern* for them. For example, studies in Los Angeles showed that satisfaction and compliance with a consultation were reduced when doctors demonstrated:

- lack of warmth and friendliness
- failure to take concerns and expectations into account, especially getting a clear prognosis from the doctor
- use of jargon
- lack of clear expectations of diagnosis and causation.

On the other hand, when doctors perform patient-centred interviews in which patients' concerns and emotions are taken into consideration, the likelihood of client satisfaction and compliance is significantly increased.

How do adherence issues relate to the veterinary profession?

One of the biggest problems with compliance in the veterinary profession is that it is not routinely measured. Without measuring compliance levels in your practice you don't know where they stand, and therefore what you need to do about them. The practices interviewed in the AAHA study generally felt they had very good compliance levels. Accurate measurement revealed otherwise.

So, how does compliance look in reality? The following real life examples of compliance issues from practice life illustrate some of the common difficulties.

Example 1: The old man and the cat

An elderly man with advanced rheumatism returned to a veterinary practice for a post-treatment check-up of his cat, which had received a recommendation of twice-daily medication with antibiotic tablets for an infected bite sore on its back. The cat was not significantly better. On questioning, the owner confessed that he had had great difficulty giving the tablets, partly because the cat was very uncooperative and partly because he had very arthritically deformed hands. Changing the medication to a liquid oral form, and demonstrating how to give this to the cat using a water-filled syringe which the owner also tried out in the surgery, gave rapid results and at a further check-up three days later the cat was well on the way to recovery.

This is an example of a motivated and concerned owner (he has brought his cat for help and returned for the check-up despite physical difficulties himself) who is simply unable to follow through the recommended protocol. By finding ways to help the owner, the cat regains its health, and the owner his peace of mind.

Example 2: The 'natural' horse owner

A colleague was asked to 'just look at' an itchy horse at a stable he visited. The horse was clearly suffering from the allergy-induced condition 'sweet itch' and was rubbed raw along the mane and tail-base. On questioning, the owner said she was treating the horse with a 'natural' mixture of tar, honey, olive oil and some other ingredients, which she'd learnt about on a (non-veterinary) 'natural horse' course. Asked why she would not use the veterinary treatment of choice – corticosteroids – she replied that she'd read on the internet about the side effects of steroids and was frightened of them. Despite a clear explanation of why a short-term course of corticosteroids would be beneficial in treating her horse, and why her treatment was actually aggravating the condition, she still elected to continue her 'natural' method. The vet was left concerned and frustrated for the horse's welfare. Only later did fellow stable members persuade the owner that for the horse's sake she must have veterinary treatment, and within a few days on the appropriate corticosteroid treatment the horse was markedly better.

Example 3: The deceitful dachshund

Bonzo, the dachshund, required medication again to help dissolve his bladder stones. His lady owner had previously given the daily tablets without problem and the same occurred again this time. Every day she dropped the tablet in the back of Bonzo's mouth and quite willingly he would seem to swallow it. However, when he revisited the veterinarian for a check-up some weeks later, the stones had not diminished in size. This was of great concern because if Bonzo had stopped responding to the medication – which his owner swore she gave him – his future looked grim. It was with considerable relief that his owner phoned the veterinarian some days later to report that whilst looking for something under the bed in the spare room she had found a little pile of white tablets. After receiving his tablets, Bonzo had apparently been sneaking off and spitting them out. After that, his owner made sure he not only got them but that he also definitely swallowed them – and by the next check-up his stones were resolving nicely.

The AAHA study quantified compliance (the term adherence does not seem to have caught on yet in the veterinary profession) in six different areas: heartworm testing and prevention, dental prophylaxis, therapeutic diets, senior screenings, canine and feline core vaccinations, and pre-anaesthetic screenings. The results were disturbing (Table 13.1).

Further investigations to identify where compliance breakdown occurs when there is a distinct health problem to be managed revealed there were three distinct stages to making an effective recommendation (Fig. 13.1):

■ recommendation from the veterinarian and healthcare team
■ acceptance of recommendation by the pet owner
■ follow through of recommendation by the healthcare team.

The biggest gap occurred in the veterinarian and the healthcare team actually making the recommendation.

Table 13.1	Non-compliance rates in the USA
Feline therapeutic diets	82%
Canine therapeutic diets	81%
Canine senior screening	68%
Dental prophylaxis	65%
Feline senior screening	65%
Core vaccines	13%

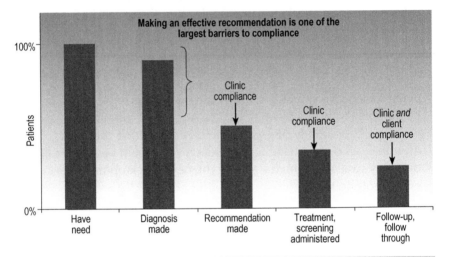

Figure 13.1 Making an effective recommendation is one of the largest barriers to compliance. (Courtesy of Hill's Pet Nutrition.)

What was the resistance? Veterinarians claimed concern about cost to clients, appropriateness of recommendation ('How should you talk about the dog's obesity when the owner is clearly obese too?') and lack of time. Clients, however, said that they were more than willing to pay for the best treatment and to buy veterinary recommended products and services – *if they were clearly recommended to them.*

So, how can veterinarians and their healthcare team make effective recommendations? For compliance to work in veterinary practice requires the following:

- That veterinarians understand their role in maintaining the human–animal bond.
- That veterinarians do not simply work on their own, but as part of a team of vet–nurse–animal owner.

Figure 13.2 Appreciating the strength and complexity of this bond between people and their pets is a very important part of the art of practising veterinary medicine. Acknowledgement Anne-Marie Svendsen.

- That recommendations are made clearly and in such a way that owners are motivated and able to act on them.
- That there is regular follow-up from the team with the owner to ensure optimal adherence.
- That adherence levels are monitored so that they can be managed effectively.

Let's look more closely at these factors.

Veterinarians and the human–animal bond

Owners have a relationship with their animal. This relationship – or attachment – is complex and provides elements of safety, intimacy, kinship, companionship, fun, responsibility, caring and constancy. For many people, pets are members of or even substitutes for their family. Appreciating the strength and complexity of this bond between people and their pets is a very important part of the art of practising veterinary medicine (Fig. 13.2).

The veterinarian is spokesperson for the health and welfare of animals. Animal owners contact us when they have a problem with their animal. This problem has caused a breakdown in the human–animal relationship – the animal is no longer eating, is vomiting, or has shows signs of pain. Owners are seeking a solution to their problem, which may be anything from healthcare advice – such as getting rid of bad breath – to major surgery or even euthanasia. To be able to help the animal requires that the vet can create a trust relationship with the owner. To do this requires competence in communication: the veterinarian's 'bedside manner' is, in the clients' eyes, at least as important as his or her knowledge.

The vet is not, however, simply treating a sick animal but helping the owner resolve the *relationship breakdown problem* that has arisen between the owner and their pet. By understanding the value an owner places on their pet the veterinarian is in a position to help the animal most effectively. This makes the veterinarian an integral part of the owner–pet bond.

Veterinarians as part of the vet–nurse–owner team

Veterinarians are trained to solve problems and do this on their own. The independent autocracy of a trained intellect is very useful at times – but it can be a handicap if the veterinarian does not appreciate the value of input from other team members, not only to enhance his problem-solving capacity but also to better communicate the resulting information to the person responsible for the animal – the owner.

Making effective recommendations

Like others in the medical profession, vets are not trained in communication skills and yet are daily in situations that need communication excellence. It is very easy for a desire to truly and effectively communicate with clients to become a desire to 'educate' them; that is, 'talk and tell' them. One of the major roles of a veterinarian is as a teacher, but good teachers do not force their views and opinions on their pupils and assume they are stupid and ignorant if they do not comprehend what is meant. Veterinarians must be willing to listen to what their clients want and be able to present their message in a way most likely to gain client cooperation and understanding. Clients need to feel *they* are in control, and that *they* are making the decisions concerning their pet's welfare, *not* that they are being pushed into something they do not fully understand.

The desired outcome of making an effective recommendation is that the veterinarian successfully persuades the client to 'buy into' the recommended treatment plan. The veterinarian needs to ask the question, 'How can I help you make this work?'. To achieve consistent success requires an understanding and application of the components outlined below:

> **Education**
> *Does the client have enough knowledge to understand the recommended treatment?*
>
> **Psychology**
> *Is the client motivated and ready to follow my recommendations?*
>
> **Behaviour**
> *How do I make it practical and easy to follow my recommendations?*

Education

> *Each of us carries around a crippling disadvantage – we know and probably cherish our product. After all, we live with it day in and day out. But that blinds us to why the customer may hate it – or love it. Our customers see the product through an entirely different set of lenses.* Education is not the answer; listening and adapting is.
>
> Tom Peters, Management Consultant

To ensure the client has enough knowledge to understand the recommended treatment requires education and training not only of the client about the problem, but also of the veterinarian and healthcare team in how they plan to work together to tackle the problem cooperatively with the owner (Fig. 13.3).

For example, to successfully diet an overweight dog requires that:

- the owner understands his dog is overweight ...
- ... and the risks of being overweight on his dog's health and future
- ... and that dietary management and exercise therapy are the only really successful methods of treatment
- ... and that weight loss will take time.

Explaining this is usually not very difficult. To do this well, the veterinarian and the healthcare team need to be agreed on how and when they will approach owners of overweight animals, what they will say to them, how they will cooperate with each other to reinforce the seriousness of the message to the owner, and then how they will help the owner achieve goal weight for the patient. However, experience shows that *education alone is not enough.*

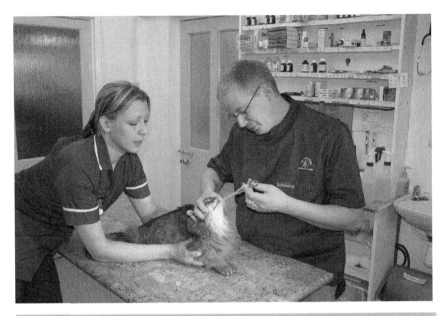

Figure 13.2 Demonstrating how to pill a cat and then teaching the owner how to do this in the clinic will help improve client compliance. Acknowledgement Anne-Marie Svendsen.

Psychology

As with the example given earlier of the 'natural' horse owner, even with the best knowledge available to them clients will not cooperate if they are not motivated and ready to do so. Understanding the stages of motivation and assessing 'client level of readiness' is critical to gaining raised adherence.

The stages of motivation

- Pre-contemplation – at this stage, the client is not thinking about changing anything – either because they are not aware there is a problem, or they have already decided not to change. Often more information is required at this stage. *Example: The owner is unaware that her dog is overweight or the consequences for the dog's health this could bring.*
- Contemplation – the client is now aware of the situation but feels unsure about appropriate action, and is reluctant to change. *Example: The owner accepts the dog is overweight and now wonders what she should do about it.*

- Preparation – client considers changing the current feeding and exercise regime (reasons for changing outweigh reasons for not) and begins to plan. *Example: Who can take the dog out more often or for longer periods?*
- Action – the client begins to implement plans. Support is often needed at this stage because changing behaviour is involved. *Example: The owner decides to enlist the help of the family to exercise dog more and will substitute some of the daily ration of diet food for the treats.*
- Maintenance – the client tries to maintain the changes made, but often lapses occur. It is important to help the client through motivation phases again to support and maintain desired changes. *Example: Ensure regular telephone contact with client by nurse, and regular revisits to clinic to weigh dog.*

Behaviour

Complying with recommendation requires a change in behaviour from the client whether it is to give twice daily medication, change a bandage daily, or walk the dog on a lead for two weeks. This is often the most difficult aspect of all to influence, even when motivation is apparently high. To increase compliance, consider the following questions:

- How can I make it practical and easy for the client to follow my recommendations? What are they physically and mentally capable of?
- How do I make it important to them?
- What practical tools could help them?
- What traps might lead to resistance?

Some ways of helping clients change their behaviour include adapting medication protocols to daily routines; for example, remind the client that when they brush their teeth morning and evening the cat should receive its antibiotic tablets, or the dog should have its medication at the times the owner watches the morning and evening news on the TV.

Which cases are suitable for compliance?

Compliance is about ensuring the animals you are treating receive the level of care you want them to have. High levels of compliance are especially important for long-term treatment of animals, for example with dental disease, diabetes mellitus, Cushing's or Addison's disease, thyroid dysfunctions, osteoarthritis, and other chronic disease conditions.

High levels of compliance are also important for patients needing major surgery, for example, pre- and post-management of spinal or joint problems, or those with operable cancers. If care is not taken with the regular follow-up of these patients then there is a high risk that complications may develop that result in unnecessary suffering and untimely death for the animal, and a disappointing and poorly functioning relationship for the owner.

Compliance is also important for shorter-term cases such as the management of bacterial infections. Owners need to understand that it is necessary for the animal to receive its complete 10-day course of antibiotics and not until the symptoms seem to be getting better, not only for the sake of best management of the disease, but also to avoid bacterial resistance developing. In these cases, ensuring the owner is able to give the medication (see example 1 above) or finding creative ways to help – which may even include daily visits to the clinic for injections if home medication is not possible – demonstrates the practice's commitment to best treatment protocols.

'Best practice' management of the canine osteoarthritic (OA) patient

Professor Stuart Carmichael of Glasgow University has developed a 'best practice' protocol for canine OA patients. He highlights that OA is a serious, progressive, painful and disabling disease that has severe consequences on the owner–pet relationship. Management of the condition to achieve good quality of life for the dog and a satisfactorily functioning relationship for the owner can only be achieved through close cooperation between the team of dog owner, clinician and nurse.

Following clinical diagnosis of OA in one or more joints, and discussion with the owner about the prognosis, the ABCDE protocol is instigated. The requirements for the individual dog in each of the categories are assessed and a form completed.

- Analgesia – does the dog need analgesia and if so what is the appropriate medication?
- Body weight – is body weight optimal? If not, what actions are necessary?
- Comfort, complications – does the dog need non-slip mats at home, a ramp to climb stairs? What happens if he does not respond to analgesic medication?

- Disease management, diet – is surgery required? How rapidly progressive is the OA? Is this a suitable patient for dietary intervention, for example using Hill's Prescription Diet J/d (joint diet)?
- Exercise – how much exercise can this patient tolerate? Is swimming an alternative to walking?

The trained nurse then keeps in regular contact with the owner to hear how the treatment plan is working and whether or not the goals of life quality and a good relationship are being achieved. The patient returns for scheduled revisits to the clinician for further clinical assessment in combination with a questionnaire completed by the owner assessing their perception of how well the patient functions in the home environment. The original form is then reviewed and altered as necessary. Together, this team creates a Best Care treatment plan for the dog.

Regular follow-ups by the practice team

Our study clearly showed that practices that involved the staff in compliance issues achieved significantly higher levels of compliance than those who did not.

AAHA compliance study

Although the veterinarian makes the initial treatment recommendation, the rest of the team are critical in ensuring the recommendation is successfully followed through. This requires good communication within the team, and protocols in place for knowing who is responsible for maintaining client contact and how it is to be done. For example, the diabetic patient may have a scheduled blood test taken by the nurse every 3 months, and the vet then phones to discuss the results with the owner at a pre-booked time.

The protocols need to be worked out by and agreed by the whole staff, which will take time. Staff may undermine compliance protocols if they do not feel that the protocols are truly in the best interest of the patients in their care.

It is also important to close the 'recommendation gap'. This means getting everyone, especially the veterinarians, to agree that they will always make a recommendation consistent with the practice's protocols without prejudging the client's level of interest in providing the best care for her pet or her willingness to pay.

Identify the specific follow-up steps and assign responsibility for each step. These include the following:

- The receptionist checks the patient's records and identifies areas of potential non-compliance, e.g. expiring vaccinations or the need for a dental revisit. She informs the client as he waits and highlights this for the veterinarian.
- Relevant educational material is kept to hand to reinforce these recommendations.
- The veterinarian makes appropriate recommendations. These are supported or further explained by the nurse as needed.
- The client books his next appointment or schedules the recommended procedure before leaving the clinic.
- Provide written instructions for home care. Almost 80% of owners want information in both verbal and written format.
- Evaluate the practice's reminder system for vaccinations, scheduled blood testing, dental revisits and so on. Much of this can be done automatically on the computer.
- Make follow-up telephone calls. In most cases, this can be done by a nurse. This is particularly important in helping an owner make dietary changes or starting a complicated medication regime.

Monitoring compliance in practice

The best way to improve compliance initially is to identify a number of key areas where compliance can fairly easily be measured and set goals for improvement. Results can be measured in terms of number of patients treated, e.g. revisits for dental examinations, product sold (e.g. clients returning to buy more diet food for the management of renal failure), or success achieved (number of dogs and cats that achieved goal weights).

Software systems are available that can help you track compliance.

What are the outcomes for you and your clients of improved compliance?

Studies within the medical profession show that by actively working to improve patient adherence, the success of patient treatments improves dramatically. For veterinarians, higher levels of client compliance represent not only improved pet health but also more satisfied clients and more sales of services and products from the clinic.

For example, improved adherence for the overweight patient means that instead of the client mumbling something about, 'Oh, we'll try giving him a bit less food at home', which is unlikely to be a successful method for the very overweight dog, the vet/nurse team sets up regular client revisits for weighing of the pet, helps the owner deal with any problems that may arise, and coaches and encourages the client to keep going. The outcome is a slimmer, healthier pet, a happy owner – who knows you really care about them and their pet, the satisfaction for the staff of knowing they are doing a good job and making a difference, and increased practice income from sales of weight management diet. In addition, the bonded client is more likely to purchase other services and products based on the practice's recommendations.

Contacting owners of pets that have been hospitalised the day after they come home and asking how the pet is doing increases compliance. Often the owner has concerns and worries they 'Don't want to bother the vet with', and are very grateful to have the opportunity to talk about them with a nurse. If the nurse can deal with issues like why the pet is very tired, or not yet eating well, and reiterates or explains instructions for medication, exercise and diet, owners will feel much more confident about being able to help their pet. They also really appreciate that the practice cares enough about them to take the time to contact them.

Summary

Improving client/pet compliance is a win–win situation for everyone. As spokespeople for the health and welfare of animals, it is the veterinarian's responsibility to do as much as possible to enable clients to care properly for their animals. Teaching the practice team about the importance of compliance, and using methods such as active listening and motivational interviewing raises understanding of the issue and works effectively to counteract it. The outcome is healthier animals, happier owners, more satisfied staff, and increased practice turnover.

14 Role of wellness healthcare in veterinary practice

Today's veterinarian measures professional success not by the number of 'interesting' diseases or syndromes diagnosed and treated, but by the number of animals in the practice that are enjoying perfect health because of diligent risk factor management by the caring team of owner and veterinarian.

Elisabeth Hodgkins, Veterinary Nutrition Consultant

Preventive healthcare (PHC) programmes have been well established in farm animal practice for many years. Recognising that disease prevention is more economically sound for the farmer than disease treatment, herd and flock health schemes have proved an effective way to maintain animal health. Preventive medicine forms the medical and financial backbone of thriving farm animal practice.

These days, the family pet is the family friend. Owners want their pet to have a long and healthy life – they want to prevent illness in their pets. Clients are better informed about their own health and they seek quality healthcare for their pets too.

Companion animal practice, however, still lags behind in an organised approach to preventive healthcare, partly because the veterinary profession itself has continued to foster the idea that the veterinary clinic is the place to bring sick pets rather than healthy ones. The universities still teach veterinarians to manage disease rather than prevent it. In practice, sheer workload often prevents active efforts towards integrating PHC principles into the daily activities. For example, in the USA and countries where increasing numbers of vets are fighting for decreasing numbers of clients, PHC programmes are much more vigorously pursued than, say, the Scandinavian countries where vets are a sought-after commodity.

Insurance companies do not pay for PHC activities such as routine dental work and pet neutering. And PHC lacks the glamour and excitement of, say, a complicated surgery or solving a medical problem.

However, better knowledge about the origins and management of many common disease conditions makes PHC more applicable than ever before. In addition, many of the PHC programmes available in practice can be largely run and managed by suitably qualified veterinary nurses, thus freeing up the veterinarians time to focus on case diagnosis and management.

What are preventive healthcare programmes?

PHC programmes are a coordinated effort to manage and prevent disease. They provide a structured approach to 'risk factor management', which is defined as examining 'those factors of sickness which can be managed or permanently removed from the still healthy individual, thereby reducing the likelihood that costly diagnostics or treatment will be needed' (Hodgkins, 1990).

PHC programmes run alongside the everyday emergencies and problems of normal practice. They interlink with each other so that, for example, an elderly cat that comes in for its annual booster vaccination can be recommended to join the senior programme, and from there be directed into the dental healthcare programme.

Programmes have in common a strong component of owner education through regular, frequent contact with clients. This not only strengthens the bond with the client and improves the animal's health, it also enhances practice income. Preventive healthcare is better quality medicine and quality medicine is profitable.

Some ground rules

There are three essential ground rules to setting up effective PHC programmes in practice.

Everyone in the practice must agree on the ethos behind the programmes and be committed to it

For many practitioners managing PHC is difficult. It is not about problem-solving – which is how vets are trained to think – but about avoiding the problem in the first place. However, it is negligent not to practise preventive healthcare at every opportunity. Giving the animal the chance

Figure 14.1 Regular vaccination is one of the routine healthcare strategies used that helps pets in developed countries live longer, healther lives. Acknowledgement: Susanne Max, Regiondjursjukhuset Helsinborg

to be wholly well through good nutrition, and a healthy lifestyle, helped by regular vaccination, neutering, good diet and regular health examinations is the most important way that we can work as a profession for the animals in our care (Fig. 14.1).

The aim of PHC programmes is to improve animal health through owner education. Gaining the compliance of animal owners is essential to the success of PHC programmes as it is the animal owner who, largely, creates the environment for the animal. This requires a sensitive approach to the owner rather than a dogmatic, 'I am right, you are wrong' attitude.

For example, obesity, is the most common nutritional disorder of pets. It results from the animal eating too many calories for its needs. Management is easy – if the veterinarian can gain the full understanding and cooperation of the pet owner. Owners often cannot 'see' that their pet is fat; they believe, 'Fat is happy'; they associate the giving of food with the receiving of love from their pet; they may have obesity problems themselves, and so on. These complex psychological factors combine to make this a tricky and sensitive issue for the veterinarian to deal with successfully.

The veterinarian must adopt the role of 'teacher' rather than 'fixer'. Client education is a long-term goal – changing client attitudes is not something that happens overnight.

Good planning is essential to success

Where programmes fail it is always due to unrealistic expectations, lack of organisation, and not having clear aims for the programme. Planning (what are our aims? who will be involved? when will we run it? how do we measure success? etc.) takes time initially but ensures a far more successful and satisfactory outcome for all concerned.

Figure 14.2
Premium quality nutrition from an early age helps ensure healthy growth and reduces the risk for nutritional imbalances that may lead to disease.

Acknowledgement: Susanne Max, Regiondjursjukhus et Helsingborg

 Existing programmes should be updated and improved before new programmes are introduced

Building up a step-by-step range of PHC programmes, starting by revising and updating the ones you currently have in the practice (such as puppy/kitten care), means that clients get the best from each programme before new ones are introduced, and that the practice does not become overwhelmed with too many new projects at once.

Types of 'wellness' programmes

There are many different programmes that can be established in companion animal practice. These include:

- vaccination
- puppy and dog health
- kitten and cat health
- behaviour management
- neutering
- obesity management
- dental disease
- senior healthcare.

Planning a preventive healthcare programme

The exact details differ from programme to programme (Tables 14.1 and 14.2) but the following approach is a logical and useful basic guide.

Ascertain the need for a programme

Veterinarians are often not sure about introducing PHC programmes into a practice, believing owners will not want them. But it is *not* adequate to rely only on your own feelings about what clients do and do not want. You do not perceive pet health as your clients do. You need to ask your clients what *they* want, and *listen* to their replies. Discussing successful programmes with colleagues in other practices can also be an encouraging pointer.

Table 14.1   Aims for specific programmes

Paediatric healthcare
To educate and inform owners about all aspects of home care of their puppy or kitten including the importance of correct nutrition, dental prophylaxis, exercise, grooming, disease and parasite control, neutering and behaviour management.

Senior healthcare
To educate and inform the owners of older animals (over the age of 5–7 years) about the control and management of age-related disorders such as organ failure, dental disease, and joint and skeletal problems through correct nutrition, dental care, exercise and screening for early detection of disease.

Dental prophylaxis
To educate and inform owners about the problems associated with dental disease and how they can be prevented through careful home management. Special attention is given to animals in high risk categories such as toy breeds, and brachycephalic breeds.

Behaviour management
To educate and inform owners about the benefits of owning a well-behaved pet, and to supply expert advice about management of behaviour problems.

Obesity management
To educate and inform owners about the risks associated with obesity and how they can help prevent or manage the condition in their pets through dietary management and exercise.

Annual health checks
To educate and inform owners about the benefits of regular screening of a range of parameters, coupled with advice about correct nutrition, and other health-maintaining factors to maintain an optimal health status for their pets.

Table 14.2 Suggestions for special equipment checklist

Paediatric healthcare
Weighing scales
Model demonstrating dental disease
Toothpaste, toothbrushes
High-quality growth diet
Preserved parasite specimens
Diagrams and specimens of external and internal parasites

Senior healthcare
Weighing scales
Refractometer
Laboratory facilities for haematology and blood biochemistry
Radiographic facilities (ECG, endoscope, etc.)
High-quality diet to meet the special nutritional needs of older pets

Dental prophylaxis
Dental sealer and polisher and/or appropriate hand instruments
Toothbrushes and toothpaste
Recommended dental chews
Model demonstrating dental disease
Appropriate high-quality (dry) diets

Behaviour management
Appropriate aids to behaviour management
Suitable high-quality diet (diet may be a significant factor in some forms of behavioural abnormality)

Obesity management
Weighing scales
Weight comparison charts
Weight-reducing diet
Weight management diets

Annual health checks
Weighing scales
Refractometer
Laboratory facilities for haematology and blood biochemistry
Model of dental disease
Appropriate high-quality diets
Diagrams and specimens of external and internal parasites

Be realistic

PHC is a long-term commitment. Establishing PHC in your practice usually represents a change in attitude not only within the practice, but also in how your clients perceive your practice. It is therefore natural that not all your clients will be immediately interested. PHC programmes not uncommonly fail in practice because of unrealistic and overoptimistic expectations about how many clients will take up the programmes, and how immediate that response will be. For example, with a senior programme, although around 40% of your clients' pets may fall into the senior category, probably well under 10% will initially take up a senior healthcare programme. On the other hand, with a good recall system you can anticipate an almost 100% response and uptake from your clients on, say, a vaccination programme over the course of the year (see below, the effect of marketing).

Reasons for starting a programme

Why are you starting a new PHC programme? Has new technical information recently been published which you want to share with your clients? Are you planning to improve the standard of healthcare offered by the practice? Is this an opportunity to enhance practice income? Do you want to justify the purchase of a new piece of equipment by incorporating its use into a PHC programme? Do you want to utilise staff time more effectively?

Aims

By assessing your true reasons for wanting to develop a new programme you gain a clearer view of your aims, and how you can measurably achieve them. In general terms your aims will include:

- improved health of the pets in your care leading to better life quality and greater longevity
- better client service through better pet care
- improved practice image through practising better veterinary medicine
- improved use of staff time and experience
- better use of practice facilities
- increased income for the practice through increased sales of services.

Work out these aims in terms of a SMART goal that is:

- Specific
- Measurable
- Action-orientated
- Realistic
- Time-limited.

Remember to identify who is responsible for implementing the programme too.

An example of a specific SMART objective for a dental health programme could be:

We aim to examine the mouth of every pet that is presented to the practice and perform dental procedures as necessary on at least 20% of them over the next year. Simultaneously, we aim to give every client in the practice a brochure about dental healthcare for their pet and will measure the effect of our dental awareness programme by response to a client questionnaire after 6 months.

Benefits

The promotion of the service needs to be in the form of the *benefits* of the service rather than the promotion of the service itself. Through promotion, the sale should be made at the programme level rather than at an individual service level, promoting the total health programme rather than a single vaccination or bag of dog food. Listing the benefits of the new programme to the practice, the staff, the clients and the pets serves two functions:

- It clarifies why you want this programme and what you hope to get out of it.
- It helps your staff identify the benefits they should discuss with the client – which is how the programme is best promoted.

First and foremost the animals in your care benefit with improved life quality and expectancy. Periodontal disease, for example, affects more than 85% of animals over the age of 3 years (Emily and Penman, 1990). It can be effectively managed by a rigorous control programme combining routine clinical examinations and home care, ideally starting from the puppy's or kitten's first visit to the surgery (Fig. 14.3).

Figure 14.3 Regular and thorough dental examinations by a veterinarian are part of a dental healthcare programme. Acknowledgement: Susanne Max, Regiondjursjukhuset Helsingborg

Figure 14.4 Obesity is an increasing problem in cats and dogs. Demonstrating obesity to an owner by weighing the pet is the first stage in obesity management. Acknowledgement: Anne-Marie Svendsen.

Around 40% of dogs in the UK are obese, and are thus at risk of developing locomotory disorders and joint disease, diabetes mellitus, circulatory problems and certain types of neoplasia. Obesity can be prevented through counselling owners about the seriousness of the disease, and instigating better feeding habits for their pets (Fig. 14.4).

In the USA, behaviour problems are still the primary reason for euthanasia of dogs between weaning and maturity. In the UK, the Association of Pet Behaviour Counsellors observe that most of the cases treated are avoidable had the pet been purchased from a better source and socialised properly with its own kind and people during critical weeks of development prior to about 18 weeks of age. Raising breeder and client awareness of the importance of having a well-behaved, well-socialised pet through running behaviour advisory programmes can help prevent unnecessary pet deaths.

Pet owners benefit from PHC programmes by having a happier, healthier pet. Through increased awareness of the risks that can lead to disease, they can make more informed decisions about their pet's health and, in the long term, save money on the potentially expensive cost of treatment of preventable conditions.

The practice benefits in many ways from PHC programmes. For example, staff gain more satisfaction from practising better medicine and enjoy the increased responsibility from more personalised client contact – and practice profit can significantly increase through more productive use of trained staff time plus sales of quality health products. These profits can, at least in part, be ploughed back into the practice for further development and improvement of client services.

What do we need?

All programmes require a committed attitude from the whole practice, appropriately trained staff, suitable client education materials (information brochures, personalised letters, demonstration models, practice photograph file, illustrative material, etc.), appropriate pet health record cards (e.g. one where the weight can be marked on a graph for an obesity programme, or where the major problem areas in a mouth can be illustrated for a dental programme), a reminder/recall system and appropriate dietary management.

Without doubt, PHC programmes are easier to run if the practice has computerised client records. Not only can clients be easily targeted (dog/cat owners, high risk breeds, senior health checks), but the remainder/recall system is also more easily instigated.

Some programmes may require an investment in certain types of equipment such as a dental scaler and polisher, weighing scales or laboratory equipment (see Table 14.2). As these can be used in many different ways in the practice, they represent a worthwhile outlay.

The cost of caring

The potential profit from setting up and running a new programme can be roughly calculated as follows.
    Outgoing expenses:

- planning time
- staff training
- staff time to run the programme
- employing an expert, for example in pet behaviour
- production of promotional literature (newsletters, handouts, reminders, posters, etc.)
- mailing costs
- purchase of special equipment (weighing scales, laboratory equipment, dental instruments)

- purchase of professional over-the counter products (diet foods, dental home care prophylactic products, behaviour management products, etc.).

Income:

- direct client uptake of services and products
- continued, long-term use of specific products such as foods, dental products, behaviour products
- indirect effect of uptake of other services and products, such as medical or surgical procedures following the primary service (e.g. vaccination leading to laboratory tests and wart removal).

The profitability to the practice is enhanced by allowing support staff to run these programmes. This not only gives them the opportunity to create their own additional income for the practice but it also releases the veterinary surgeons for procedures more suited to their skills and training. In addition, clients are often more willing to talk freely to staff members and are more likely to ask them about other services available for the better health of their animals.

Fee-setting

The fee charged for the programme should accurately reflect the time and expertise involved. Fees are often used as a measure of quality, so a high fee often represents high quality to the client. However, setting the fee is a major stumbling block to establishing PHC programmes in many practices. Do not be ruled by your own 'fee comfort factor'. Calculate all the costs involved and express this as a package. Explain the *benefits* of the programme and how it can help the health of the pet to convince interested owners of the value of the fee. Remember that you are appealing to the 80% of people whose buying decision is not ruled only by price, but who consider value and benefits too.

Marketing

Don Dooley, Veterinary Management Consultant, once wrote: 'The services that veterinarians think their clients don't want, most clients *won't* want. Why? Because they don't *know* the services are available' (Dooley, 1992). For the new programme to work, clients must know about it. The response to any programme depends partly on how enthusiastically you and your staff market it. For your staff to be keen and committed they require an understanding of the programmes' aims, and additional coaching in how to market them to clients. For example, relying solely on a targeted letter to clients will probably give less than a 10% response rate, whereas a letter plus a phone call from a trained member of staff can boost the response to a much higher level. Some or all of the following methods of promoting a programme to your clients can be considered:

- Train your staff to identify opportunities to *talk* to clients about the new service.
- Make a display in the practice using promotional literature and posters.
- Target mail information to clients.
- Use reminders (written and telephone).
- Print articles in the practice newsletter.
- Encourage features on local TV and radio stations – local newspapers may be interested in a brief article promoting the concepts of preventive health.

The importance of client education

PHC programmes are, essentially, client education programmes, teaching animal owners that many conditions are preventable rather than simply treatable. A common example of the success of owner education is how regular vaccination has reduced the incidence of canine hepatitis, leptospirosis, distemper and parvovirus.

Where specific disease conditions have been pinpointed it has been relatively easy to focus on their prevention, for example hereditary eye disease, hip dysplasia. But problems such as inappropriate behaviour and ageing changes are 'grey' topics that are less specific, and more difficult to measure. Ageing, of course, is not preventable and ultimately results in death. However, ageing changes can largely be *managed*, which can give the older animal a better quality and more comfortable life. Topics like these offer special challenges to communicate the benefits of PHC programmes clearly to clients.

When and where?

When are you going to carry out the procedures in the programme? Can the animals be booked in for quieter times in the day such as late morning and early afternoon, perhaps during the middle of the week? Will the animals need to be admitted? How long will the procedures take? Whose time will be involved? Is there a separate room where the veterinary nurse can carry out examinations and client discussions? Should you aim to start this programme in a quieter period of the year?

Different programmes take different amounts of time and may need to be performed in different places. For example, pet behaviour counselling needs around 2 hours per consultation, a high degree of owner involvement and often a home visit, whereas a senior health programme mainly uses trained support staff time in taking samples, and giving much of the general healthcare advice. Be careful not to limit yourself by restricting yourself only to the times immediately convenient to the practice – these are often quiet times *because* they are not convenient to owners.

Developing a protocol

A protocol for the programme is essential. It should be clearly and concisely worked out. Consider the following points:

- How to identify the pet for whom the programme is suitable.
- How to explain the benefits to the owner and gain their commitment.
- How the owner will participate, for example what they do at home such as dietary management, teeth-cleaning, training.
- The role of the veterinary surgeon.
- The role of the support staff.
- The role of external experts.
- Recommending healthcare products and their use.

Medical and treatment decisions lie with the clinical staff, but support staff will have valuable suggestions on how to make the programme run smoothly and effectively. A trial run of the programme in its entirety using a colleague's pet or a cooperative client can iron out any problems before introducing it into the practice.

Personnel training

Well-informed and motivated staff – and that includes the veterinarians – are vital to the success of a PHC programme. Motivate staff by involving them in the programmes from the beginning, and empowering them to run them according to goals they have helped define.

Educate staff using both internal and invited external speakers. For example, the representative from a vaccine company can describe the use of the vaccines for a vaccine programme, or a veterinary nutritional expert from a pet nutrition company can explain the importance of dietary management in a senior, obesity or puppy programme. Discuss the best laboratory tests to perform with the university experts; invite a pet behaviour specialist to work with the practice. Recommend relevant scientific papers that staff members should read; talk to colleagues who are running similar programmes.

Discuss the application of the new knowledge in practical terms. How can your staff best use this information? Can you delegate the day-to-day management of the programme to a staff member? How can this information be phrased in client communications? Is it practical (and ethical) to perform every single recommended test? Can you confidently interpret results? How do you handle client objections? How do you identify opportunities to promote the programme? Find out the potential problems and pitfalls and work out how you can overcome them. By finding answers to these questions *before* you even start, your programme has more chance of success.

Finally, reward your staff with praise and a share of the profits.

Measuring the effect of the programme

There is little point in setting up a new programme if no method is used to measure how effective the programme is, and how practice income is improved. The effect of the new programme can be determined directly from the number of clients that take up the new service, and the increase in related product sales. Indirect measurements include calculating support staff productivity levels and through questionnaires to measure client satisfaction.

Summary

PHC is challenging and profitable and is also practising better medicine. PHC benefits animal health through disease prevention and helps bond clients to the practice.

15 The future of veterinary business

Being a futurist is about being able to read trends and make predictions about likely outcomes of current activities on future business. There are many current activities that can and will affect the future of veterinary practice in the next decade or so including global and local legislation, the effects of managing and preventing zoonotic pandemics, the continuing struggle of universities for funding for veterinary research and training, changing pet ownership trends and many, many more besides. For simplicity's sake, I have chosen to concentrate on four I believe are very important. They are:

1. The importance of having good business management skills.
2. The effect of women in the profession.
3. Changes in the human–animal bond.
4. Knowledge management and serving the client.

1. The importance of having good business management skills

What is the successful practice? 'Success' is a subjective term, so some years ago, in an attempt to define 'success', eight general criteria for veterinary clinics were examined in 54 'successful' North American veterinary hospitals (unpublished report, courtesy of Hill's Pet Nutrition, Inc.). The results are summarised below.

Criteria for comparison of 'successful practices'

- *Practice mission:* over 80% shared a common vision and had stated goals.

- *Personnel management:* over 90% supported/provided further education for support and professional staff.
- *Client service:* over 95% offered medical recalls and client education programmes, and all provided a range of preventive healthcare programmes.
- *Quality of medicine and surgery:* over 80% felt they aggressively sought to learn and implement new procedures, equipment and products.
- *Community and professional involvement:* over 80% were active in different ways in the community.
- *Practice growth:* over 80% had used a practice management consultant, and all had a multi-user computer system.
- *Quality of personal and professional life:* nearly 100% felt they had an excellent quality of personal and professional life.
- *Financial performance:* average transaction fees, profit per veterinarian, and other financial parameters were all higher than the national average.

What these figures clearly show is that good business management skills are an integral part of 'success' in veterinary practice, and that success is achieved through the people in the practice.

In fact, the fundamental challenge facing veterinary business leaders of the future is to create a culture that supports and encourages all employees to tap into their deepest levels of productivity and creativity by finding personal fulfilment through their work.

As we have seen earlier, the multi-faceted, single-handed veterinary owner may also need to include 'business management expert' amongst his roles in his practice, but practices of four or more vets are increasingly realising the value and effectiveness of employing a good practice manager for this role. In addition, new forms of veterinary practice ownership are rapidly emerging including the 'corporate' and the franchise where most business management is centralised away from the practice, leaving the veterinarians to do what they are best at – practice veterinary medicine.

Good business management skills are needed to create the business in which good veterinary medicine can be practised. This does mean that even for the vets who are being 'only' vets, having at least a basic knowledge and understanding of how a business functions, including the key activities such as the importance of planning, budgeting and monitoring results, is necessary for both their personal and also the practice's success. Whilst these days some vets still choose to learn by trial and error, whilst others may choose postgraduate study, how will veterinarians of the future gain this knowledge?

Improving university preparation for life in practice

The majority of veterinary graduates go into veterinary practice. They leave university with excellent technical competence but usually lacking in the interpersonal, communication, leadership and business skills necessary for success as a practitioner. In the words of management guru David Maister:

> *Perhaps it is time for our schools and professional firms alike to stop teaching students that they are the best and the brightest, the special elite in the noblest profession of all (whatever that profession happens to be). Maybe schools and firms should find ways to teach more about what it is to serve a client, and about how to work with people whether they be your juniors, your seniors or your colleagues.*

The American Veterinary Medical Association (AVMA) accreditation guidelines for veterinary schools state that to prepare the graduate to enter careers in veterinary medicine, an understanding of professional ethics, communication skills, the delivery of professional services to the public, personal finance, and business finance and management skills should be integrated throughout the curriculum. In reality, many universities find that the intensive training needed to become a veterinarian often leaves little time for elective courses in these areas.

As one university spokesman expressed it, 'Our job is to produce veterinarians not MBAs'.

One exciting way of addressing this is to incorporate leadership training in the first year of the veterinary curriculum, as is done at the new Veterinary Leadership Experience (VLE) programme in the USA. In 2005, 70 veterinary students representing 33 of the 34 veterinary schools in the USA, participated in an intensive 5-day curriculum that worked on developing the skills of leadership, teamwork and interpersonal communication. The background to this programme was interesting: Myers–Briggs analyses of veterinary students had shown that the predominantly female students did not generally show the empathetic, socially oriented, more typically female behaviours of women in an average community, but tended to be introvert, driven, independent and intellectual. These skills serve well in pursuing an academic career, but can be barriers to success in the working environment of a veterinary practice where, for example, good communication skills with staff and clients are essential. On the VLE programme, new undergraduates learnt to adapt their natural autocratic and independent tendencies to become better team players with improved interpersonal skills – training that will serve them equally well through their student days as when they get into practice.

Veterinary students leave university with huge student debts – in the UK typically around £25 000 – and deep concerns about the chances of getting a good job as a new graduate. Even if they do manage to find a job, starter salaries are low – especially compared to other professions – which makes the weight of student debt even heavier.

New graduates are often bursting with knowledge and enthusiasm, but are often unrealistic in their expectations of what they can achieve. In addition, practices employing vets under the 2 year graduate mark are taking a risk: they can actually end up losing money and becoming less competitive than those employing the more experienced young veterinarian. Few young graduates receive job training on routine procedures such as the vaccination regime in the practice, basic surgical procedures, and sales of drugs and diets. Fewer still receive training in basic business management skills including a thorough understanding of their function as income generators in the practice. However, those two first years are critical for the young veterinarian's future success, both in anchoring their medical and surgical skills, but also in continuing the development of their business management skills.

Hopefully, in the next decade we will see a spread of programmes like the VLE to more universities as well as increased opportunities for students and young graduates to learn the business skills needed for success in their future lives.

2. Women in the profession

In 2006 it is estimated that the profession will be at least 50% female in most developed countries. In future years the profession will become even more 'feminised' – a reflection of the current extremely high level of female undergraduates.

Although women may be as ambitious as men, a few years into their work life they typically develop different requirements for their job than men in achieving a work–life balance. The needs for balancing the demands of having and managing a family with those of having a career mean that many women choose to work part-time. This may be supported by traditional family structure, as in Germany where the husband is the main breadwinner, which means that married women veterinarians do not need to work more than one or two days per week. Or it may be that generous governmental support of mothers, as in the Scandinavian countries, means women are entitled to prolonged, paid maternity leave and very flexible working conditions when they return to work. This breaks with the traditional male paradigm of a single veterinarian having full time employment. In fact it actually creates jobs. To manage this situation well requires employment flexibility in practices, and means there is either a need to train more veterinarians or to learn to utilise nurses and other support staff better to counteract the effect of so many veterinarians working part-time.

Veterinarians in most countries are required to provide 24-hour service for sick animals. This puts unsocial, unnecessary and unacceptable demands on the modern veterinarian and many are opting out of 'on call' work as a result. A solution in city centres is local emergency/night clinics which are manned in the unsocial hours to provide high standards of 'out of hours' care as well as relief for practices which function during normal working hours. In rural areas, sharing of the out of hours work between practices can reduce nights 'on call' to an acceptable level.

The 'feminisation' of the profession has other effects too. Studies in Canada, Australia, the USA and the UK show that female veterinarians on average charge less for services and receive lower incomes than their male counterparts. Women have been accused of being less 'business minded' than men, and this has been cited as a reason why men are less likely to be attracted into the profession. However, the real reasons are more complex:

- Women typically have more difficulty than men in setting a value on themselves and charging properly for the services they provide. This reflects a need for an improved understanding of business management and how the purpose of a business – selling services and products to create profit – should be separated from the emotional clouding factors of the service providers.
- High student debts, low starter salaries and low self-value make it more likely for women to have problems with getting loans to set up their own clinics.

- Rules governing practice ownership are changing as the market is changing. Non-veterinary ownership – for example, ownership by veterinary nurses – incorporating and franchising are becoming more popular.
- Women practitioners are less likely to want to buy into a practice because they do not want the commitment of a more-than-full-time business.

A partnership is not a career move

Setting up your own plate or becoming a partner by buying into a practice was often seen as the ultimate goal for a veterinary surgeon. Today's graduates see this neither as a career move (in fact, it is actually a business rather than a career move) nor as a wise investment. Partners are often financially worse off than assistants, and are required to make heavy sacrifices to quality of personal and family life, work excessive and unsocial hours, and commit themselves to one geographic location for an indefinite but usually long period of time. In addition, partnerships can be harrowing to live with and almost impossible to leave.

So, if women will shortly be dominating the profession, it is clear that the whole paradigm of working as a veterinarian needs to change. Perhaps being a good vet is not about selfless dedication '24/7', but about finding quality of life and having time for family and other personal activities. Perhaps it is about having confidence in other people and realising the importance of sharing skills and delegating responsibilities – which will mean employing someone you trust to do the 'business management bit' rather than being macho and doing it all yourself. Perhaps it means learning to proactively and proudly market and promote the services and products we sell rather than passively and politely waiting for clients to call by.

Personally, I think the 'feminisation' of veterinary practice will radically – and positively – change practice as we know it today.

3. The human–animal bond

What is man without the beasts? If all the beasts were gone, man would die of great loneliness of spirit, for whatever happens to beasts also happens to man. All things are connected.

Chief Seattle, 1855

People are genetically programmed to benefit from contact with animals. Although the way many people live today does not always make this easy it is very important never to lose sight of the fact of what animals contribute to our society, and how much we need contact with animals to thrive.

Veterinarians are part of the human–animal bond. They are responsible for providing the expertise and practical care of animals living intimately with humans and under human management. However, veterinarians are not only responsible for animal health and welfare. Because of the very close association between people and animals, through caring for animals, veterinarians also contribute to human and society's health and welfare.

In modern society, people have largely lost contact with the fundamentals of healthy living and good animal husbandry so that increasingly pampered pets have become a substitute for normal, healthy relations between humans, and demands for cheap meat, milk and eggs have justified society's turning a blind eye to animal exploitation.

I sincerely hope that the future trend with the greatest impact on the profession will be the radical revision of our – we veterinarians – attitude towards our stand on animals and their welfare. There is already general pressure from people and the legislators to change animal welfare regulations, particularly in the farm and production animal sector, but also for horses and companion animals. As more knowledge becomes available about the true needs of animals and more expression given to their rights, I sincerely hope cruel practices such as long distance transport of animals for slaughter in conditions reminiscent of the transport of human slaves only a few centuries ago, cage and intensive rearing of pigs and chickens, inappropriate husbandry practices such as continuous stabling of horses and separation of mothers from offspring before weaning, and breeding pets that cannot breathe, walk properly, or reproduce themselves normally will become a thing of the past.

As the world becomes – metaphorically – smaller and the population becomes – literally – larger, I sincerely hope veterinarians are amongst those that take up the cause against practices that exploit global resources such as cutting down irreplaceable and ancient rainforest on one side of the world to grow the grain to fatten the feed lot cattle which will make a rich nation's hamburgers on the other; or against practices that allow uncontrolled use of antibiotics and other drugs, leaving both the human and animal population of the world open to the risk of devastating disease; or against practices that go completely against Nature and natural methods such as genetic manipulation and cloning.

Veterinarians have an ethical and moral responsibility to educate and inform animal owners about 'best practice' animal care and welfare. I sincerely hope that an increased awareness of the power of compliance will raise the veterinarian's recommendations to a whole new and powerful status that will benefit animal – and owner – alike. As Lonnie King, Dean Veterinary School, Michigan State University, said in his Keynote address to the Association of American Veterinary Medical Colleges (AAVMC) just a couple of years ago: 'The most serious challenge to veterinary medicine is to re-establish its social responsibility.'

4. Knowledge management and serving the client

Knowledge is increasing at such a rate that in another couple of decades it will be doubling every 30 seconds. Access to this knowledge via the internet is also increasing at lightning speed. What effect might all this knowledge have on the future of the veterinary profession?

Clients will become more demanding as they learn about advanced medical and surgical achievements for people and want them for their own animals. The demands to be able to offer more and more sophisticated life-saving services will drive the 'cutting edge' of veterinary medicine.

As the human population itself fights against the effect of ageing and learns more about the benefits of healthy living, so will people become more interested in preventive healthcare for their animals. This means veterinarians need to be better at providing these services.

The growth of knowledge challenges the discipline of traditional scientific thinking – the very backbone of veterinary practice. Clients are increasingly aware that there are other – perhaps even better ways – of practising medicine and curing disease. As they search for alternatives for themselves to symptom-based Western medicine(a style of thinking that emerged from the study of the dead body) and turn increasingly to holistic Eastern medicine (which evolved through striving to understand the flow of energies through a living body), so will they expect this for their animals. Veterinarians who continue to deny the value of integrating Eastern medicine into their practices will be left behind by those who can embrace practices such as using herbal medicines, chiropractic, homeopathy, acupuncture, Raiki and other holistic and currently less conventional healing forms.

Summary

The most significant challenge facing the veterinary profession today is not competition or recession, but rather our own ability to change the habits that got us where we are today.

Thomas Catanzaro, Veterinary Management Consultant

The only constant feature of today's business world is change. Change by its very nature is not static, so we constantly face new challenges. I believe the most important challenge we face in ensuring the future success of veterinary practice is ourselves, the veterinary profession. Change will continue to go on around us all the time – we need to review *our* ability and willingness to respond to change.

Change is something to be excited about. It offers chances to try new things, to be creative, and to develop. Let's learn to embrace change and enjoy life!

Appendix **1**

Telephone skills

What are telephone skills?

Telephone skills are:

- The ability to behave courteously, politely and effectively during any telephone interaction.
- The ability to create business both directly (e.g. an appointment) or indirectly (e.g. goodwill), thus using the telephone as an effective marketing tool.
- Ensuring time spent on the telephone is productive and not wasted. Wasted time represents wasted money for the practice (ineffectual use of staff time, telephone bills) and can be a source of irritation and frustration to your clients.

Standard answering technique

A good answering technique that everyone in the practice is trained to use helps communicate an image to the client of a team of efficient, service-oriented animal care professionals, and gives an excellent start to a relationship. A well-proven standard method is:

- Answer within three rings (clients are time-pressured, and they are also often worried about their animal). Answering promptly shows you respect their time and concern (*not*, as one vet I met thought, that you are not a good practice because you have nothing else to do than answer the phone!).
- Adopt a pleasant, helpful, positive and efficient attitude. And don't forget to smile – it can be heard down the phone!

- Greet the caller, identify the practice and yourself by name, and ask how you may help the caller.
- Screen the call and deal with the query: for example, book an appointment, give the necessary advice, refer to the person requested, etc.
- Never treat any call as routine – to the caller this particular call may be very important.
- If appropriate, write the owner's name (address), telephone number, pet's name, sex, nature of problem and other relevant details as a memo to deal with later. Read the details back to the caller to make sure you have them correctly.
- If it is necessary to put the caller on hold, ask them if it is convenient first, then check back with them every 20–30 seconds to ensure they know they are not forgotten. Apologise for keeping them waiting.
- At the end of the call, check that you have answered all their questions, and thank the caller for phoning.

Improving the service

I phoned a consumer advisory agency and asked for a Miss Smith. The receptionist told me she was off sick. Could anyone else help me with my problem? I asked, and explained briefly what it was. No, she answered. When should I try contacting Miss Smith again? When she's better, I was told. You can imagine my level of satisfaction with the firm – but I have also phoned veterinary practices and had similar responses from receptionists!

Some pointers to improving the telephone service you currently offer include:

- Prepare a basic script for how to answer the telephone. Ensure *everyone* in the practice follows the same basic telephone technique. Check this by tapping and recording calls (with their knowledge) and discussing the quality of the call with them. Did they really follow all the steps? The point of having a script is that it gives a quality standard rather than everyone answering in their own unique way.
- Have *memo pads and pens fixed* near the telephone so that they are readily accessible for taking notes.
- Have a *reference folder* near the telephone at all times which gives the answers to common questions and outlines practice protocol on common proceedings.
- While the client is on hold, *use a message* on the answer machine, which gives details of the services offered by the practice.

- Have a *timer* next to the phone and learn to restrict routine calls to 3–5 minutes. Telephone conversations longer than this might include planned discussions with clients about treatments or laboratory results, or clients grieving the loss of a pet. However, most calls longer than 3–5 minutes are ineffective and cost the practice not only in wasted time, lost clients (who give up waiting) and staff frustration, but also in increased telephone bills. This latter is especially important as many calls out from the practice are now made to mobile phones, which can be very expensive.
- Consider alternatives to booking appointments by telephone such as enabling clients to request appointments via email. Although emails have to be answered, their advantage over telephone calls is that they are not as urgent and can be answered at times when front-desk business is a bit slower.
- Some clients phone for advice, which can be time-consuming over the telephone. Ways to deal with this are to answer common questions on the practice website, or to have a special telephone line where callers are charged per minute.
- Use *simple language,* especially for explaining medical or surgical procedures and do not use slang. Post out or email information, as needed, for example pre-anaesthetic routines, treatment protocols or welcome packs to new clients.
- *Think about your choice of words*: 'Fluffy has settled into the ward' sounds much better than 'Fluffy's sitting in her cage'.
- Use the *client's name* during the call to personalise it.
- Do not make *personal calls* where clients can see or hear you; use a private line.
- Ensure *adequate staffing* at peak times so that the telephone is not neglected.
- If you have to *phone a client back*, do it at the agreed time.
- Instigate fixed veterinary telephone times where either the client can phone in to speak specifically to the veterinarian, or the veterinarian can phone the client at a pre-booked time. The advantages of the latter system is that others in the practice can book these times for the veterinarian in advance, the veterinarian can be well prepared by having the client's records already open on the computer in front of her, and calls are restricted to 10 minutes because they are booked by appointment.
- *Price quotations* given over the phone should always be recorded (in the client's records with a signature and date) unless they are for fixed price items or procedures.

- To improve efficiency, *plan* what you are going to say, and get references you may need to use to hand, before you make an outgoing call.
- Develop *client questionnaires* to identify the best and worst aspects of your current telephone service, and to give a base to work from in improving your standards. *Regularly reassess* your telephone service as part of your overall service to clients.

Using the telephone as a marketing tool

Some callers are just shopping around for the best price. They can be converted to loyal clients by a well-trained receptionist. A conversation can be extended to take an interest in the client and gain a commitment from them. The receptionist must portray value and a caring image by voice alone. The following guidelines can turn a phone shopper into a client:

- Greet the caller.
- Before answering the caller's question about price of a service, ask them about their pet – name, age, breed, vaccinal history. Be friendly and interested.
- Tell the caller what this practice offers and why it is unique. Explain why your services are the best for them and their pet. Keep cost at a low profile – sell the client the benefits of your services. It may be appropriate to send information through the post, but phone and see if it answered her queries a few days later.
- Make the appointment.
- Reaffirm your interest in the client and their pet by saying you look forward to seeing them on the specified day.
- Thank them for calling (remember – they can choose to ring elsewhere!).

Appendix 2

Planning and managing effective team meetings

Team meetings are an essential activity for a healthy team. Meetings can include everything from a quick chat in the corridor to a formal meeting of all staff in the practice. They should be an extremely effective way of improving communication in a practice, but all too often they are total time-wasters.

Meetings are called for a variety of reasons:

- *Information dissemination:* for example, new information about a vaccine.
- *Problem-solving meetings:* for example, there is a problem with the telephone service that needs a solution.
- *Creative-thinking meetings:* for example, how can we inform clients about our new dental health programme?
- *Miscellaneous.*

Meetings can be made inspiring, stimulating and successful by sticking to the following guidelines:

Ten golden rules for effective team meetings
1. Keep meetings short – maximum 1 hour.
2. Start and end on time.
3. Have a predetermined agenda (see below) and stick to it.
4. Control the meeting by ensuring members do not dominate the meeting and that everyone has a chance to contribute.

5. Only involve those who are necessary but keep everyone informed of the outcomes.
6. Rotate chairmanship of the meeting so that everyone in the practice has the opportunity to organise and chair meetings.
7. Make sure all the relevant information (facts, figures) is available – if necessary prepare handouts.
8. Involve everyone in the meeting by asking for their contributions.
9. Ensure people stick to the subject under discussion and that their remarks are relevant.
10. Use written minutes which are circulated to and signed by all members of the practice.

Meeting agenda

Everyone in the practice should have the opportunity to contribute to forming the agenda; for example, by having a sheet of paper in the staff room where suggestions can be written for topics for discussion. The chairperson should then select the five or six issues that can be included in the meeting.

In addition, every agenda should include:

- *Achievements and mistakes:* ask the team to briefly outline achievements and mistakes since the last meeting. This gives the opportunity to praise successes and assess errors.
- *Follow-up* from the last meeting on what was decided. Has everyone done what they promised they would do?
- *The new action plan* for the week/month. This is not an opportunity for complaints, but for positive suggestions and ways of improving systems in the practice to be put forward.
- *Rewards and recognition:* praise and reward those who have done a good job. Make sure everybody gets some sort of recognition.
- *Professional development:* ask a team member or invite a speaker in to share some interesting information. It could be on a new surgical technique, a new diagnostic test, or a better way to answer the telephone. Videos and audiotapes can also be useful in this context.
- *General announcements* – to save time these can be typed up beforehand and distributed. Comments can be invited.

Appendix **3**

External lecturing

Another way in which veterinarians communicate with clients – who may be animal owners or colleagues with referral cases – is through lectures and presentations. There is an art to giving a good presentation, and while it is not possible to describe it in detail here you *can* improve your presentation technique by attention to the following points:

- Identify your audience clearly, for example their technical knowledge, age, interests.
- What message are you conveying? Is this a technical presentation to colleagues? A marketing presentation about herd health for farmers? Information about correct nutrition for breeders?
- Identify size of audience – a powerpoint presentation is ideal for a large group but may be too formal for a group of six.
- There are many ways to plan an effective presentation but one of the simplest is the abcABCabc method. Identify three key points you will talk about in your introduction (abc), expand on them in detail in the main section (ABC), then summarise them briefly (abc). Repetitious? People need to see or hear something at least 20 times before it 'sinks in' and causes a change in their behaviour!
- Prepare your presentation carefully, and practise it out loud so that you can give it fluently.
- Be prepared to answer questions.
- Keep it short and use a variety of media to convey your message. People's concentration span is becoming shorter and shorter so long powerpoint presentations are seldom effective. Use support aids such as skeletal models or live animals, or demonstrate techniques such as bandaging or clicker training.

Appendix **4**

Process mapping and quality control

Process mapping is a workflow diagram to bring forth a clearer understanding of a process or series of parallel processes. It is a series of connected steps or actions to achieve an outcome, and has the following characteristics:

- A starting point and an end point. This is the scope of the process.
- A purpose or aim for the outcome.
- An internal or external customer.
- Rules governing the standard or quality of inputs throughout the process.
- It is usually linked to other processes.
- Repeatability.

A map allows you to examine a business process clearly, without the 'distraction' of the organisational structure or internal politics. As with process charts, the usual approach is to map a process 'as is' (to identify the current status of a process), to use this as the basis of analysis and review – in terms of identifying process steps that are the (potential) cause of bottlenecks, delays, barriers and errors – and to create a map of the re-engineered process to aid in 'selling' identified process improvements.

Examples of processes in veterinary practice include:

- diagnosing and treating lameness
- vaccinating a pet
- admitting a pet for routine surgery.

The primary aim of process mapping is to improve the level of service to the client. Through working more effectively, not only is the client

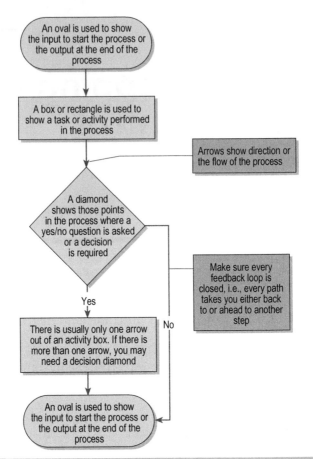

Figure A.1 A typical process flow chart explaining the different box shapes used in creating a chart.

more satisfied (and therefore more likely to return) the practice is also more profitable.

A process can be compared to the flow of river. Stones and natural bends have shaped and slowed down the flow of this river. Just as a water engineer might clear the river's path so that it can flow most effectively, so a process mapper removes the obstacles and hindrances that reduce the effectivity of a process in a business.

Clients are looking for seamless solutions to their problems. Process mapping aims to clear the work flow to be able to serve the client in the best possible way. Usually this means real clients – the pet owner, but in many of the supportive processes it is colleagues and workmates who are the 'clients'.

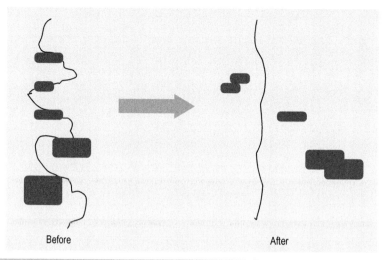

Figure A.2 Removing the rocks that hide the flow of a stream: how process mapping works.

Process mapping both makes working methods more efficient, but also builds an attitude of serving the next in the chain in the best possible way (because you yourself are a link in the whole chain too!). When you look at the complete processes you can begin to see how complex many of them are and how easy it is for problems to happen.

Support processes in veterinary practice are things like taking X-rays or laboratory tests as part of making a diagnosis. For every support process there is a customer (in the clinic) with needs. The biggest problem in a process is often the transition from one section or department to the next. On the borders it can be very unclear who is responsible for what. Process mapping highlights the importance of one person being responsible for the whole process, e.g. a vet or nurse who follows the animal through the whole process, and also that the results produced are measurable.

Appendix 5

Setting fees in practice

Financial planning

The purpose of financial planning is to take control of the financial development of the practice to create the practice of your vision. At its most simplistic, financial planning consists of:

- deciding on the profit you would like to generate
- calculating the costs in the practice
- calculating the income necessary to cover the costs and generate the profit you want.

Outgoings (costs) include staff salaries, heating/lighting/maintenance costs, drugs and other stock items, food and accessories, property rates, taxes and insurance, and so on.

Income is generated from professional fees and the sale of professional goods and medicines. It is influenced by the level of professional fees set in the practice, the number of cases seen, and the amount of goods and medicines sold.

Fee-setting is a controversial issue but it is an important part of the healthy, positive attitude of the responsive practice. Although it is beyond the scope of this book to look in any more detail at financial planning for veterinary practice, the issue of fee-setting is examined in more detail.

Fee-setting

Clients are more fee sensitive than they used to be, which does not mean they automatically seek the lowest fees. Careful attention to fee-setting can bring substantial returns to a practice, helping to attract clients away from other practices, and to obtain clients who might otherwise have avoided a particular service because they feared it would cost too much.

Fee-setting involves multiple considerations:

- What are the objectives of fee-setting?
- What strategies are available?
- What are the tactics for implementing fee-setting?
- How should fees be changed and how often?
- How can fees be negotiated, invoiced, and collected most effectively?
- Identifying and eliminating the emotional clouding factors to fee-setting.

Determining the objectives of fee-setting

Practice life-cycle

The objectives of fee-setting depend on what the practice wants to achieve with its fees and where it is in the practice life-cycle (see Chapter 2). Thus the 'expert' practice will set high fees but expect relatively few clients, whereas the efficient practice will set lower fees but anticipate a high client throughput.

Market penetration

A practice may want to penetrate a particular market and therefore needs to make itself distinctly different from the competition. For example, a practice may find low fees advisable initially if:

- The market appears to be highly sensitive to fee levels, and therefore a low fee will stimulate a more rapid market growth.
- A low fee would discourage actual and potential competition.
- A low fee would not be viewed by clients as an indicator of poor quality work.

However, if none of these conditions applies then fee-cutting would not be the technique to use, and other methods of market penetration or other objectives should be found.

For most veterinarians, their main objective in fee-setting is to charge a fee that is fair and enables them to cover their time and expenses, and generate a profit that allows them a comfortable (but not extravagant) standard of living. Their reputation as being fair and competent matters more than making lots of money.

Strategic options

There are two key elements to a fee strategy:

- the average fee level
- the fee presentation approach.

The practice needs to decide how low or high it wants its fees to be, on average, in comparison to other practices, and how it will present these fees to the client.

There are three basic techniques for determining the average fee level:

- calculating the cost per procedure
- demand-orientated method
- competition-orientated method.

The cost per procedure is often a good base to begin from in fee-setting and can be used to create price lists of procedures, and the price of drugs and disposables. These are then combined in different ways for different cases to produce the final fee.

Demand-driven fees are primarily those where clients can fairly easily 'shop around', for example the cost of vaccinations, neutering, worming, basic examination. They are also routine, common procedures which therefore have relatively fixed overheads.

Competition-determined fees are calculated in relation to neighbouring practices and their charges. There may be a deliberate decision to set fees above or below those of the competition.

In reality, a mixture of all three is used so that, for example, in calculating the fee for a routine procedure such as a bitch spay, the fee to the client would be lower than, say, surgery for a gastric torsion. This is because a spay is a common operation that is relatively standard, is often presented as a fee package (the total cost of a bitch spay including intravenous fluids, pre- and postoperative care is £x) and one that clients will phone around practices to get price quotations on. A gastric torsion is not routine, not standard and cannot easily be 'packaged' because it is highly individualised.

Selecting a fee-presentation approach

In veterinary practice there are three main methods of fee presentation:

- time and costs
- fixed sum
- mixture of the two methods.

Fees that are calculated on the basis of the time and costs involved are variable and often more profitable than those routine procedures that have a fixed fee. This is because they reflect the true time and costs involved rather than an estimated average, or the down-valuation of a demand-driven fee.

One major disadvantages of the time and costs approach is the uncertainty and consequent dissatisfaction it creates in clients. The client must make a decision based only on an estimate (provided by the professional) of the total cost of the procedure. Misunderstandings over what a procedure will cost is one of the most common communication problems that arises in practice (see 'Preventing bad debts', below).

Another major disadvantage is the tendency of veterinarians to 'shave' the bill to reduce it to a level that they *personally* find acceptable. This is done by 'forgetting' to charge for minor procedures, and disposables. This can represent huge losses to the practice (see 'Identifying and eliminating the emotional clouding factors', below).

The fixed sum method alleviates client uncertainty over fees and can also be used to 'hide' high hourly/daily rates that clients may have difficulty accepting (as they do not earn these amounts). On the other hand, the procedures can create a lower profit margin and there must therefore be a constant drive to ensure the volume of work that will create the profit.

In practice, a mixture of the two methods is generally used. Fixed sum fees are used for the 'shop around' procedures whereas the time and costs method is used to calculate individual, less routine procedures.

Tactics for fee-setting

The offering of discounts to clients is common in veterinary practice. It is usually done for clients who:

- require services in a 'slow' or quiet period of the year
- have a large number of pets and buy a large volume of services
- need the services to support an animal charity or trust.

Carefully used, it can be a very powerful method of cementing the trust bond with a favoured client. Wrongly used, it loses profit and implies the practice charges too high fees anyway.

Another common tactic is the 'high estimate'. Estimating a fee then adding a factor of 25–50% serves two functions:

- if the estimate was, in fact, too low there is already an in-built safety factor and the final fee is not a surprise to the client

- if the estimate was accurate, the client has the bonus of a pleasant surprise.

Referral and second opinion fees should always be higher than ordinary fees. Clients seek professional expertise: this should be charged for accordingly.

Initiating changes in fees

Whatever the fee policy chosen it is always necessary after a period to change fees to account for inflation, costs, demand for services and competitive factors. The fee change can be general or specific. It is sometimes an advantage to use selective fee changes so that the most sensitive items (the 'shop around' procedures) have little or no alteration in price.

There is always a fear associated with increasing fees that clients will be frightened off and business will decrease. This can be managed in a number of ways:

- Having frequent small increases in fees (½–2% every 2 months) so that it is difficult to spot increases. This also has the added advantage that it keeps the fees on a level with inflation.
- Changing the fees at the time when the maximum level of work is anticipated such as in the summer.
- Ensuring staff are informed about fee changes.
- Monitoring client response to the fee changes – it is said that if less than 5% of clients complain about your fees they are probably too low!

The effect fee changes will have on clients is extremely difficult to measure. People tend to ignore or avoid information about fees prior to the purchase of a service, paying most attention to this information after the services have been received. This is classically seen when an emergency patient is rushed in and the distraught client will 'pay anything' for treatment, only to complain later that the bill is too high. People are prepared to pay high fees for professionals with outstanding reputations. Fees are an important part of the development of the trust bond with the client, and may be more significant in deciding whether or not the client will *return* to a practice than for making the initial visit. Fees are also a measure of quality of service expected by a client.

The fee structure can change as part of the long-term development plans of the practice. Thus a relatively low-price new practice may become the most expensive practice in the area as their style changes, and their client base stabilises.

Fee communication and collection

The most important point to bear in mind when collecting fees is to *avoid negative surprises*. Careful preparation of a fee estimate which the client sees and accepts, updating the client if there are any changes in the original estimate, and breaking down the final bill into its component pieces can help make the process of fee collection be as painless as possible.

Itemising

Itemising all the procedures carried out on the final invoice has both advantages and disadvantages. On the one hand, it educates and informs the client about what was done to the animal, and helps create trust with the practice because nothing is hidden.

On the other hand, itemising gives more room for client query.

Preventing bad debts

It is important to have an established, effective policy for fee collection to avoid bad debts. Such a policy could include some or all of the following:

- For procedures over a certain value, clients sign written estimates to indicate agreement with and acceptance of the costs involved. The client is kept fully informed of any changes in the estimate and may be required to sign new estimates.
- A portion of the costs are paid before the procedure is performed. This is an especially sensible policy in areas where client credit-worthiness is dubious.
- When clients join a practice they are required to complete a personal history form that includes details of their bank and credit cards.
- Make payment by major credit cards possible.

Bad debts are not the only way money is lost from fees in practice. Probably the most important way in most practices is through improper charging, i.e. missing services and procedures that have been performed.

Identifying and eliminating the emotional clouding factors

Veterinarians, like many in the caring profession, are heavily influenced by emotional factors in relation to fees and fee-setting. Some of these factors are:

- a low self-value based on setting extremely high professional standards for themselves

- a fear of money: money is not something professional people need to talk about
- personal ethics
- need for money
- fear of client perceptions
- inability to attach a real value to a service
- an in-built, fixed, personal ceiling that influences all other decisions.

Support staff are not immune to these clouding factors either. It is an important part of successful practice policy to teach staff how to talk about fees to clients. They should be able to talk confidently not apologetically about fees, be knowledgeable about how a fee is calculated and be able to handle objections to fees without embarrassment.

Computers play an invaluable role in fee calculation and collection. Not only can they generate and alter the price list as necessary, but they can also act as the passive 'third person' when it comes to charging ('The computer says it costs ...'), which can take pressure off staff.

It is very important that clients feel they get value for money. If the practice is to charge the highest fees in town, clients must feel they get the best service from that practice (see Chapter 8). Remember, fees are the clients' view of the value of service they receive.

Appendix **6**

Practice promotional literature

Practice promotional literature is all of the papers or documents that you produce in the practice for client or business use. It promotes or represents the practice and is one of the many methods of communication used in practice. It is very important to produce literature of a high standard that reflects the professional standards in the practice.

It is worth seeking professional help to design the literature for your practice. Home-produced literature can lack professional finish and quality. Commercial advertising firms often give very reasonable quotations for logo-design, production and printing costs and can give invaluable advice about paper quality, typestyle, etc. They are often a significant time-saver for the practice as well.

The following is a brief summary of all the different types of practice promotional literature available, with notes on aims and effective presentation of each.

Client information sheets

Function: to give clear, specific instructions/information in simple terms about disease management or pet care.

- To give the owner more understanding of particular health problems.
- To give owner advice on home care.
- To give answers to common questions.
- To inform owners of the benefits of new or existing services/products in the practice to the benefit of themselves and their pet.

Information sheets can be personalised with the client's and the pet's name and with information specific to their particular problem.

Examples of topics suitable for handouts

- Neutering
- Vaccination
- Giving medication – eardrops, eyedrops, pills
- Pre- and post-general anaesthetic care
- Managing surgical drains/bandages/sutures
- Prevention of dental disease
- The importance of home dental care
- Internal and external parasite control
- Obesity management
- Senior health
- New puppy/kitten care
- Specific diseases – renal failure, diabetes mellitus, diarrhoea and vomiting, liver failure, etc.
- Emergency care/first aid
- Euthanasia and grief counselling
- Nutrition
- Dealing with common behavioural problems.

How to use handouts

- Fewer than 15% of clients will read a handout if it is just taken from the rack.
- More than 85% will read it if they are handed the leaflet with the words: 'This is important information (about the health of your pet): you should take time to read it. Please feel free to ask us any questions you may have.'
- Include appropriate leaflets in an information pack; for example, a puppy pack could include leaflets on nutrition, vaccination, worming, neutering, pet insurance, and the facilities in the practice.
- Provide an appropriate leaflet explaining the use and value of the product when a particular product is purchased, for example diets, shampoos, parasiticides.
- Mail to selected clients.
- Use leaflets as part of a product display.

Newsletters

Function: to inform and update clients with new information of benefit to themselves and their pets. They are particularly useful to market the benefits of owning healthy animals.

A newsletter could contain some of the following:

- seasonal information – fleas, fireworks, heatstroke, hot cars, grass seeds, hair shedding
- practice-specific information – new staff, new services
- preventive healthcare information about different programmes, for example dental, obesity, vaccination, senior, puppy care, behaviour
- ongoing series, for example caring for your kitten, cats of the world
- interesting cases – to demonstrate challenges in practice and practice facilities
- client question and answer page
- 'client corner' with photos of the owners and their pets
- forthcoming events, for example an open day, National Pet Week.

Advantages:

- excellent concept
- can be mailed to every client, handed out in the practice, used at meetings, etc.
- often can be partly or wholly sponsored by veterinary companies in return for advertising
- may have outside authors contributing, local photographers, etc. at no extra cost
- can be successfully organised and run by a member of the support staff.

Disadvantages:

- may be difficult to find the time and motivation to keep producing
- can be costly – printing, mailing, time
- not always easy to measure the impact, for example increased uptake of services
- can you be sure people read them?

Practice brochure

Function: to encourage clients to use the practice by describing the practice and all the services it offers in terms of the quality of care and the benefits that the client and their pets receive.

Consider:

- cost of production – what is your budget?
- how will you measure the impact on your clients?
- size, appearance, paper quality and colour, contents, message, number of pages, glossy/matt, photos/illustrations, logo, number to print, how soon out of date? full colour/some colour/black and white?

To include:

- front/back page – practice logo, practice details, map
- practice mission statement
- number and qualifications of staff
- specialist/referral facilities
- major services in the practice expressed in terms of benefits to the client and their pets, for example X-ray, ECG, laboratory, anaesthetics facilities, diathermy, cattery, kennels, operating theatre(s), dental facilities, reception, isolation ward, qualified veterinary nurse care
- appointment system/open surgeries
- payment policies.

It is tempting to produce a high-quality, full colour, glossy brochure but this will be extremely expensive. Smaller, less glossy productions can be just as effective but with a big cost saving.

How to use a client brochure

- Give to new clients on first visit.
- Give several brochures to referring clients.
- Send brochures with statements and reminder cards.
- Mail brochures to all clients in an area when the practice first opens.
- Display in reception and examination room.
- Give brochures to prospective clients via family and friends.
- Give out brochures when lecturing.
- Hand out on open day.

Reminders

Function: to remind clients a service or health check is due, for example dental, vaccination, senior check, pet health check, diabetes mellitus, renal assessment, skin problem.

Consider:

- addressing the reminder to the pet
- personalising a pre-printed card by using the pet's name
- using humour to make it eye-catching so that it is not just thrown away: mailing it in an envelope may have the same effect
- giving brief information outlining benefits of the particular service to owner and pet
- including a simple questionnaire to encourage questions about pet health

- requesting a urine sample as an introduction to a senior programme
- including name, address, and phone number
- giving a time for a pre-booked appointment to encourage the owner to phone and change it and thus making contact with the practice.

Client information pack

Function: to give the new client, or new puppy/kitten owner an introductory pack of information about the practice consisting of several brochures that explain the services it offers, and how to care for their pet.
Information to include:

- practice brochure, or at least practice details (name, address, telephone number, opening times, payment method, etc.)
- caring for your pet (species specific)
- specific information on vaccination, worming, neutering, dental care, senior health, etc.
- dietary recommendations
- practice newsletter
- recommended boarding kennels/catteries, grooming parlours, etc.

Client registration form

Function: to gain information about a new client and their pets; to raise concepts of preventive healthcare to the owner from the first meeting.

The details you obtain from this form can simplify the assessment of your client base, help you identify services that are needed, help with target mailing, and so on.

The questionnaire should not be too long or complicated. The practice name and logo should feature prominently, it should be confidential, and it should finish with, 'Thank you for your cooperation'.
Questions you may wish to include:

- Name, address, telephone number, and contact number of owner.
- How did client hear of the practice, for example Yellow Pages, practice sign, client recommendation ('Who may we thank?').
- Name, age, species, breed of pet.
- Health status of pet: neutered, vaccinated, last wormed.
- Any known disease or allergy problems with pet.
- Is pet on any medication?
- Weight of pet.

- What is pet fed?
- Does pet have any behaviour problems?
- 'We believe preventing disease is as important as treating it. Which of the following preventive health programmes for your pet would you like to know more about?' List ...
- Any other pets? List ...

Sympathy/birthday/thank you for the referral/ welcome to the practice cards

Function: to convey a particular, personalised message from the staff of the veterinary practice to create the feeling that you really care about the pets and their owners.

Consider:

- handwriting the owner's/pet's name and the appropriate message
- using the personal signature of one or all of the members of the staff
- addressing the birthday/welcome card to the pet
- including a small gift, or discount voucher for a healthcare product from the practice.

Clinical examination form

Function: to simplify and standardise history and record taking for the benefit of the practice, client and referring veterinary surgeon.

Forms can be produced for:

- general health examinations
- skin cases
- senior health checks
- dental examinations
- ophthalmology
- neurological assessments
- gastrointestinal problems
- cardiology, etc.

The general health forms can be used on a daily basis to standardise clinical examinations. Copies of them can be given to owners upon completion as:

- proof of a thorough examination
- opportunity to stress that certain problems were identified during the examination which may need further investigation.

The other forms are used for:

- referrals to other veterinary surgeons
- guides for examinations of body systems, especially when the user is not doing these regularly.

The forms should include:

- practice name, address, telephone and fax numbers
- practice logo
- space for the client's and pet's details and relevant history
- simple diagrams where appropriate
- questions that work logically through a system
- space to write comments, observations, etc.

If the client is personally taking the pet to a referring veterinary surgeon the practice can provide a simple, pre-printed map of the location.

Client questionnaires

Function: to gain information about the client's view of the practice with the aim to improve the practice to better suit the client's needs.
Subjects for questionnaires:

- service both in general and specifically
- assessment of the newsletter
- understanding of particular articles in the newsletter, etc.
- how the clients first found the practice
- monitoring the effect of changes made in the practice
- interest in new services.

Questionnaires can be anonymous or signed, targeted or random. Properly designed and used, they are probably the most effective way of finding out what your client really wants.
Use the information generated to:

- compare branches of your own practice
- improve your services
- make changes in the organisation and running
- identify what your clients really want.

Questionnaires can be:

- mailed out to clients
- completed while waiting
- included in a newsletter as the response element.

Business documents – stationery, invoices, health certificates, business cards, compliment slips, envelopes, etc.

Function: to transact written business.

All these documents should include the practice logo, name, address, fax and telephone numbers. Invoices can also have seasonal information about services available in the practice.

Posters

Function: to promote services and goods to clients within the practice using a simple but powerful image or message.

Posters can be home-made or supplied by companies. They must have high visual impact to be effective so should not include a lot of text. They should, of course, only be displayed if the products or services they advertise are recommended by the practice.

Subjects suitable for posters include:

- health programmes, for example dentistry, senior, puppy parties
- 'behind the scenes' displays of the practice showing practice facilities
- forthcoming events
- to raise awareness of new diseases or epidemics, etc.

Appendix 7

Conducting market surveys

Superior performance ... [in client service] ... – however you measure it – is a matter of meeting your customer's requirements. And you can't meet these requirements if you don't know what they are. Not what you think they are or what you want them to be, but what they really are. How do you learn what they are? Very simply, you ask your customers what they want, need and expect, in a variety of ways. Then listen and act.

Cannie and Caplin, *Keeping Customers for Life*, 1991

Market surveys can range from small, in-practice questionnaires to a full investigation of your current and possible market by outside experts. The basic questions you want answers to are:

- Why do your clients come to you?
- How do they value your services and products?
- What do they like and dislike about your practice?
- How do you compare to your competitors?
- What do you do that annoys, infuriates or really pleases them?

These can then be adapted for a focus subject (such as the need for an obesity clinic; better telephone service).

The most commonly used types of client insight research are described below.

Direct personal contact with clients

It is very easy to ignore or dismiss as unimportant what clients are saying to you in a practice situation, but by consciously listening to them and asking probing questions you can find out what they really want. Often it is quite different from their apparent reason for coming to the practice.

Random phoning of clients who have been into the practice in the last few weeks can also give information about their impressions and what they want from their practice.

Staff contact with customers

Staff who are trained to listen are invaluable at picking up information from clients. They not only have the most direct idea of what is going on, but they probably have excellent ideas of their own too. Clients often chat more freely to staff members, so encourage all staff to pay attention to what clients say – then be prepared to use this information to make changes in the practice.

Feedback

Feedback is a common form of formal client research. A typical example is the card found in hotel rooms with a number of questions pertaining to the service in the hotel. Feedback provides very useful information but there are several points to remember:

- Keep systems, for example questionnaires, as short and simple as possible.
- Use behaviours that measure satisfaction; for example, would the client recommend the practice to a friend? What is the level of satisfaction with waiting time for appointments on a 1–5 scale?
- Share results of feedback systems so that everyone in the practice knows what clients think – good or bad.
- Tell clients you value their opinion because you really want to do something about the level of service you offer them.

Client questionnaires

Simple and effective client questionnaires can easily be prepared in the practice as long as the following guidelines are used:

- Focus on one problem area at a time, for example reception service, postoperative release of pet, routine vaccination service.
- Keep questions short and simple.

- Use predominantly closed questions (requiring a yes/no answer), or ones that have graded answers (What do you think of … on a 1–5 scale?).
- Use some open questions to learn what people think is important.
- Avoid asking more than 5–6 questions to ensure cooperation.
- Explain what the questionnaire is for.
- Thank clients for their help.
- Keep clients informed about progress.

Example of a feedback questionnaire

Here at Rosewood Veterinary Hospital we would like to improve our telephone service to you, our valued clients and patients. Please help us assess our current service by circling your answers to the following questions:

1. Do you have difficulty contacting the practice?
Yes/No

2. When you last phoned the practice, how quickly was the telephone answered?
<3 rings   3–5 rings   >6 rings

3. Was the person who answered
Friendly and helpful?   Indifferent?   Not helpful?

4. (a) *Were you kept waiting on hold?*
Yes/No
   (b) If 'yes', how long for?
   <1 minute   1–3 minutes   >3 minutes

5. What suggestions would you make to help us improve our telephone service?

A questionnaire like this would give information on how well the phone is answered, and whether you need more incoming lines (or staff to handle calls). Other specific questions could ask whether the client was phoned back in the promised time, whether they felt all their questions were answered, and for how long they thought their conversation lasted.

There is an advantage to using external organisations to do client surveys – answers are likely to be more honest. However, bad answers or complaints should not be received in a negative light: they provide an opportunity to improve the service to clients.

Evaluation

Research helps you evaluate your ongoing programmes by providing information for assessing your performance. This information can then be used to make decisions about working towards performance goals.

For example, an airport opened information booths to help travellers with problems or questions. As these were not very successful they investigated further. Researchers found that most of the passengers were satisfied with the service they had received – but only 5% of all passengers had used the booths because **the rest did not know where they were.** *Airport officials improved the visibility and advertising of the booths and more passengers were then aware of them and could use them.*

Sources for information are:

- your clients
- non-clients because they are potential clients and can give you a different perspective on things than your present clients
- staff who are in constant touch with clients and are an excellent source of information.

Of course, ask comparable questions of each group.

A thought in closing: The US Office of Consumer Affairs conducted exit surveys of 200 customers of a well-known Washington retailer. The choices were **very satisfied, moderately satisfied, moderately dissatisfied** *and* **very dissatisfied.**

> *Fifty-four per cent of the respondents said they were very satisfied … [But] How many of the customers giving … [the moderately satisfied response, not a bad rating] had a specific complaint about something that happened in the store? All of them. And how many of the 92 customers who were less than very satisfied … complained to anyone in the store? Zero. Not one of them said anything. And why not, do you suppose?*
>
> *When asked they said, because they expected mediocre service, because they didn't believe anything would be done if they had complained, and because the store's level of service was about the same as that of its competition.*
>
> *In summary, if you're just content to retain market share … [these results] may be good enough – at least until your competition offers better service.*
>
> Cannie and Caplin, *Keeping Customers for Life*, 1991

References and further reading

AAHA (2003). *The Path to High Quality Care – Practical Tips for Improving Compliance.* AAHA, Colorado.

Armstrong, M. (1990). *How To Be An Even Better Manager* (3rd edn). Kogan Page, London.

Barrett, R. (1998). *Liberating the Corporate Soul.* Butterworth-Heinemann, Boston, MA.

Blanchard, K. and Johnson, S. (1982). *The One Minute Manager.* Fontana, HarperCollins Publishers, London.

Blanchard, K., Carew, D. and Parisi-Carew, E. (1993). *The One Minute Manager Builds High Performing Teams.* Fontana, London.

Blanchard, K., Oncken, W. and Burrows, H. (1990). *The One Minute Manager Meets the Monkey.* Fontana (Harper Collins), Glasgow.

Bloom, M. (1994). Have you sorted out your contracts of employment? *Veterinary Business Journal* **3**, 44–45.

Bone, D. (1988). *A Practical Guide to Effective Listening.* Kogan Page, London.

Bower, J., Gripper, J., Gripper, P. and Gunn, D. (2001). *Veterinary Practice Management* (3rd edn). Blackwell Science, Oxford.

Bradford, D.L. and Cohen, A.R. (1984). *Managing for Excellence.* John Wiley, New York.

Bradford, L.J. and Raines, C. (1992). *Twenty-something: Managing and Motivating Today's New Workforce.* MasterMedia, New York.

Bush, B.M. (1992). Obesity in small animals, its causes, diagnosis and treatment. *Veterinary Practice Clinical Review* **1** (6), 1–2,4,6–7.

BVA (1988). *BVA Guide to an Agreement Between Principals and Assistants.* BVA Publications, London.

Cannie, J.K. and Caplin, D. (1991). *Keeping Customers for Life.* Amacom, New York.

Catanzaro, T.E. (1991). Two outside forces that will change the way you practice. *Trends* Oct/Nov, 26–28.

Coleman, K. (2001). *Giving Students the Business: How Do We Help Future Veterinarians Succeed Financially?* Veterinary report, University of Illinois at Urbana-Champaign, Summer 2001, Vol. 25, no. 3.

Collins, J.C. and Porras, J.I. (1996). Building your company's vision. *Harvard Business Review* Sept–October, 64–77.

Covey, S.R. (1989). *The Seven Habits of Highly Effective People.* Simon & Schuster, New York.

Covey, S.R. (1992). *Principle-centered Leadership.* Simon & Schuster, London.

Denny, R. (1993). *Motivate to Win.* Kogan Page, London.

Desatnik, R. (1987). *Managing to Keep the Customer.* Jossey-Bass, San Francisco.

Dooley, D.R. (1992). Negativity gets you nowhere. *Veterinary Economics* July, 46–49.

Downing, R. (2000). *Pets Living with Cancer.* AAHA Press, Lakewood, CO.

Drucker, P.F. (1966). *The Effective Executive.* Harper & Row, New York.

Drucker, P.F. (1968). *The Practice of Management.* Pan Books, London.

Drucker, P.F. (1994). The theory of business. *Harvard Business Review* Sept–Oct, 95–104.

Drucker, P.F. (2001). *The Essential Drucker.* Harper Business, New York.

Egan, G. (1990). *The Skilled Helper: A Systematic Approach to Effective Helping* (4th edn). Brooks/Cole, Monterey, CA.

Elkins, A.D. and Elkins, J.R. (1987). Professional burnout amongst US veterinarians: How serious a problem?. *Veterinary Medicine* **82**, 1245–1250.

Emily, P. and Penman, S. (1990). *Handbook of Small Animal Dentistry.* Pergamon Press, Oxford.

Geneen, H.S. and Moscow, A. (1985). *Managing.* Granada, London.

Gerber, M.E. (2001). *The E-myth Revisited; Why Most Small Businesses Don't Work and What To Do About It.* HarperCollins, New York.

Goleman, D. (1996). *Emotional Intelligence.* Bloomsbury Publishing, London.

Goleman, D. (1999). *Working with Emotional Intelligence.* Bloomsbury Publishing, London.

Graham, J.R. (2003). Marketing murder: 13 great ways to kill your company's marketing. *Petfood Industry* March, 8–11.

Gunter, B. (1999). *Pets and People: The Psychology of Pet Ownership.* Whurr Publishers, London.

Hackman, J.R. (1994). Commenting on *The team that wasn't. Harvard Business Review* Nov–Dec, 22–38.

Hackman, J.R. (1995). Can empowerment work at Sportsgear? *Harvard Business Review* Jan–Feb, 26–28.

Harvey-Jones, J. (1989). *Making it Happen.* Fontana Paperbacks, London.

Hayes, R. and Watts, R. (1986). *The Corporate Revolution.* Heinemann, London.

Hill, J. (1993). First years in practice: experiences of young graduates. *Veterinary Record* **132**, 521–522.

Hodgkins, E.M. (1990). Bringing wellness to companion animals. *Partners in Practice* **3** (3). PO Box 148, Topeka, Kansas.

Huggett, J. (1988). *Listening to Others,* Hodder and Stoughton, London.

Hunt, J. (1981). *Managing People at Work.* Pan Books, London.

Jevring, C. (1993). Do your support staff lay golden eggs? *In Practice* **15** (4), 198–201.

Jevring, C. (1994a). Improving your telephone technique. *Veterinary Business Journal* **4**, 22–25.

Jevring, C. (1994b). Expanding the role of the veterinary nurse. *In Practice* **16** (2), 101–104.

Kanter R.M. (1997). *Frontiers of Management.* Harvard Business Review Books, Boston, MA.

Kotler, P. and Bloom, P.N. (1984). *Marketing Professional Services.* Prentice-Hall, Englewood Cliffs, NJ.

Kotler, P. and Clarke, R. N. (1987). *Marketing for Health Care Organisations.* Prentice-Hall, Englewood Cliffs, NJ.

Kotter, J.P. (1995). *Leading Change.* Harvard Business School Press, Boston, MA.

Kotter, J.P. (1999). *John P. Kotter on What Leaders Really Do* (Harvard Business Review Book). Harvard Business School Press, Boston, MA.

Kübler-Ross, E. (1970). *On Death and Dying.* London, Tavistock Publications Ltd. Republished (1993) Routledge, London.

Lagoni, L., Hetts, S. and Butler, C. (1994). *The Human Animal Bond and Grief.* Saunders, Philadelphia.

Lambert, A. (2005). *Mystery Shopping: A Unique Look Through Your Client's Eyes.* Conference proceedings. Management Symposium, BSAVA.

Legislation Affecting the Veterinary Profession in the United Kingdom. Royal College of Veterinary Surgeons, 32, Belgrave Square, London SW1X 8QP.

Little, G. (1992a). How to merchandise a practice. *Veterinary Practice* July, 8–10.

Little, G. (1992b). What's wrong with selling? *In Practice* January.

Loder, M. (1985). *Feminine Leadership.* Times Books, New York.

Lofflin, J. (1992). Merchandising: it works for him. Does it work for you? *Veterinary Economics* May, 37–51.

Maister, D.H. (1993). The power of practice leadership. In: *Professional Service Firm Management* (5th edn). Maisters Associates Inc., Boston.

Maister, D. (1997a). *True Professionalism.* Free Press, New York.

Maister, D. (1997b). *Managing the Professional Service Firm.* Free Press, New York.

Maister, D.H. (2001). *Practice What You Preach.* The Free Press, Simon & Schuster, New York.

Maister, D. (2003). *Management: What It Really Takes.* Online. Available: **www.davidmaister.com**

Maister, D. (2005). Professionalism in consulting. In: Greiner, L. and Poulfelt, F. (eds) *The Contemporary Consultant.* Thomson-Southwestern, Mason, OH.

Manning, P.R. (2003). Consultation technique in general veterinary practice. Masters Research Thesis.

McCurnin, D.M. (1988). *Veterinary Practice Management.* J.B. Lippincott, Philadelphia.

McKenna, P.H. and Maister, D.H. (2002). *First Among Equals.* The Free Press, Simon & Schuster, New York.

Mintel Report (2005). *Pet Food and Pet Care Retailing – UK.* May.

Morgan, N.A. (1991). *Professional Services Marketing.* Butterworth-Heinemann, Oxford.

Nohria, N. *et al.* (2003). What really works. *Harvard Business Review* July, 43–52.

Obholzer, A. and Roberts, V.Z. (eds) (1994). *The Unconscious at Work: Individual and Organisational Stress in the Human Services.* Routledge, London.

Oldcorn, R. (1989). *Management.* Macmillan, London.

Pease, A. (1984). *Body Language.* Sheldon Press, London.

Peters, T. (1989). *Thriving on Chaos.* Pan Books, London.

Peters, T.J. and Waterman, R.H. (1982). *In Search of Excellence.* Harper & Row, New York.

Pettit, T.H. (1994). *Hospital Administration for Veterinary Staff.* American Veterinary Publications, Inc., California.

Pritchard, W.R. (1989). *Future Directions for Veterinary Medicine.* Pew National Veterinary Education Programme, North Carolina.

Ravetz, G. (2005). Who's interviewing who? Matching expectations in the selection process. Management Symposium compendium.

Receptionists Rule OK (1992). Proceedings of symposium, Hatfield, Herts.

Royal College of Veterinary Surgeons Guide to Professional Conduct (1993). RCVS, 32, Belgrave Square, London SW1X 8QP.

Sheridan, J. and McCafferty, O.E. (1993). *The Business of Veterinary Practice.* Pergamon Press, Oxford.

Shilcock, M. (2003). *Interviewing and Recruiting Veterinary Staff.* Pocket Practice Guide, Threshold Press, Newbury, Berks.

Shilcock, M. and Sutchfield, G. (2003). *Veterinary Practice Management, a Practical Guide*. Elsevier, Edinburgh.

Silverman, J., Kurtz, S. and Draper, J. (2005). *Skills for Communicating with Patients* (2nd edn). Radcliffe Publishing, Oxford.

Stewart, M.F. (2003). *Companion Animal Death*. Elsevier Science, Edinburgh.

Swift, B. (1994). How to communicate with your employees. *Veterinary Business Journal* **3**, 9–11.

Tannen, D. (1992). *You Just Don't Understand*. Virago Press, London.

Thomson, K. (1998). *Emotional Capital*. Capstone, Oxford.

Tracey, B. (1995). *Advanced Selling Strategies*. Simon and Schuster, New York. *Veterinary Times* (2005). **35** (34), 1.

Vivian, M. (1994). Tightening up on stock control. *In Practice* **16** (5), 282–285.

WHO (2003). *Adherence to Long-Term Therapies: Evidence for Action*. World Health Organization, Geneva.

Women in the Professions (1990). Report by UK Interprofessional group, Working party on women's issues, June.

Index

Printed and bound by CPI Group (UK) Ltd, Croydon, CR0 4YY

08/05/2025

01864672-0001